PROVEN STRATEGIES FOR
SUCCESS IN SPORT, LIFE AND MENTAL HEALTH

Brent Pope is an ex-rugby player and professional coach from New Zealand, but is well known in Ireland for his work as a rugby pundit for RTÉ television over the past two decades. Brent is also an accomplished children's book author and in 2012 penned an award-winning autobiography entitled *Brent Pope: If You Really Knew Me.* As well as appearing in numerous crossover television programmes from cooking to singing, Brent has also curated his own Dublin art gallery for outsider artists and in 2013 created his own fashion brand label called POPE. Brent is an ambassador for many Irish mental health charities, and is one of Ireland's leading advocates and speakers on mental health, having himself suffered crippling anxiety. Brent is currently juggling a successful television, art and fashion career with a return to full-time study in the field of psychotherapy.

Jason Brennan is a psychotherapist specialising in depression, anxiety, grief, loss, panic, acute stress and obsessive thinking. Originally from Ireland, Jason completed a BA in Psychoanalysis before moving to Wellington, New Zealand to become a Certified Transactional Analyst. He has provided training and coaching for large corporate and government agencies, executive teams, military and emergency services personnel including police, ambulance, fire and national defence force support. As a mental skills coach for the Super 18 Hurricanes rugby team he contributed to their first championship win in the club's 21-year history and has gone on to provide mental skills coaching support for soccer, rugby, cricket, tennis, motor sports, netball and hockey teams. He has written articles for the 42.ie and he has a special interest in mental health in sports and for quality of life. He lives in Dublin, Ireland with his wife and two children.

www.thewinningmind.net

Further contact information is provided in the resources list at the back of this book.

WIN

PROVEN STRATEGIES FOR
SUCCESS IN SPORT, LIFE AND MENTAL HEALTH

BRENT POPE
& JASON BRENNAN

HACHETTE
BOOKS
IRELAND

First published in 2018 by Hachette Books Ireland

Copyright © Brent Pope and Jason Brennan

The right of Brent Pope and Jason Brennan to be identified as the Authors of the Work has been asserted by them in accordance with the Copyright, Designs and Patents Act 1988.

All rights reserved. No part of this publication may be reproduced, stored in a retrieval system, or transmitted, in any form or by any means without the prior written permission of the publisher, nor be otherwise circulated in any form of binding or cover other than that in which it is published and without a similar condition being imposed on the subsequent purchaser.

Cataloguing in Publication Data is available from the British Library.

ISBN 9 781 47366 7037

Typeset in Cambria by redrattledesign.com
Printed and bound in Great Britain by Clays Ltd, St Ives plc.

PAC Ego State Model, from *Transactional Analysis in Psychotherapy* by Eric Berne, used with permission of the author's estate
Excerpt from *Coach Wooden's Pyramid of Success* by John Wooden and Jay Carty. 2005. Published by Revell, a division of Baker Publishing Group. Used by permission of publisher.

Hachette Books Ireland policy is to use papers that are natural, renewable and recyclable products and made from wood grown in sustainable forests. The logging and manufacturing processes are expected to conform to the environmental regulations of the country of origin.

Hachette Books Ireland
8 Castlecourt Centre
Castleknock
Dublin 15, Ireland

A division of Hachette UK Ltd.
Carmelite House
50 Victoria Embankment
London EC4Y 0DZ

www.hachettebooksireland.ie

Laois County Library
Leabharlann Chontae Laoise
Acc. No. 18/3439
Class No. 302.14
Inv. No. 14626

This book is dedicated to the wonderful winners in my life who continue to make me more successful each and every day – Vanessa, Ella and Killian.

JB

To my brother Mark.

And to all the brave people who have experienced mental health issues in their lives, yet chose to push through the stigma and barriers and make their lives as fulfilling and enjoyable as they can. Your weakness is your strength.

BP

Contents

List of Interviewees

Seán Óg Ó hAilpín
Beauden Barrett
Tim Bateman
Suzie Bates
Chris Boyd
Bernard Brogan
Zinzan Brooke
Ollie Campbell
Dan Carter
Eamonn Coghlan
Dane Coles
Lar Corbett
Victor Costello
Ken Doherty
Damien Duff
Bernard Dunne
David Gillick
Shane Horgan
Sir A.P. McCoy
Lieutenant Colonel Rian McKinstry
Jenny Murphy
Paul and Gary O'Donovan
Ronan O'Gara
Derval O'Rourke
Conor O'Shea
Eddie O'Sullivan
Sonia O'Sullivan
Gary O'Toole
John Plumtree
Alan Quinlan
Dean Rock
Tania Rosser
Richie Sadlier
Ben Sigmund
Nehe Milner-Skudder
Conrad Smith
Haidee Tiffen
Victor Vito

'I had already started to experience the power of the mind in sport'

Brent Pope

Prologue

When I was about four years old, I was told by my father that I would be appearing for the local Marist under-fives team the following Saturday morning. This was to be the beginning of my lifelong journey as a rugby player, coach and commentator.

Throughout that week I kept imagining what the match was going to be like; I was so excited that I hardly slept a wink. The days went by until the morning when I got up early, put on my bright green jersey, white shorts and green socks, and eagerly awaited my father in the kitchen. After a while, there was still no sign of him, so I went down the hallway and knocked on my parents' bedroom door, quietly asking when would we be leaving for the game. My father's reply came back quickly, in a rather drowsy and, I suspect, slightly annoyed murmur: 'Brent, for God's sake go back to bed – it's only Thursday!'

What I didn't realise then was that I had already started to experience the power of the mind in sport. In my own way, and as a very young child, I had already begun using the mental skill of *visualisation*, repeatedly imagining the game in my head long before I actually played it. Years later, as a teenager, I would use this technique again, this time in a more targeted way, going through the motions of scoring the winning try in our back garden, or repeatedly making the game-changing tackle on an old sawdust-filled tackle bag hanging from a tree.

I vividly remember too how, at 12 years old, I crept through a small hole in a fence in the local showgrounds to watch the Lions team of 1974 play in Ashburton, the small rural township in New Zealand where I grew up. I marvelled at the skills of Ireland's Mike Gibson, and of the blond-haired English winger David Duckham; I was spellbound by the antics of the mercurial Welsh wizard Barry John. I then went home and tried in my own small way to emulate these heroes – side-stepping all around the perimeter of our garden; or fighting with my brother Mark for possession of a rolled-up sock in hallway rugby contests, where the try-line was the door at the other end of a long passageway.

Even later, when I became a representative player, I continued to use similar self-invented strategies, which today would be recognised as mental skills techniques. I visualised myself winning matches; pulling on the famous black jersey of the All Blacks; being the very best that I could be. I would also write down, and revise, my goals for practice and performance, and check in with them every day – was I any closer to achieving my targets; how could I be a better player – not just physically, but mentally; what did I need to do to have the competitive edge on the next player in my position.

I was fortunate to meet Jason a few years ago and was immediately intrigued by how he was working as a mental skills coach with a number of All Black greats, helping them improve their game. It fascinated me that these already great players kept coming back for more: they had a thirst for more knowledge about mental skills and how these could give them a greater advantage. Jason could not tell them how much to train in the gym or on the paddock, or what that physical training should consist of – but what he did give them was a better way to train their minds, a better way to think about success and failure, disappointment, setbacks, focus and long-term goals. A better way of using an arsenal of mental skills to consistently enhance their performance on the field, become more accomplished athletes and more effective teammates.

Even though I received virtually no formal training in mental skills during my time as a professional rugby player, all my life I have known instinctively that the mind drives the body forward, and not the other way around. Two sportsmen may be of roughly equal size, aerobic capacity and physical compatibility – yet one will succeed where the other fails and carry the day when the other gives way. I quickly realised that the difference was down to whoever had the stronger mindset, the more steadfast will to succeed, the greater ability to push themselves beyond physical pain and psychological barriers. It was down to whoever was mentally tougher.

One of the important questions we will explore in this book is how the mindsets of those who are successful are different from the rest – in sports, in business or simply in life generally. Is it the capacity to stay calm during periods of adversity or pressure; is it the resolve to set yourself ever-higher targets or standards for performance? Is it the ability to channel all the psychological resources you have so as to influence the outcome from the inside and become supremely successful?

No two athletes, musicians or business people are ever the same, and there is no single, easy psychological formula for success that will work for everyone. However, what is certain is that we can draw knowledge and know-how from athletes, and key players in other walks of life, who have succeeded on their own terms. We can listen to their experiences and learn from the techniques and strategies they have found to be of most use in specific situations, and in general ways too. We can then create our own formula for success; our own winning strategies in our sporting, business and personal lives.

In the interviews Jason and I carried out with high-profile athletes and sportspeople – Sonia O'Sullivan, Seán Óg Ó hAilpín, Ronan O'Gara, Dan Carter, Sir A.P. McCoy, Damien Duff, Conrad Smith and Zinzan Brooke to name but a few – we probe some of what makes them tick. We seek to understand how they used, and continue to use, mental skills to overcome obstacles and achieve excellence, and become the elite sportspeople that they are today. While we have sought insights and wisdom from the very best in the world of sport – those who are literally at the top of their game – this learning and knowledge will not just be of interest to the elite athlete or competitor: it will also be of value to anyone in any area of endeavour who dreams bigger, who wants to push the boundaries of achievement, of what is possible.

The very best rugby players I played with over the years, from international greats to ambitious club players, have always had that extra something – that supreme mental fortitude. Did they always succeed? Of course not, and in an important chapter later in this book we talk about how it feels to fail or to lose hope or confidence – the down days – and how best to cope with them. We also look at how to overcome mental blocks, so that we can move forward and enable ourselves to be the best we can.

It goes without saying that, even if you have all the physical and psychological attributes necessary for success, whether in sport or life generally, elements like luck and injury can still play a huge part in how far you can go. This is exactly what happened to me when my biggest sporting opportunity came – last-minute injury meant that I missed my chance of selection for the mighty All Black team, just a few days out from the start of the 1987 rugby World Cup.

As I will recount later in this book, that disappointment would come back to haunt me with a vengeance, uncovering some mental health difficulties I hadn't previously been aware of, and becoming just another factor that would lead me to many moments of despair and depression. Following that injury, my biggest and most urgent priority was to simply get my head right, to achieve enough balance and stability to be able to function in everyday life. It was no longer about how to cultivate a winning rugby mindset, but about basic survival, as I fell victim to anxiety and panic attacks and my mind gave itself over to thoughts of failure. At my lowest points, I even questioned the value of being alive at all.

And so, in these pages, we will hear from sporting stars about their experiences of mental health and how they dealt with issues such as loss, grief and disappointment. Jason will be sharing some good advice and practical techniques and strategies for dealing with more serious issues, such as depression and anxiety. It is a testament to a new generation of understanding and empathy that waiting rooms, which ten years ago would have failed to attract a single person, are now full of those who want to know more about the mind and its ability to change, recover and grow throughout life.

I believe that everyone, regardless of their ability and even their level of excellence, has an innate desire to grow. This thirst for self-realisation and development, which goes beyond our instinct for simple survival, can drive us to be better people and to lead fuller lives. Jason will explore this drive in greater depth, looking at how we can release the energy and motivation it can generate to fulfil our full potential. This book is about how best to achieve results, whether you are seeking to maximise your abilities and talents as a sportsperson or in another professional field, or simply want to lead a more fulfilled life generally.

Jason and I did not want this book to read like rocket science. Our vision was that it should be a mix of practical techniques and useful strategies, accompanied by real-life sporting stories demonstrating how mental skills can really work. A helpful book that any young sports player, indeed any young person, could pick up and get something out of; a book that would also appeal to seasoned athletes, or in fact those seeking success in any area of life; a guide that would provide valuable pointers to all of us to enable learning and growth, and help us get more out of our chosen pursuits, and life in general.

Brent Pope – sports analyst, mental health advocate and entrepreneur, January 2018

Introduction

The top sportspeople, coaches and leaders Brent and I interviewed for this book have been incredibly generous in sharing their varied insights and experiences. Over and above this, and along with Brent's own deeply courageous contributions, many of the strategies, skills and learnings shared in this book are the result of my years of experience both as a mental skills coach for high-level athletes and as a practising psychotherapist. I have been lucky enough to be able to spend time in the company of some great sportspeople, as well as clients, who have shown great strength of character in seeking support and guidance at times in their lives when they were feeling low, afraid, lost and distressed.

Mental skills are not just for the elite, and not just for sportspeople either. This book is about bringing what works so well in sports, and what works so well in the therapy room, into other areas of life and achievement. Many of the techniques I use as a mental skills coach – including some of those I personally developed – I first encountered as a psychotherapist. Techniques that were designed to help clients to better manage themselves in the moment, to cope more easily with their overwhelming feelings and thoughts, and to better deal with extreme levels of stress and the fallout of emotional trauma.

One of the major motivations Brent and I had in putting together this book came from our awareness of there being a need for some accessible, user-friendly and holistically based mental skills training in many contexts. From my experiences of having worked with players and teams from a variety of sporting disciplines and at all levels – amateur players starting off, professional athletes at the height of their achievements and players reaching the end of their careers – it has become obvious that there is still little grounding in basic mental skills techniques and strategies on offer. Even in the highly successful sporting outfits where the mental aspect of performance is regarded as a priority, the corresponding level of investment, when compared to other aspects of the training on offer, still falls very short. One of our hopes is that this book will go some way towards bridging this gap in practice.

During my time as a mental skills coach in New Zealand, I worked with, among others, such rugby teams as the Wellington Hurricanes and the Wellington Lions, the New Zealand White Ferns cricket team and the Wellington Phoenix soccer team. Sadly, while in New Zealand, I witnessed a number of fine young athletes at the height of their athletic talents and sporting careers fall in a very spectacular and public way, often finding themselves decimated by drugs, gambling, physical violence or risky sexual behaviour, and suffering the consequences in the form of criminal charges, major depression, panic disorders and even, tragically, suicide.

Introduction

Today, young men and women are entering the world of professional sport at an ever-younger age, as global sporting franchises look to recruit fresh talent to take the first steps on the road to sporting superstardom. The result is that young, inexperienced players are faced with greater expectations, more pressure and tougher competition than previous generations had to cope with, along with potentially greater early success and the spoils that go with that in the form of money, celebrity and excess. In 2017, for example, footballer Neymar da Silva Santos Júnior was signed by Paris Saint-Germain for €222 million – the biggest transfer fee in football history. Neymar was 25 years old.

Along with all the other pressures, the exponential growth of the use of technology in recent years has created a whole new set of demands on young sportspeople. Now players are routinely expected to revisit their most recent performances on iPads and tablets; after each game, they are instantly sent footage and breakdowns of their performance stats to review and learn from, enabling them to instigate immediate improvements to their future play. One day they may wear glasses and headsets for virtual reality reconstructions aimed at putting them right back into the replaying of their actions, allowing them to physically re-enact what they did and what they should have done.

While this use of technology is par for the course these days, and indeed fantastically useful in helping to evolve the way sports are coached and skills are trained, for the player it also means a lot more screen time and self-analysis, and with that, more psychological and emotional stimulus than ever before. In most sports, multimedia and social media are now also a major part of the territory. The use of this kind of technology can be extremely effective in enhancing a player's or team's profile; on the other side of the coin, however, social media has brought with it the pressure of 24/7 public scrutiny of the private lives of high-profile players and an expectation of constant availability for their fans.

Outside of sport, advances in technology have meant that young people, children included, are also having to deal with many more relentlessly stimulating stressors than previous generations. All of us, in fact, find ourselves subject to far greater levels of visual and auditory stimulation than ever before, in all aspects of our lives. Huge numbers spend many hours of their free time scrolling through Facebook, Twitter, LinkedIn, Snapchat and so on.

Today, our children are experiencing much of their world through screens; and in doing so, they are increasingly removing themselves from living life at first-hand. The same applies to adults – we only have to look at how people experience concerts and live music events now: not directly but indirectly, through their phones, removing themselves from the in-the-moment emotional and sensory experience. In the process, they are undoubtedly losing something of the quality of the real experience – and indeed of themselves as people.

This attachment to technology is also an inevitable feature of the business world today. The multiple use of technology is outpacing our ability to understand and assimilate the continuous stream of new information now bombarding our brains. The result is that the brain is often left over-stimulated, overloaded with information and with an uncomfortable sense of being technologically and psychologically dependent or left behind. I have worked with many clients who are struggling with pace overload and 'change fatigue'. A very common experience in business environments these days is 'email saturation', where our brains do not yet know how to cope with all of the information and demands for our attention coming from so many different sources.

In all of the above, the role of mental skills and the use of psychological strategies is today more valuable and necessary than ever in helping our bodies, our minds and our emotions deal with all the new challenges technology has brought with it.

In my work as a registered psychotherapist, I have spent much valued time sitting with, listening to and connecting with people, who came to me at times of great distress in their lives – when they were brave enough to seek external help. In the course of the therapeutic journey undertaken with each one, we sought together to bring deeper meaning to these painful life experiences, helping to heal the hurt and to unlock what lay at the heart of the issues some of these individuals had been struggling with over many years. As a result of this process, many clients experienced what they often described as a 'freeing up' in themselves, which in turn enabled them to make key decisions in their lives and paved the way to greater fulfilment in their relationships, greater achievements in their professions and a greater degree of contentment in their lives in general. I have also experienced this 'freeing up' countless times in my work with athletes, as we used mental skills techniques to help them to quickly unlock their talent and potential, or to enable them to regain their abilities and self-belief and get back on track after a challenging time.

Like Brent, I have a firm belief in the innate desire to grow and develop which lies in all of us as human beings. I have seen for myself the contribution that mental strategies and techniques and greater *self-awareness* can make in this area, helping athletes, high performers and indeed anyone in any field get closer to realising their true potential. Our hope is that the great insights of those we interviewed for this book, as well as some of the personal stories that Brent and I will share, will help connect the science with the real-life experiences, sporting and otherwise.

Here we have tried to avoid too much theory, and instead worked to make each chapter and the explanation of the techniques and processes as practical as possible. Our hope is that anyone will be able to pick up this book, look up the topic or exercise which interests them most and learn something they can quickly and easily implement in their regular routine. The invitation is for you, the reader, to work on yourself too – not just to passively read, but to actively engage and learn more about yourself and what you may be capable of achieving.

Jason Brennan – mental skills coach and psychotherapist, January 2018.

Authors' Note

Although a lot in these pages will help you in winning a race, the act of reading this book is not a race! You don't need to rush it. You don't need to try everything all at once, neither should you immediately say *no* to something that you think you may have tried before and given up on. In getting to know yourself more, which this book will give you the opportunity to do, it's important to *take your time*.

Later in this book Brent talks about the importance of getting out of your comfort zone. We invite you to start doing this here. If something feels uncomfortable at first, this means you are trying something different. Or perhaps that you are trying some familiar things, but in a different way. Allow the experience to settle in your mind and body – get used to it. Don't worry about 'getting it right', it's not about that. It's about acquiring a new skill; learning a new behaviour; adding a new element to your routine. Review it, see the results you are getting. Take the opportunity to learn, grow and push your own boundaries. This is where the growth really happens.

To help you slow down as you read this book, we have placed the above symbol at certain key points in the text to act as a reminder to pause, take a break and have a think about what you have just read. This in itself embodies the very valuable mental skill of *active reflection*, which means taking the time to assimilate experiences and think about what we can learn from them.

The symbol is a Celtic knot. One interpretation of its meaning is that the three corners of the triangle represent the mind, body and spirit, which are interconnected at all times and potentially the source of a seamless and boundless flow of energy. In this context, the circle in the middle, where the mind, body and spirit elements overlap, represents your *personal life experience*: all the unique events and circumstances that bind your life together and have made you who you are today; the individual unique journey that has brought you to where you are now. Brent and I chose this symbol because it has resonance for us both, in its association with the Gaelic heritage of Ireland, the country of my birth and Brent's adopted homeland.

However, you don't have to take on board the deeper significance of the symbol to be able to benefit from it as you read this book. Whenever it appears on the page, simply hit 'pause' and stop reading. Put the book down and take some time to reflect on what you have just read. If it relates to a question you have been asked, simply stop, think about that question and see what comes up for you. Write down whatever occurs to you; if you can, get it down on paper or in your mobile phone notes – or even as a text to yourself. If there is no specific question, simply take some time to think about what you have just read. How does it relate to you and your experience? If anything interesting or surprising occurs to you, make a mental note of it or jot it down somewhere.

In doing this, you will be familiarising yourself more and more with one of the most important mental skills of all – the process of *active reflection*. In a fast-paced, ever-changing world, it is one of the most neglected practices these days, but one of the most valuable. So, even as you begin to read this book, your mental skills journey has already begun!

PART ONE

Steps to Success

ONE
What Are Mental Skills?

'To help me get the best out of my performance, I would always reduce how big the task was in my mind. Instead of thinking about how enormous it was, I stayed in the present moment and focused on what I could control'

Derval O'Rourke

Mental Skills aren't about shutting yourself off in a room and trying to focus for hours and hours. For me, it is just about having ways of dealing with pressure points in games, being mentally prepared and ready for when they come. Having a few strategies and techniques to call on helped me be more consistent later in my career.

Victor Vito – former All Black flanker with 33 caps; 100 games for the Hurricanes

My coach at that time didn't want us talking to psychologists. It's my single biggest regret. That I didn't have a psychologist type, who could have realised that I was beginning to get too obsessed with the whole sport, and that I had no outlet.

Gary O'Toole – retired Olympic swimmer (represented Ireland at Seoul and Barcelona) and swimming commentator; practising orthopaedic surgeon

Brent

Years ago, a professional golfing coach told me a story which always comes to mind in any discussion about mental skills. He'd noticed that a young, inexperienced golfer he was coaching at the time had a habit, when playing anywhere near a water trap, of reaching into his bag to get the oldest, most cracked ball he could find.

The next time it happened, the coach asked the young player why he was doing this. The answer came without hesitation: 'It's a water trap – I don't want to waste a brand new ball!' You can probably guess what happened next, when the guy hit the ball. Yes – he put it exactly where he worried he would: in the water!

His mind had already said, 'If that's where you think this ball will go, then I'll make sure I take it there.' The body then followed the mind. His swing became tight due to his nervousness around the water; instead of looking in a positive way beyond or beside the trap, to where he needed the ball to land, all of his focus was on the very place he wanted to avoid – the water. So it's hardly a surprise that this is exactly where the ball landed. 'The body flows to where the mind goes,' as they say.

It's a simple story, but for me it perfectly captures the importance of the mental aspect of any performance situation; it's a powerful illustration of the huge effect the mind can have on the body, and what happens when mind and body are not properly aligned. Quite often sportspeople who find themselves outside of their normal comfort zones cannot perform. Why? Because their minds want to bring them back to a place where they are used to feeling in control. You can just about bet on the fact that an inexperienced athlete who finds themselves unexpectedly leading a race or a big tennis match, or ahead on the final day of a prestigious golf tournament, will end up losing. This is because the mind is saying, often subconsciously, 'I don't feel good with all this pressure; I'm not used to it – so let me take over and put us back to where we feel comfortable again.'

Rising Irish golfing star Paul Dunne first came to prominence at the 2015 Open Championship where, at just 22 years of age and playing as an amateur, he was sensationally tied for the lead after three rounds. Speaking at the time about going into the last round as joint leader, he admitted, 'It's going to be a new feeling for me. I'll be out of my comfort zone.' Despite nerves very understandably undermining his chances of immortality on this particular occasion, Dunne approached this unanticipated challenge with the perfect winning mindset: 'By the end of this week, I'm going to be a much better player than I was at the start of the week . . .' One of the secrets of consistent success is to constantly step out of your comfort zone – and having the right mindset and mental skills at your disposal are what enable us to do this.

In November 2013, the Ireland rugby team were leading the All Blacks in Dublin's Aviva stadium as the final moments of the game approached. It looked like a historic victory was within reach for the Irish – but then they gave their rivals one last chance. The All Blacks of course seized the opportunity and scored, defeating Ireland within the last few minutes of play. Why did this happen? Well, the Irish found themselves out of their usual comfort zone against the All Blacks. In some regards, they believed they had done enough to win and against another team they probably had done enough. Even if one Ireland player had stepped up and deliberately slowed the play down – yes, he might have given away a penalty, even a yellow card for a deliberate foul – but this could have still given the Irish team enough time to get better organised defensively. But it didn't happen, because the Irish had never been in that position against the New Zealanders before. The All Blacks on the other hand had won plenty of games in the last few minutes of play, and they knew what they had to do: just maintain possession of the ball, and let Ireland panic. I remember asking some of the All Blacks after the match what their captain Ritchie McCaw had said to them when it looked as if they may lose. He had said, 'Ireland will give us one more chance, you must be ready to take it.' They did.

After this huge disappointment for Ireland, their coach Joe Schmidt established a training routine where he would push the team really hard with a couple of minutes of ball retention skills practice at the end of every session. He decided to do this because that was exactly the time it took for the All Blacks to win – two to three minutes at the end of the game, when the Irish team had switched off and allowed themselves to get tired. In this way, Schmidt was teaching his players that if they were ever in the same situation again, they would know not to make the same mistakes. The next time the two teams met, in Chicago in 2016, Ireland famously beat the All Blacks for the first time in more than a century. It seems unlikely to be just a coincidence. Schmidt clearly recognised the value of continually reaching beyond established comfort zones and thereby creating a fresh, success-oriented mindset.

DEFINING MENTAL SKILLS

> To help me get the best out of my performance, I would always reduce how big the task was in my mind. Instead of thinking about how enormous it was, I stayed in the present moment and focused on what I could control. I would identify the factors that I could control to help my performance, like my warm up routine. I would think about the factors I could not control, which I then tried to block out. My competitors, for example. I always tried to keep things very simple and stuck to my messaging. I had one or two things to concentrate on.
>
> *Derval O'Rourke – former sprint hurdles athlete in the 60 and 100 metres hurdles, Irish national record holder in both events*

Throughout this book you will hear the many athletes we interviewed – like New Zealand's Victor Vito and Ireland's Gary O'Toole or Derval O Rourke, above – talk about 'mental skills', as they share with us the preferred techniques and strategies that have helped them handle all aspects of competition. Their insights will cover such areas as pressure, mistakes, winning, losing, focus, concentration, relaxation, setbacks, success, media attention and many other challenging experiences which are part and parcel of the world of high-performance sports.

So, what are mental skills? As the name implies, they are simply skills for the mind, skills to help us raise our mental game for performance. They can all be learned and actively developed to enable our minds to work better with our bodies, especially in relation to physical performance. In today's demanding sporting environment, the learning and development of such psychological abilities and aptitudes is now regarded as an essential element in achieving consistently high standards of performance.

As we will show in this book, these techniques, skills and aptitudes are transferable to many other contexts, and will help improve performance in business, in the arts, in our personal lives and within important relationships. Other benefits include the achievement of more consistent long-term success and a greater sense of personal fulfilment and satisfaction. Mental skills work to improve not just our performance but our wellbeing too.

The key mental skills I use on a day-to-day basis dealing with teams and professional sportspeople are ones that people can easily apply to everyday life and, as you work through the book, I'll go into these in more detail: how they can be applied and how you can train your mind to be able to react and deal better with situations – and indeed life. Even something as simple as listening to music can be applied as a mental skill once mental awareness of the process is present. Of course, there are a lot more mental skills to be explored than those covered in this book. In my work as a mental skills coach and psychotherapist, I have identified the different skills and processes that can be learned, practised and developed in order to help with performance. We will look at some of these core skills in the chapters ahead. You'll also find them explained in more detail in the Glossary of Mental Skills at the end of the book, along with the other mental skills not specifically covered in this volume.

In general terms, mental skills fall into two broad categories:

1. practical techniques and strategies
2. psychological qualities and capacities that can be acquired through a process-based approach. Process-based simply means having a familiar process to go to and repeat each time.

Practical techniques, for example, include *goal-setting, visualisation* and the use of *imagery, grounding* and *centring, reframing* and *mindful meditation, encouraging self-talk, anchoring* and *critical-moment focus strategies.* Examples of process-based capacities include *progressive thinking,* ongoing *positive mental attitude, intrinsic motivation, optimistic thinking, mental resilience, high self-esteem, emotional fluency* and *potentialising.*

> Potentialising is making a decision to do something that will release energy to grow a person's experience, furthering their abilities and increasing knowledge of their performance - what they can actually achieve.

When you are starting off, learning and practising three to five of the core mental skills is plenty, and already enough to help you achieve greater success. (Of course, you can add to your repertoire at any time.) Such skills, when routinely practised, have the effect over time of rewiring the neural pathways of our brains, thereby working to enhance our self-confidence, self-esteem, powers of focus and concentration, and our physical mastery of our sport or other areas of expertise. They will also help to reduce the prevalence of negative thought patterns, tendencies towards self-doubt, low self-esteem and other undermining modes of thinking.

When delivering a mental skills programme in a sporting context, I find it simplest to break the range of techniques, processes and strategies into a further four categories – and for the purposes of this book, we will do the same, in a very general way. These categories relate to the four stages of performance.

The Four Stages of Performance

1. The long-term preparation for performance
2. Immediate, pre-performance preparation
3. Actual performance on 'match day'
4. Post-performance assessment and evaluation

Or, in other words: daily or regular training and practice; what you can do just before a big game or match; what you can do during the game; and what will help after the performance is over.

While of course some of the key mental skills will work across the board at all stages of performance, many are more likely to be used during specific stages. For example, skills like *goal-setting* and *contracting* will help athletes in their ongoing, long-term preparation and training, and in establishing their long-term aims and ambitions. As will techniques such as *active reflection* and processes such as having a *positive mindset, potentialising* and the development of *mental resilience*.

In the immediate, pre-performance phase, skills such as *grounding*, *centring* and *meditation* will enable sportspeople to manage more effectively their thoughts, their feelings and their physical responses to anxiety and nerves, giving them better control over themselves and their bodies. Meanwhile, skills such as *goal-setting* and *visualisation* will help them to focus on what specifically they want to achieve from the upcoming performance.

During performance itself, drawing on such techniques as using *trigger words, controlled breathing, anchoring, centring* and *performance enhancing thoughts* will enhance your chances of success moment by moment. These mental skills help by: allowing you to become more present during the heat of competition; enabling you to recognise and shut down thoughts that are negative and potentially detrimental to performance; allowing you to filter out external distractions, such as noise from the crowd, or attention – positive and negative – from fans or media.

And finally, following performance, techniques such as *reframing* and *perspective thinking,* or capacities such as *active reflection* and *optimistic thinking,* and strategies such as *connecting* with important others will help a sportsperson better review what their strengths and weaknesses were during a game. These will also enable someone to more effectively manage the emotional fallout of mistakes and failures – and even of success, which can sometimes feel overwhelming too, as we will see in later chapters.

As both Brent and I have already said, almost all of the mental skills we will take you through in this book can equally be used in non-sporting contexts, including business, the arts, leisure activities and interpersonal relationships. Broadly speaking, our experience of any activity which entails an element of performance at its core can be enhanced by the use of mental skills, so equally the mental skills listed above such as *anchoring, optimistic thinking* and so on can just as easily be applied in any challenging situation you find yourself, such as:

- Giving a business or classroom presentation
- Testifying in court
- Performing as a solo instrumentalist with a symphony orchestra
- Taking a driving test
- Auditioning for a role in a drama production
- Giving a best man's speech at a wedding
- Doing a live radio interview
- Cooking a meal for 20 people for an important family occasion
- Doing an important job interview
- Participating in a military or police operation
- Making an important sales call
- Giving a eulogy

In business, mental skills will help you improve your presentation skills, facilitate meetings with more ease, evolve a more effective leadership style, improve team dynamics and develop more productive relationships across the board – all with the net result of achieving better outcomes.

In relationships and parenting, mental skills will help you reduce stress reactions and respond in more measured ways, cultivate mindful interactions, develop deeper compassion and enjoy a deeper sense of connection with the important people in your life. You will be more able to slow things down, so that you have more space to reflect on what you are saying and can better assess whether what you are communicating is actually what you want to say.

By giving us greater *self-awareness* and more control over our thoughts, feelings and actions, using mental skills in all these contexts will help not only in performance situations, but will also improve our quality of life as a whole and the degree of satisfaction we feel in whatever we do and in how we interact with others.

Once you have built up a range of techniques and strategies, you will have them readily available at any time and in any situation imaginable. From a high-pressure finals match or an important speech, to the more mundane challenges of regular training sessions on a cold and wet winter's day or getting the kids ready and out the door quickly on a dark and chilly weekday morning, these skills will be with you – your own powerhouse of fuel whenever you most need to lift your energy and move forward.

With the demanding pace of business and life these days, having these skills in our armoury could be regarded as not only useful, but even essential in allowing us to cope – and indeed to grow – through the pressure to perform, strive and succeed.

> What I'd say to young players is just to recognise the importance of [mental skills]. And one thing I learnt, and a lot of people outside of sport don't probably realise, is that [they are] skills and so can be developed. It's not just something you're born with. Take handling pressure. It's not like some people can

handle pressure and some people can't. It's a skill, and you . . . can get better at it over time. You just have to invest time in it and recognise that everyone feels pressure at different times in a game and there are techniques to deal with it. You've just got to find the ones that suit you.

Conrad Smith – professional rugby player, former All Black centre with 94 caps; 126 games for the Hurricanes; qualified lawyer

I think it is the cog that you need to play well. Mental skills are very much overlooked a lot of the time. You've got a lot of physical attributes you bring to the game, that you work with your coaches on. But if you're not right upstairs, in terms of how you are approaching the game and how you are preparing for matches, you're already on the back foot. In professional sport, the pressure just mounts mentally. How prepared you are for this pretty much determines how far you are going to go in the game.

Victor Vito – professional rugby player, former All Black flanker with 33 caps; 100 games for the Hurricanes

TWO

The Mental Skills We Need to Win: in Sport, Business, Life

'The best performers are almost never the most talented, but they have an internal reason for succeeding'

Eddie O'Sullivan

Brent

I recall hearing not so long ago a radio interview with CJ Stander, the South African rugby player who plays for Munster, Ireland, as well as for the Irish and British Lions in 2017. At one point he was asked about the time, earlier in his career, when he was on the verge of having to either convert to hooker or give up his dreams of being a professional rugby player altogether. Did he think that if he had decided to go back to his parents' 500-acre farm in George on the Western Cape he would have enjoyed it?

Stander replied that while the prospect of returning home to the farm and working alongside his father was a fantastic option, he could never have forgiven himself for not going to the 'ends of the earth' to see how far his rugby talents would take him. If he had given up rugby at that point, it would be the one regret he would have always had. So with his parents' support and a contact from Munster rugby, he moved to Ireland to give rugby his best and possibly last shot – the rest is history. Stander is respected and has been well received as an adopted Irish sportsperson, even going so far as to learn Ireland's national anthem before his first cap for his adopted country.

For Stander, the picture in his mind was always there – his vision of playing international rugby, which he'd had since his early childhood. He was not going to stop at the first hurdle.

In November 2016, Stander scored a try in Ireland's historic win against the All Blacks, the first such win for Ireland in 111 years of competitive rugby. It was one of the great moments in the annals of Irish sport and, for the young South African, a remarkable high point in a career that was so close to being given up altogether just a few years earlier. Now Stander holds the winning picture – which was once merely a long-held dream – and all because he had the mental skillset and determination to make his dream a reality.

Ambitions in rugby don't come much bigger or better than this, and there are thousands of Standers in this world in so many different sports. The ones who succeed are those that persevere and just won't give up. In my own sporting career, I was always personally inspired by the final lines of Rudyard Kipling's poem, 'If—':

If you can fill the unforgiving minute
With sixty seconds' worth of distance run,
Yours is the Earth and everything that's in it . . .

These lines summed up for me my own realisation that, if I did everything within my power to give myself the best possible chance of success, then later in life I would be able to sleep soundly, knowing that I had left no stone unturned in trying to realise my dream. Life can still be a roll of the dice, but being mentally prepared to, as Kipling says, give it the full 60 seconds' run, can make a world of difference not only in terms of tangible results, but also to your own sense of achievement.

This book is about winning – in sports; in business; in whichever type of activity you choose to excel in; in life itself. In the course of these early chapters, we will be looking at what attributes and qualities are key to achieving success in almost any field, and what separates consistently high achievers from those who do not consistently perform so well. We will also see how we can foster and develop these behaviours and approaches in ourselves, using a broad range of the mental skills the world's top sportspeople draw on to gain the competitive edge. It's also worth noting that throughout this book we look at the definition of winning from a personal perspective and how that will mean different things for different people – it's not always about which team triumphs on the day, or who gets gold. Winning, as you will read, means many things.

THE FOUR D'S

In my work as a mental skills coach, having spent a lot of time working with and observing high-performing athletes, I have come up with my own simple model of the four key attributes necessary for success. I call these the Four D's:

1. Drive
2. Direction
3. Discipline
4. Determination

Whenever I take on new clients – individuals or teams – to create a basic mental skills programme, I find that the Four D's make a very useful guide for us to refer back to as we navigate the main areas that anyone wanting to improve their performance needs to consider.

D FOR DRIVE

> The best performers are almost never the most talented, but they have an internal reason for succeeding.
>
> *Eddie O'Sullivan – former head coach of the USA and Ireland national rugby teams*

In Brent's account of CJ Stander's story at the top of this chapter, we can see that one very important contributor to his ultimate success, which kept Stander going through thick and thin, was having a long-held dream which went back to his childhood days. It was this vision – of becoming a top-performing world-class rugby player on the international stage – which gave him the confidence and strength of mind to ignore the advice of his coach in South Africa to give up professional rugby and do something else. It was this same dream that fuelled his determination to push through this discouraging period in his career and find the drive to explore another avenue in his bid for sporting success.

Many of the top sportspeople we interviewed for this book had similar insights to offer about what lay at the heart of their drive for success:

> I think my school-playing days – secondary school – brought the competitive person out in me. That was the first time that I experienced sport at a high level, playing against the best

players from other parts of the country. This stood to me later on in my career for Cork at senior level. At my peak I relished the challenge. I loved matching up against the best players, knowing that if I nullified them, this meant I was doing my part for the team. There were times when I had to play against the biggest names of the sport, and I cherished these challenges. I didn't always succeed, but . . . never making it easy for an opponent was a victory in itself.

Seán Óg Ó hAilpín – former hurler and Gaelic footballer; winner of three All-Ireland hurling titles with Cork

[At 12 years of age], when I saw my fellow Irishman Alex Higgins win the 1982 World Championships, I thought, 'That is my dream!' I dreamt of it from that day onwards. When I got to the final in 1997, one of the things that kept me really calm was that I had dreamt of it for so long. I just saw myself winning it. I saw myself lifting up the cup and giving it a kiss, just like Higgins did, and it gave me a calmness.

Ken Doherty – ex-professional snooker player; snooker commentator; 1997 world snooker champion

Growing up, I was well aware of my dad's success and profile. As a kid, all I ever wanted to be was a Dublin footballer. I wanted to kick frees for Dublin. This was because I loved the sport, and that my dad had done these things.

Dean Rock – Gaelic footballer; winner of four All-Irelands with Dublin

I loved the fact that Dad had made friends for life during his career with Dublin; how he was respected in the community. I wanted that respect. [My brother] Alan helped motivate me as well. I saw him make the Dubs as a 19-year-old, and I wanted that feeling

> too. I wanted to reach the top in my sport, to walk out onto Croke Park on All-Ireland finals day. That's every young player's dream. It took a while. I didn't debut until [I was 24], which is late in the modern game – but having to work so hard made it even sweeter.
>
> *Bernard Brogan – Gaelic footballer; winner of five All-Irelands with Dublin*

What's evident in these testimonies is that each of these competitors had a very clear picture of the ultimate goal they wanted to achieve – the destination, if you like – right from the outset, and often from a very young age, long before they started their sporting careers in earnest. There's a common saying often used in personal development work, which goes like this: **'If you don't know where you're going, any road will get you there.'** It's actually a paraphrased line from Lewis Carroll's *Alice's Adventures in Wonderland*, when Alice asks for directions but says she doesn't know her destination. The point being made is – how can you pick a road to somewhere when you don't really know where you are going? For this reason, one of the first things I ask individual athletes, coaches and teams beginning any kind of mental skills training is to clearly identify what their ultimate goal is, and then to dig a bit deeper and work out *why* they want to achieve this.

While the effort to understand our inner drive takes a little time, it is time very well spent. Once we are clear about our purpose, we will find that anything we do thereafter falls into place more easily and more quickly. When our goals resonate with who we are, our body, mind and emotions all line up to release positive, galvanising energy, and we get things done. This lining up is called *congruency*.

Understanding what you want and why you want it – your own inner drive – requires *self-awareness* and *active reflection* – two cornerstone mental skills that will serve you well at all stages in your quest for success and high performance. The key insights and the rewards they bring can be accessed by simply taking the time to check in with, and listen to, ourselves first – since so many of the answers we seek are already within us.

ACTIVE REFLECTION EXERCISE

This is always best done in a quiet setting, somewhere without too much external noise and where you won't be disturbed – at least for a time anyway. Start with a few deep breaths as you begin to 'zone out' of the external environment and focus your attention inwards. Begin by asking:

- What am I trying to achieve (in sport/business/the chosen activity)?
- Why am I trying to achieve this?
- What will it mean for me to achieve this?
- How much do I really want to put into achieving this?
- What will satisfy me most: to improve slightly; to be much better at this activity; to be my absolute best; to be *the* best at it?

High performance is about stretching ourselves by creating goals that are not easily achievable – the more ambitious goals that will release a greater drive to succeed. The first step to releasing this powerful energy is to bring a picture of what success for us represents into sharper focus. Help your mind see it as clearly as possible. Take your time, this stage is important.

When we are just starting out in a sport or in another undertaking, we don't always know exactly what we are capable of, and so it can be difficult to envisage a very specific – and realistic – endpoint for our efforts. With personal potential, however, starting with ourselves is always the best option. If we can personally maximise the potential of a situation and bring the best of our ability to bear in that moment, then we are activating our drive and moving towards our optimum performance. This is what it means to *potentialise* our energy, and we will be talking more about this later in this book.

Top performers always strive towards bringing out their best at every opportunity – often they will refer to this as 'pushing myself', 'embracing the challenge', 'giving it my best shot'; it's what Brent in the opening to this chapter describes as giving it the 'full 60 seconds' run'. Beyond big-picture goals and long-held dreams, all high achievers share this drive to *potentialise* opportunities, *potentialise* their abilities and try their best. Again, almost without exception, all the top athletes Brent and I interviewed freely admitted to having this trait. Here is what just a few of them said:

> From a young age we always wanted to win, and we would try to never compromise on that. We know that many other people in

the world also want to win, so we always have to try really very hard, or else winning won't be an option.

Paul and Gary O'Donovan – Irish rowers; European gold (2016) and Olympic silver (2016) medal winners

I was always driven and focused. Prepared to go that bit further than the next person to succeed. Even when I broke records, I refocused on breaking them again. If that meant driving all night to win a race, then I would do that. I always set goals and then set about seeing how I could break them.

What makes [retirement] easier is that I never had regrets. I never left anything behind. That's the best thing I can say about my career – no regrets . . . I was never content with losing, I always wanted more. Every day I would ask, how can I do better?

Sir A.P. McCoy – former horse-racing jockey; champion jockey 20 times; knighted for services to horse racing in 2016

I was lucky, I guess – Mum and Dad were grafters, hardworking people, and I just inherited that. I guess it was in my genes – I always just wanted to be the best I could be, and to that end I worked incredibly hard. In fact, even when I was 37 and back playing for Shamrock Rovers, I still wanted to work at being the best player I could be.

Damien Duff – former professional footballer; football coach; 100 caps for the Republic of Ireland

As a kid, I always was quite determined . . . I always had the mental attitude that I am going to give it my all. I didn't like losing; I never liked it and always tried as hard as I could . . . If I got a 40 break, I wanted to get a 50 break the next frame.

Ken Doherty – ex-professional snooker player; snooker commentator; 1997 world snooker champion

So, wanting to do your *best* is a key part of a high-performance mindset and a crucial, easily identifiable element in the drive for success. In the next chapter, we will look at how, as individual performers, we can set about pinning down and further defining what this means – making it more concrete, measurable, and therefore a more attainable mindset.

D FOR DIRECTION

A deeper understanding of what it is we want to achieve and why we want to achieve it will release positive, dynamic energies in the form of excitement, enthusiasm, passion and a sense of purpose, which will strengthen and consolidate our drive to move forward. Having this greater clarity, about where we are going, will also help in terms of 'future proofing' – meaning that during times of hardship, frustration or doubt, it will be easier for us to check in with our long-term dream, or vision for success, re-engage with our direction and keep going with renewed purpose. Keep on track, so to speak.

Once you have your 'big-picture', long-term goal in mind, along with a deeper understanding of why you want to achieve this, it's important to spend time working out *how* you will get there – to set your *direction* and create a detailed roadmap of that path. This will include the practical processes you can put in place to bring it within your reach, and 'milestones' along the way by which you can measure and get a sense of your progress. This is the mental skill of *goal-setting*, which is absolutely key for any kind of consistent, long-term success

– in sport and, indeed, in all other fields of activity. Former rugby player Alan Quinlan spoke to Brent about the huge difference this approach made for him during his time at Munster Rugby:

> I was really intrigued by goal-setting because when I got into Munster, I never really had placed [much] emphasis on that before. I only really started that with my own individual goals, like, 'I want to play for Ireland'. I started writing stuff down and then asked, 'Well, are they attainable?' Breaking them down and starting to think about stuff to work on. And realising 'Well, this one is the hardest one', to be on the British and Irish Lions . . .
>
> When I had that as a goal, I had a process to get there: my attitude, my fitness, and so on. I found goal-setting very helpful to me . . . If we at least set [a] target, then we can start making small steps towards that – it might take a bit of time . . . But you can then measure your success!
>
> *Alan Quinlan – former professional rugby player; 27 caps for Ireland, 212 appearances for Munster; rugby analyst*

We will hear more from Alan in Chapter Four – which looks at how successful teams function – when again he talks about how *goal-setting* at Munster really helped with team confidence and focus.

Irish Olympic athlete Sonia O'Sullivan also gave Brent some fascinating insights into how she used *goal-setting* on a more detailed level, in approaching individual events, to help keep her firmly on course on the road to becoming a champion:

> I used to write a plan before a race, drawing up how I felt I could approach the race and get the best result. Trying to focus on what

> *I* could do, rather than looking at the other athletes and what they might be able to do. I had to think about the process and how I could get the best possible result from each race. Sometimes you lose sight of the step-by-step process and make mistakes, so then you have to go back to the drawing board and work with the basics.
>
> *Sonia O'Sullivan – Irish track and field Olympic silver medal winner; world record holder*

EXERCISE: PRACTICAL GOAL-SETTING

As we have said above, *goal-setting* is essential for all types of performance, and is a key mental skill to develop in helping us to achieve results. Our minds like to be put to work and have achievable goals to focus on and measure. The sense of satisfaction we feel when we work to accomplish these is enriching for our spirits and good for our self-esteem. Here's a simple guide to *goal-setting* which I use in initial mental skills sessions with individual athletes and teams.

First, figure out what you want to achieve and in what ways you want to improve your performance. Create a picture in your mind of what the end result will look like, once it has been achieved, what will be different, what you are looking at and put this down on paper. Try to imagine the feelings associated with this success.

Now, write out as specifically as possible all the steps along the way towards your 'big-picture' goal. In fact, in doing this, you are breaking down the big task you have set yourself into a sequence of mini-goals. These interim goals can be big or small and achievable over varying timeframes – hours, days or months, and so on. Ideally, they should lead into each other – like stepping stones. Each smaller goal, and indeed the end goal itself, needs to fulfil the following 'SMART' criteria to really work:

S	Specific
M	Measurable
A	Achievable
R	Realistic
T	Time-bound

Time-bound means to include timelines as you plot each step of the way towards your ideal end result, if possible noting specific dates and what in concrete terms you want to have achieved by when. Now write down how you will acknowledge the achievement of each step. Having some way of marking and celebrating your smaller success along the way will help to keep you motivated and on message. As you work out how you will track your interim progress, don't forget to plan for setbacks. The key here is not to dwell on what might go wrong, but to anticipate likely obstacles and have a plan in place which you know will help to get you back on track and keep you going forward. We will look in more detail at the importance of planning for setbacks later in this book.

As we have said previously, *goal-setting* is an invaluable skill, not just for sport but for any performance situation, and indeed for life itself. Whether your aims and objectives relate to increased revenue, personal fitness, weight loss, mental health recovery, being a more contented person, happiness or improving the quality of your relationships, the same principle applies – all goals benefit from having a plan to act upon. This key skill is not of course reserved for big, long-term plans or dreams, but used to enhance our general quality of life, time management and daily sense of achievement. Each day we are faced with choices and we can set mini-goals in terms of what we can get done, where we want to be and by what time, what *needs* to get done and the type of energy we bring to these experiences – at work, at home and with our family. This is something many of us do as a matter of course anyway, and so in that sense, we all already have a degree of experience and competence in this area, which we can draw on when looking at bigger life ambitions and aspirations by simply bringing more conscious attention to bear upon them.

A deeper, more holistic approach to *goal-setting* will also include an honest assessment of what factors or attitudes might be getting in the way of achieving our dreams and ambitions – again, the mental skills of *active reflection* and *self-awareness* are invaluable in this context. For many of us, unconscious elements are often working to undermine our efforts, or even to sabotage them. In later chapters we will be looking in depth at the most common ways we can unknowingly undercut our own success.

D FOR DISCIPLINE

Of the four D's, Discipline perhaps adds the greatest long-term value. It is this D that gets us up and out into the cold, the dark, the snow or rain, to go to training, to work, to do the school run, to go to that class, to finish that exam – especially when our minds might try and convince us otherwise. Discipline saves us from ourselves, when our internal *self-talk* tries to persuade us that staying in a warm bed or eating stodgy comfort food or just having a few more beers won't do any harm to ourselves or our training regime or to our efforts to diet or get fitter. Most of us find that we have to exercise discipline with ourselves to some degree as we go about our daily lives, in terms of getting household chores done, answering emails, taking the dog out for a walk, not staying up till the early morning watching TV, so that we aren't too tired to go to work the next day – and so on.

Every day we are faced with multiple choices, whether just going about our daily lives, in business or in our multiple interactions with other people. We have to make decisions about what we are going to do, eat, drink; and how we interact with others. Today more than ever, excess stimulation, multiple distractions and opportunities for consumption are available to us 24 hours a day, seven days a week. In this sense, we are always being offered opportunities to practise discipline and to challenge ourselves, in big and small ways, for our own health and wellbeing.

Not only is being disciplined an essential quality to guard us from self-sabotage and self-destructive behaviours, it is also an absolutely key component when it comes to a high-performance mindset and achieving ambitious, long-term goals and aspirations which require us to push far beyond our comfort zones and into the outer limits of our capacities. Every single top athlete Brent and I spoke to for this book was adamant about the necessity of sheer hard work when it comes to high performance – here's what some of them said:

When I was training in my days in England, I would hardly leave the club . . . Even as a coach today for the under 15s, I'm brutally honest with them – I tell them how hard they will have to work to achieve their dreams, and even [then] that . . . it can all come down to luck and timing too, playing a good game in front of a scout, whatever. In the end, all you can do is work hard . . . it's about work ethic and grounding.

Damien Duff – former professional footballer; football coach; 100 caps for the Republic of Ireland

All the top sportspeople are the hardest workers.

Sir A.P. McCoy – former horse racing jockey; champion jockey 20 times; knighted for services to horse racing in 2016

Yes, [I felt fed up] lots of times. Playing three to five hours every day can be very monotonous. [But] I always knew that if I didn't do it, the other guy will be doing it, and I'm not going to be sharp enough. If I go to tournaments, I will be wasting my time.

Ken Doherty – ex-professional snooker player; snooker commentator; 1997 world snooker champion

Everyone knows that in order to gain mastery over – and continually improve in – a particular skill, repeated practice and preparation are a very big part of the equation. Discipline comes into play when we feel our motivation flagging, when we are fed up of practising or discouraged because our progress is slower than we might have hoped. Discipline is essential in a broader sense throughout a career in high-performance sports, helping athletes to maintain focus and the energy of enthusiasm once the initial excitement of doing well begins to wear off. New Zealand rugby great Conrad

Smith had some insights to offer when I spoke to him about the importance of sustaining focus ('staying switched on') through mental discipline:

> Later on [in your career] you notice it's the mental side of [staying] switched on. Getting up for games – it's easy at the start of your career, but after 50 or 60 games, you sort of lose a little bit of the buzz, which is just natural, [but] you have the mental challenge of preparing for those games. [Keeping switched on is] something that never stops and is massive and I think probably separates good athletes from great sportspeople.
>
> *Conrad Smith – former All Black centre with 94 caps; 126 games for the Hurricanes; qualified lawyer*

The same is true in any area of life, whether it's sports, business, community or personal relationships. Or even when it comes to reading this book! It's often easy to kick off a challenge (or start to read a book) when we are first fired up with enthusiasm – but in terms of any long-term and really worthwhile undertaking, goal or purposeful pursuit, there will come a time when our initial momentum or response to the challenge loses energy, loses its shine and the task becomes harder to stick at. As Conrad says above, this is only natural, and simply part of the process. But being able to keep going anyway, when the road becomes a little steeper, is where discipline comes in.

Discipline is a word we very often associate with the military, where repeated practice and drills are all part of a very structured way of life. The reason discipline is so important here is that, when dealing with life-and-death situations, it is crucial that each individual knows what to do, and that the group as a whole can rely on this when faced with such challenges. Among the crack teams in this field, few are more ambitious, committed and high performing than the SAS – Special Air Service. This is reflected in one of their key values: 'The Pursuit of Excellence'. When I spoke to Lieutenant Colonel Rian McKinstry, the current Director of Leader Development for the New Zealand Defence Force and former SAS commanding officer, he explained the key importance of discipline in everything these elite teams do.

> In a military context, we talk about drills. The aim of a drill is to help a solider become proud, alert, obedient (to training), and [this] provides a basis for teamwork . . . We train a lot! Individual training and collective training. Learning muscle memory and reaction times. Practising, practising and practising. Every time, fine tuning; turning it into a drill. We spend a lot of time training individually. Getting it right individually first, and then as a team. When we go on military exercises, it is all about collectively bringing it all together – the same way a sports team might do on the field.
>
> *Lieutenant Colonel Rian McKinstry – ex-Commanding Officer, New Zealand Special Air Service; Director of Leader Development for the New Zealand Defence Force*

Discipline can of course take many forms, depending on the activity being engaged in and the area in which we are working to achieve something. Anyone who is involved in any kind of long-term quest for achievement, be that in business, sports, the arts or the sciences, will need to exercise discipline in order to achieve ongoing, sustained success. You might think an international rock music icon would be the last person to recognise the value of discipline – but take a look at this compelling insight from the late David Bowie, which appears in the 2016 documentary *The Man Who Changed the World* (dir. Sonia Anderson), about the importance of maintaining focus in this sense:

'I am very disciplined. Discipline doesn't mean you make sure you have breakfast at 8 o'clock in the morning and you are out of the house at 8.30 a.m. Discipline is that if you conceive something, then you decide whether or not it's worth following through with. If it is worth following through to its logical conclusion and [you decide] to do it, you do it to the BEST of your ability. That's discipline.'

Bowie's creativity, talent for reinvention and ground-breaking output in a career spanning many decades may seem light years away from the world of military special ops – but the capacity for discipline at work in both cases is remarkably similar.

Self-discipline is something that can be learned and improved upon over time with continued practice. One simple way of approaching this is to try to deliberately integrate small ways of being disciplined into our everyday lives. Here are two basic exercises which will help with this – the first of which uses the mental skill of *meditation*.

DAILY DISCIPLINE EXERCISE

Each day we can take a mindful approach to how we want to be, including how we want to start or end our day. A good way of doing this, depending on what our schedule permits, is by simply setting an alarm on our phone to prompt us at regular intervals to stop what we are doing, take a break, slow down and calm our minds. Depending on what you are doing, you could set an alert to go off every hour, or every few hours – or you may want to set aside a short time every morning and evening to take this mental time out. It's a good idea also to set a time limit on how long you want to set aside to focus your mind in this way. Especially when you first begin, allocate just a short time, maybe 5 or 10 minutes. As you continue this daily practice, you will be able to increase the length of time – up to a maximum of, say, 20 minutes.

We can reinforce the effect of this simple practice by creating a *trigger word*. Using *trigger words* is a powerful mental skills technique which enables us to summon up a state of mind or a feeling just by internally repeating a single word or phrase. Creating the association between the word, the feeling and the physical sensations is a matter of repeated practice, until simply saying or thinking the word will trigger the feeling. When working on developing discipline, we can intensify the effect of the trigger word by choosing to use the word 'discipline' itself.

Start by focusing on what you know you are good at and are always doing – yes, breathing! Bring yourself strongly into the present moment by simply acknowledging this, by saying in your mind with each inhalation, 'I am breathing in,' and with each exhalation, 'I am breathing out.'

Take a few minutes to settle your breathing into a calm, steady rhythm; longer breaths are better. Now you can introduce the word 'discipline' into your mind, repeating it internally with each in-breath. If you find your mind wandering, simply bring it gently back to the word 'discipline'.

The more we repeat this simple practice, the more the quality of calm and focus we achieve in these quiet times, which will spill over into the rest of our everyday lives.

If, later, we find ourselves thinking of doing something that will be detrimental to our goals, we can stop such thoughts in their tracks by internally repeating our trigger word, 'discipline'. As a result, we will find that our breathing slows and we will experience the feelings of calm and wellbeing we have come to associate with the word during our time in *meditation*. This makes it easier to walk away calmly from the self-sabotaging situation. Whether our goal is keeping to a healthy diet, a fitness plan, a training regime, or to improve our interactions with others by connecting better, having more compassion or being more positive, this simple daily practice of *meditation* on a trigger word will be invaluable. As well as helping us advance our goals, being able to control unhelpful behaviours by using conscious discipline brings a deep sense of satisfaction in its own right.

COLD SHOWER DISCIPLINE

Although it may sound like a fairly drastic measure, building our discipline and endurance by putting ourselves through a somewhat uncomfortable physical experience can help us to learn how to better control our reactions. This in turn builds the important mental skill of *self-regulation*, which involves being able to manage our immediate physical and emotional responses – essential for high performance of any kind. We will look at the skill of *self-regulation* in more detail in later chapters.

This exercise in discipline involves experiencing the cold. Set yourself the goal of having a cold shower each morning or evening for the next 5 to 10 days. It's kind of like a test, but one you choose to impose on yourself. As you step into the stream of water, don't simply dive in to get it over with quickly – instead, prepare your mind first.

Start by slowing down your breathing, and then take a few moments to breathe deeply, as shown above. Now, repeat to yourself, 'I am greater than the cold' – this will help to prepare and prime your mind, and build your confidence. Next, on an out-breath, slowly walk into the water, continuing to manage your breathing at the point at which your body reacts to the cold.

The more you practise, the easier it gets!

D FOR DETERMINATION

> In players, I first look for the obvious – such as technical ability, focus, drive. But then it's about resilience and what they had to overcome to be here. Their determination: why are they still here? These players are better able to handle pressure situations. They are better able to cope with adverse situations that occur in games and off the field.
>
> *Conor O'Shea – former professional rugby player; 35 caps for Ireland, 127 appearances for London Irish; head coach of the Italian national rugby team*

The final D is Determination – a quality which all high achievers share. Determination is where we stand our ground, show our strength, fight for what we want and believe in, for what we believe we deserve and for what we are able to achieve. It is an energy many of us experienced a lot as young children – when we could see in our minds something we really wanted; when we refused to give up or give in, but persisted in our efforts to make that thing happen. Stubbornly so, our parents likely thought – but we knew what we wanted and wouldn't stop until we had it.

As adults, we can tap into that same kind of energy, but channel it (perhaps more constructively) to help us achieve more well-considered aims and long-term goals. Like persistence and perseverance, determination is a very powerful attribute. Going back to the story Brent tells about CJ Stander at the opening of this chapter, we can see that it is a trait that this young South African rugby player has in spades, and one which enabled him to block out the discouraging voices. Let's leave the final word on this to the legendary US coach and Basketball Hall of Famer, the late John Wooden. In his ground-breaking book *Coach Wooden's Pyramid of Success: Building Blocks for a Better Life*, he defined the essence of determination as follows: 'It is the ability to stay the course, even when that course is most difficult, and the obstacles seem insurmountable. You do not quit. Be persistent. Be determined. Be tenacious. Be unrelenting. The road to achievement is rocky, hard, and long. Things easily achieved are rarely long-lasting or significant.'[1]

THREE

Winning: What Does It Mean?

'Winning to me is a result of doing a good job'

John Plumtree

Winning to me is a result of doing a good job. There are different types of winning, like players being selected for higher honours. Success is also important to me personally, as it means I am doing a good job and this is important to me, as it is for many other people . . . Winning is also about believing in your processes and not being scared to seek help. Being prepared to change if required, for example, to get that win. To achieve success.

John Plumtree – assistant coach of the Hurricanes (New Zealand); previously worked with the Irish national rugby team and the Sharks (South Africa)

I go out to win every game, but it's not something I think about in each moment . . . It's more about focusing on my performance. If I can do that right, if I can nail each task in the moment, the performance will take care of itself. I love winning, it's the most satisfying thing . . . the icing on the cake . . . I work hard all week, all year to win.

Beauden Barrett – All Black fly-half with 62 caps; plays club rugby with Hurricanes

In 2017 in Sweden, where my family and I were living at the time, the national football association's Council of Representatives took steps to 'ban' the practice of appointing winning teams in all under-13 football leagues – meaning that now it is no longer possible for teams with children up to the age of 12 to become champions in competitions. Surprisingly, perhaps, the main reason for this decision had less to do with the children than with their parents. The purpose of these measures was to curb the prevalence of what the Swedes refer to as *tavlingshets* at young people's football matches. *Tavlingshets* can be translated in this context as 'competitive agitation' – where parents, during games, become too het up about their children's teams winning or losing, leading to an atmosphere of negative, aggressive competitiveness rather than one of healthy, friendly rivalry. At this level of the game in Sweden, as elsewhere, most of the coaches of these teams are themselves parents of one or more of the team members. The Swedish Association's decision was aimed at controlling the negative competitive behaviours in the parent coaches – that is, in the adults, not the children.

I am sure many of us have witnessed the behaviour of certain parents, screaming and shouting instructions, and sometimes even having a pop at the referee, as they stand on the sidelines of their children's sports matches. They are the same people who will overreact to the final scores, with displays of unseemly triumphalism if their child's team wins or anger and frustration if the result is less favourable. Not a great example to be giving to their children, of course – very questionable indeed. In Sweden – as in other countries, no doubt – before this measure was introduced, it wasn't unheard of for parents to be banned from attending their children's games due to their inability to manage themselves as spectators. Clearly lacking the mental skill of *self-regulation*!

A number of people have welcomed the Swedish association's decision – and it will surely help to moderate the atmosphere at children's football events. Yet, to my mind, the measure is a questionable one. What will the long-term consequences be? Who could really be losing out here? What messages will it send to children about winning and losing, and indeed about competition itself? By removing the possibility of winning, will valuable opportunities for providing and receiving constructive feedback be missed?

Professor Carol S. Dweck of Stanford University, one of the world's leading researchers and authors on motivation, writes about 'messages about failure', and the inherent risk today of over-protecting children: 'Children need honest and constructive feedback. If children are "protected" from this, they won't learn well. They will experience advice, coaching, and feedback as negative and undermining. Withholding constructive criticism does not help children's confidence; it harms their future.'[1]

So, simply removing winning and losing from the equation is not necessarily helpful to the children. Neither does it address the real problem – the ill-adjusted attitude of the parents. Behaviour like theirs is usually the result of a historically poor processing of loss and disappointment, coupled with messages around unhealthy competing. In acting in these inappropriate ways, they are not passing on to their children a healthy model of success, but rather an unhelpful model of not knowing how to cope with failure. Loss, failure and making mistakes are all natural, and unavoidable, and

PROFESSOR DWECK'S GROWTH VERSUS FIXED MINDSETS

Also in her book *Mindset: The New Psychology of Success*, Professor Carol Dweck identifies two starkly opposing mindsets that can make the difference between children who seek to achieve their potential and those less likely to do so. Her findings were, she writes, that the most successful and most resilient children, who handled setbacks and failure best, were those who, when faced with not being able to complete a task, responded in a 'shockingly positive way', saying things like, 'I love this challenge', regardless of the prospect of not being able to 'perform' perfectly. These children had a basic understanding that their 'abilities can be developed'. Professor Dweck called this a growth mindset. This was in stark contrast to the children who regarded the possibility of not being able to complete the same task as 'tragic' and 'catastrophic', and who clearly felt themselves to be 'up for judgement'.[2] Noting their tendency to dramatically over-personalise such situations, she observed that many of these children would often 'run from difficulty', as opposed to facing into it. To sum up these tendencies and approaches to life, she coined the term fixed mindset.

When it comes to winning and high performance, having a growth mindset – being open to making mistakes, being prepared to take risks and move beyond our comfort zone – is an essential part of the formula for success.

very important aspects of competing and indeed learning itself. No fulfilling and ultimately successful long-term career in sport was ever built on never losing, or always winning.

FEAR OF WINNING

We talked in the last chapter about the importance, for anyone striving for high performance, of digging deeper to understand what drives us. This helps to keep us in touch with our long-term goals, especially when times are tough – but looking a bit more closely at our motivations can also help uncover thoughts and feelings which may be preventing us from fulfilling our true potential. Again, this is where the mental skill of *active reflection* really works.

It may be a surprise to know that many professional athletes and successful business people have had to struggle with an unconscious *fear of winning* in the course of their careers, and, while they can achieve an impressive level of success by running on talent alone, they may often have the feeling that something, on some level, is holding them back. In a recent conversation with Brent, as part of the research for this book, ex-professional footballer Richie Sadlier talked very openly and honestly about this:

> I remember I was very low in self-confidence. This was the biggest challenge for me internally. I don't remember having any conversations with a coach or a teacher . . . where I was given

> the opportunity to tease out my responses to certain situations and the causes of them, or how I could handle them better . . . I had talent, and often on the pitch in most cases things would go well for me. But I also carried with me this voice in my head that always questioned my worthiness. A little presence on my shoulder saying, 'You're going to get found out here, you know you are!' I approached many games with this negative mindset. So low was my confidence that I had to become as motivated to prove [the voice] wrong . . . I would chase those moments of peace which would only come by the voice shutting up. For me, the only way then to succeed was to succeed on the pitch.
>
> *Richie Sadlier – former professional footballer; 145 appearances for Millwall, capped for Ireland; football pundit*

Although Richie was clearly very successful in his football career, he always had a sense that had he been able to really get to the heart of this lack of confidence in his own abilities, things would have been easier for him to handle, and he would have actually enjoyed the game more:

> After I finished playing, people would ask me, 'If you had your time again, what would you do differently? Do you have any regrets?' [And] what I would always come back to was, I would've loved [to] have worked with a psychologist, just to see – could I have done something to create more of the days where it was easy and fun? And reduce the days where it felt like this insurmountable challenge that would leave me feeling inadequate . . .

When I chatted to former Irish rugby star Ronan O'Gara about this issue, he also admitted to having similar feelings of self-doubt as a young player:

> When I was young, going back 20 years – as a 20-year-old playing for Munster, playing with a lot of legends – there were a lot of doubts like, 'Am I good enough to play at this level?' That happened for nearly two years. Then there was the constant assessment with goal-kicking, and the pressure that comes with goal-kicking. It can be such an easy skill and then [on] other days, such a difficult skill.
>
> *Ronan O'Gara – former professional rugby player; rugby coach; 128 caps for Ireland*

Many talented athletes who are hampered by these unconscious blocks can find themselves experiencing a repeated sense of disappointment, frustration and even anxiety and panic. Do you recognise yourself in any of this? If so, it is definitely worthwhile trying to identify and confront possible hidden fears of this kind. In my work as a mental skills coach and psychotherapist, I have witnessed on many occasions the way in which *committing* to this process has enabled high achievers to experience huge breakthroughs in performance terms, by allowing them to shift their thoughts and connect with and release their energy to achieve – and to actively enjoy winning, enjoy success.

COMPETING WITH THE UNCONSCIOUS

As we have said, competing can be a difficult and emotive issue for many people – not just in sports, but in all walks of life. The reason for this is that many of us were told early on in our lives, by parents, teachers and coaches, *not* to want to win, *not* to actively compete with others. We were told that taking part was enough; that it is not winning or losing but participating and enjoying the game that counts. While the intention among parents and mentors here is well-meaning, unfortunately these messages can create an unconscious conflict for the young person, which can play out in an upsetting way later in life.

While messages about taking part and enjoying sports or any competition are spot on, setting them up in direct opposition to winning and being naturally competitive is not. A young person can enjoy taking part and *also* enjoy competing and wanting to win. Presenting them with a choice between either participating or competing/winning risks creating an unconscious fear of winning and, by extension, possibly a fear of competing itself. This can lead to a child not wanting to participate at all, preferring to opt out altogether, unsure of what to do with the concept of competing, not having a healthy frame of reference for it, and not knowing how to react when others compete against them. The ulterior confusing message they can hear from adults is 'Don't compete – don't win', 'too risky', so they don't.

Every child has a healthy competitive side, which can be nurtured or repressed. This competitive side is obvious in any playground. The question is how to work with it, as opposed to simply denying it exists. Sport is a very obvious example of competition, but children naturally compete with each other in all kinds of ways. When they opt out altogether, they are limiting themselves and missing out on discovering more of what is possible, on discovering more about themselves and understanding more about the learning process.

An inherent aspect of sport is competing! For anyone wanting to improve their sporting ability it is essential that they enjoy competing and accept and fully embrace it. But when, as children, we have picked up conflicting messages about competing, this can hamper our ability to perform at our best and enjoy being our best, and can undermine our potential and getting to know our true abilities.

Take a moment and have a think about what competing means for you.

COMPETING AND BEING COMPARED TO OTHERS

Another reason why many people feel uncomfortable, or at least not entirely positive, about competing is because in their minds competition is very much tied up with the idea of comparison with other people. Objectively, it is true that competing with others necessarily involves our performance or abilities being in some way measured against theirs. For a lot of us, the idea of being compared to other people can be upsetting, and can have a lot of emotional weight attached to it. Such feelings usually stem from early experiences of being *unfairly* compared – to siblings, other children or grown-ups – in a critical and undermining way. Consequently, negative thoughts are generated by the prospect of being compared again as adults, given the upsetting emotions we experienced as children when being told we weren't as good, talented or intelligent as others, and were made to feel that we were inadequate in some way.

When it comes to performance, however, once we are able to take the old emotions out of the equation, we can recognise the ways in which comparing ourselves with others can be a helpful exercise and serve a useful purpose. If we want to do something really well, we can learn a great deal from others who excel in that area or activity – simply by observing what approaches they take and techniques they use to help their performance and seeing and learning from what works so well for them. In this way, we are using comparison more by way of research, to help us further our own goals. Comparison in this sense is not a value proposition, just a way of gathering helpful information.

BEING MEASURED AND BEING EVALUATED

Measuring our efforts, and having our efforts measured by others, is generally key to performance in any field. Much like comparison, however, it is another aspect of competition and business life, namely *performance appraisals*, which many people can find challenging. Again, this is often because of unpleasant memories many of us have from childhood, and particularly our schooldays, of being assessed, measured and evaluated in a less than empathetic way by teachers and parents. The emotions associated with these negative experiences, or perceived negative experiences, are still in our memory banks and we can still feel them in our bodies. When faced with situations as adults where we are being evaluated in some way, these old sensations can be reawakened, meaning that we get bombarded with negative thoughts and unpleasant feelings, spooked by the idea of our work and, by extension, *ourselves* being measured.

What can really help here is being able to make the clear distinction between *measurement* and *evaluation*, and once more, trying to take the emotion out of the equation. Evaluation suggests that we are attaching value to a result or set of results, and it is this sense of worth or merit that can psychologically undermine many of us, triggering old negative self-talk about not being good enough or worth as much as others. Measurement, however, does not need to be *psychologically* connected to the idea of value or worth. It is simply the process of establishing relevant physical facts connected to a performance – higher, farther, faster, slower and so on.

From a mental health perspective, when we add too much emotion to what we are doing or not doing well, we can unfortunately attach aspects of our sense of self to the activity. Doing this makes us vulnerable, because it makes us feel that our performance is a reflection on us as people, with something to say about our worth as human beings. This is why so many people struggle with criticism – they feel it is an attack on their sense of themselves. Having a healthy performance mindset however is being clear that measurement is measurement – simply a means by which we can improve, or highlight a lack of improvement in, our chosen activity.

Winning: What Does It Mean?

To help you work out your own feelings about winning, competing and comparison, here are some simple questions to think about:

- What are all the thoughts and feelings associated with winning for you? Write them down.
- When did you first come across winning and losing?
- Who are the key people that gave you these messages about winning?
- What are your strongest memories about losing and about being compared to others?
- What are the feelings these memories bring up for you? Write them down.
- How would you like to think about winning, about success?

If you want to dig a little deeper into this kind of *active reflection*, have a look at the PAC model, on the next page, which will particularly help you in identifying and dealing with difficult feelings and unconscious conflicts arising out of childhood experiences.

Going Deeper with Self-Awareness – the PAC Model

This is the PAC model and these circles correspond to the three Ego States present in us all: Parent (P); Adult (A); and Child (C).

P

C

Ego States

The Parent, Adult and Child (PAC) Ego State model is a psychological framework model which helps us understand human functioning and human relationships. It was developed by the Canadian psychiatrist Eric Berne in the late 1950s, as part of his Transactional Analysis theory, and forms the basis for his human development, personality and communication theory[3].

Each Ego State represents where we invest energy at any given time; this changes during the course of our daily activities. Ego States contain information in the form of thoughts, feelings and behaviour patterns that relate to our unique experiences as individuals throughout our lives.

The Child Ego State holds within it thoughts, memories, ideas, behaviours, feelings and sensations we experienced in our childhood. The Parent Ego State maintains sets of instructions, behaviours, ideas, experiences and feelings related to and learned from our parental figures. The Adult Ego State represents what we are learning and experiencing in the here and now, with access to reliable information that we have acquired from our many previous experiences and based on our present-moment processing of information.

As we grew, learned and developed, so did our Ego States, storing information about who we are and what we experience in our minds and bodies. A bit like installing various elements of software to form our own unique personalities. We then share our personalities through how we communicate with others from each of these three Ego States.

With awareness, we can influence how we communicate ourselves in a way that is more in tune with who we are and how we want to be with others. Rather than simply accessing and replaying old software over and over again, this allows us instead to proactively install and integrate new, updated software as we evolve through our lived experience. Choosing the energy we want to be bringing and investing each day helps us achieve our true potential as humans and get more from activities and life.

If, in the process of asking these questions, you discovered that you have conflicting feelings around winning, competing or success – what in psychology is referred to as a ' non-winning script' – there is some necessary psychological work to be done. The good news is that we can all rewrite our scripts, allowing ourselves to achieve more and enjoy better results and greater success in performance.

WINNING SCRIPTS

Winning is not just what the scoreboard says at the end of the game, this is too narrow a definition. Winning is actually about successful behaviours being repeated over time – succeeding through planning, through intent and through action execution. This new narrative sounds like:

'Winning is about succeeding. I am successful when I do what I set out to do. I am winning when I use my energy to achieve what I planned to achieve, through my own actions.'

'I can feel satisfied, because I did all that I could do to execute my plan in achieving my goals.'

'I am a winner because I am trying my utmost to do what I can to complete my goals to the best of my ability.'

'I want to succeed. To do this, I need to know what I have to do to succeed. Once I know this, I need to do all I can in taking those steps to success. When I have done this, I will know that I can feel satisfied.'

'Winning feels good. I like winning because it is about having successfully achieved something. Success is good. It is healthy for me to want to be successful in what I do.'

These are all examples of winning mindsets. These new narratives put success in our hands and within our reach. We determine what we focus on. We choose to *potentialise* any situation, and to square up to our challenges head-on. Faced with the decision to do something or not to do it, the easy, 'fixed mindset' approach is not to act on it; to simply opt out. An open, 'growth' mindset is to enjoy the participation, regardless of the outcome, because the experience was *real*. The knowledge that we have given something our very best shot has an intrinsic value of its own, which we can take pleasure in.

BRINGING OUR BEST

Winning in sports, and in life, is about consistently bringing our *best selves* to our role, and about working continuously to improve our competence and our contribution. **Winning is continually improving whatever we are doing, to the best of our abilities.** In sports, the word 'best' is used a lot – we talk about best practices, personal bests, what is best for the team, what makes for the best teammate and so on – all of which is common currency in a business context too. We bring our *best selves* when we:

- know what the successful behaviours we need to bring are
- are familiar with our strengths and potentialise them often
- approach what we do with passion, a sense of fun and an open curiosity

- proactively look for areas we can improve
- know who the support people in our lives are and connect with them often

WORKING OUT WHAT WINNING MEANS FOR YOU

Winning isn't everything, but wanting to is!

Vince Lombardi, legendary US football player, coach and NFL executive

We can now see that winning is actually a highly subjective concept, and that it can be much more than, for example, getting the highest score in a competition, or more than simply 'not losing'. Yes, it is true that winning a game or a tournament is never guaranteed. This is not new. What might be new, however, is the mindset that winning might be much more than the simplistic, black-and-white understanding of it we grew up with. Success for someone might involve having the ambition to think big, to want more, and going about trying to make this happen with a willingness to learn and grow at every opportunity.

Winning could also be the intrinsic satisfaction you get in setting a target and working very hard to reach it; being willing to take risks and make mistakes and learn from them: the journey as a goal in itself. Winning is a far more powerful and useful concept when it is opened up to greater possibilities. As well as being highly competitive and supremely driven to win, the most successful high performers also carry within them a recognition of the innate value of the continuous effort to get there. Former world champion snooker champion Ken Doherty summed this up very well when talking to Brent about what winning has come to mean for him:

> My son plays tennis now, and I always try and tell him [that] I don't just care about the end result: 'When you go out onto that tennis court, I don't care whether you win or lose – what I don't want you to do is give in.'
>
> Always do your best. Always give 100 per cent, because if you [do this], it doesn't only apply to sport but to life itself. If you give 100 per cent, at least you can go to bed happy – with a clear conscience. If you go out there and throw in the towel too early, give up and don't play with spirit, that's the worst thing in the world to see – on a tennis court, a soccer pitch, a rugby pitch.
>
> Keep your head held high, play as well as you can and give it your best. If the other fella is better than you on the day, then shake his hand and say well done, and that's it.
>
> *Ken Doherty – ex-professional snooker player; snooker commentator; 1997 world snooker champion*

FOUR
Working to Win in a Team

'We made a collective agreement that everything we did would point towards winning'

Chris Boyd

My years at one club were a bit more difficult – I just became negative about everything, and to be honest, looking back, that was probably some of my own doing as well. I never flicked the positive switch. I trained just as hard, [but] I was just slightly more negative.

I worked hard, trained hard, gave everything I had – I always did – it was just different in my mind. What you think, you become . . . It was a kind of negative environment, not just for me, but it seemed [like there was] a negativity about the club in general – and when that gets ingrained, it's hard to get it out. Again, I guess I should have switched that on myself, thought more positively myself.

Damien Duff – former professional footballer; football coach; 100 caps for the Republic of Ireland

Damien Duff's honest insights, on the previous page, into his time at one of the big English football clubs clearly illustrates the truth that sometimes the success or failure of a sports team is not just about the talent and ability of any individual player within that team. A team may have prodigiously talented players on board, but that doesn't always mean they will work well as a group or will automatically go on to achieve great things.

We can all think of teams – be it in sport, business or within community ventures – that never seemed to fulfil their potential, and where a lot of negative energy was at work. Teams whose members made repeated errors in performance, blaming each other when something went wrong and lacking enthusiasm for what they were doing. Teams where a culture of backbiting and negativity prevailed, and destructive and unproductive behaviours were the norm, often referred to as 'toxic'. The kind of teams no one really wanted to belong to.

On the other hand, most of us will recognise a good team when we see it. Teams where there is a great dynamic, and a forward-looking energy to get things done, where individuals get a chance to thrive while the group as a whole flourishes. Where people supportively have each other's backs and are quick to encourage someone who is flagging or not performing at their best, while also acknowledging their teammates for a job well done. In business, these are the teams that will go the extra mile for each other, where team members turn up to after-work functions to support their colleagues, not because they feel they have to, but because they want to. They are the teams people want to be in, with leaders that people want to work for.

Can you think of a team like this?

Unsurprisingly, these types of teams are invariably the ones that perform the best, consistently achieving shared aims and goals. According to Patrick Lencioni, US business speaker, thought leader and author of the international bestseller *The Five Dysfunctions of a Team* teamwork remains the ultimate competitive advantage – because it is both so powerful and so rare. So, to be successful in a team enterprise in any field, getting the dynamic of the team right is one of the most important things to work on.

In this chapter, we will look at what makes a successful team, including how to put in place the basic systems and structures needed to ensure that things run smoothly, and how to go about creating one of the key ingredients in any winning team – a positive, productive and continually learning and evolving team culture. We will also see how things can be turned around in a team that has been underperforming. So, if your team has been less than successful in the past, the good news is that, with the right approach, a winning change is very much possible!

While the key examples we will be considering are in the field of sport, the same kinds of principles and strategies are relevant to any kind of team – whether in business, community or, indeed, in your own family unit.

In a work context, being able to function in a team, and as a team, has become more important than ever in recent years. This is because the way most companies operate has changed considerably over the last few decades. Historically, the majority of the work done in a business was carried out by a number of competent key individuals, with far less reliance on teams. Figures suggest that in the 1980s, team-based work would have accounted for something like 20 per cent of a company's output. In a typical scenario these days, however, pretty much the converse is the case – with 80 per cent of a company's work being done by teams. So, having the ability to work effectively as part of a team is more important than ever before. Individuals need to quickly learn how to get on with each other, how to put personalities and 'egos' aside for the greater good of the teams' goal and for overall productivity and lasting success. They need to be more willing to help out and support fellow team members, and trust that others will do the same for them.

> A winning culture is created by many things – like a great leadership group and an environment where players can thrive. The development of each individual is so important, as is the development of talent that is coming through . . .
>
> *John Plumtree – assistant coach of the Hurricanes (New Zealand); previously worked with the Irish national rugby team and the Sharks (South Africa)*

TEAMS AND TEAM CULTURE

In the simplest terms, a team can be defined as 'a group of people with a full set of complementary skills working together to complete a task, job, or project'.[1] Equally simply, a 'team culture' could be said to be 'the collective beliefs and behaviours of a group of people working together to achieve a common goal'.

A team culture really works, and a team becomes more than just a collection of individuals when a strong sense of mutual commitment creates a synergy, a positive energy to work together as well as possible – a sense of belonging. The end result is a collective performance greater than the sum of the performances of its individual members. More generally, culture underpins and determines how a team functions – well or not well, productively or unproductively. Culture then is the unconscious *glue*, the bonding element that keeps teams working better together, for longer, in good times and bad.

Clearly, one of the key requirements for a team to function well is that all its members share a common goal and common purpose. Although it might seem almost too obvious to mention, any team in which there is a lack of clarity among its members about what they are doing and why they are doing it will fail to operate successfully.

All of the world's top sports coaches, those working with the most successful elite teams, know that defining a key goal is crucial when rallying a team and creating a successful team ethos. In this regard, Chris Boyd, coach of the Hurricanes professional rugby team in New Zealand, had some very interesting and relevant insights to share when I spoke to him recently.

Working to Win in a Team

In 2015, Chris faced a very difficult, albeit exciting, challenge, when he was asked to take over as head coach of the Hurricanes. It was a daunting task because, while the team had a number of very talented players signed up, the Hurricanes had been falling short of success for some time – in fact, in the 19 years of their existence, since their founding in 1996, they had made it to a final only once, despite a history of having world-class players!

I was fortunate enough to work with this great talent as the mental skills coach with the Hurricanes for the 2014–2016 seasons, beginning just a few months before Chris's arrival as head coach. In our recent conversation, he told me how he set about turning things around for the team, right from the very start of his tenure:

> There has always been plenty of talent [in the Hurricanes], but I had a personal opinion that they didn't have enough self-belief around the fact that they could win. When I came on [board], we made a collective agreement that everything we did [would] point towards winning a championship
>
> *Chris Boyd – head coach of the Hurricanes: Super Rugby champions in 2016, runners-up in 2015*

As Chris went on to explain, this 'collective agreement' didn't just involve the coaching team – as might be the case in a lot of professional teams – but it extended to, and required the engagement of, the whole team, including all the players and everyone else who worked closely with the Hurricanes. He outlines how he managed to get everyone's 'buy-in' so early on:

> The most important time was when we had a team meeting in our very first camp. We set the scene around what we were going to achieve. The very first slide [in my presentation] showed the picture of success, the captain holding the [Super 18] trophy. [Then I said,] 'I need to check in that everyone agrees, that in everything we do . . . [that] all our language . . . is about winning. That we're not here to make up numbers, that we're not here just to perform – [but] that we're here to win.'

We can see here that, in galvanising a new spirit of positivity, success, focus and belief, a winning mindset grew within the team, and Chris called on the key mental skill of *goal-setting*, reinforcing a sense of the team's ultimate aim – to win the Super 18 trophy – with the powerful use of *imagery* and a picture of what success would, quite literally, look like. Once he had established the parameters of what the 'big picture' goal for the team would be, he set about nailing down, with the whole team's input, the small picture of success and the process of how they would set about achieving it:

> We picked into that and we asked, 'What is it we need to do consistently to win? . . . We're going to win, but what does that look like? What are the behaviours we need to exhibit?' . . . [And] they came up with . . . a barrage of things that were important to do, to win: 'It looks like preparation, it looks like organisation, it looks like commitment, it looks like relentless homework.'

Crucially, Chris made sure to involve the whole team – every single member – in these decisions and the plan going forward. By doing so, he allowed everyone to have a say, and a stake in the common goal and how to achieve it – he knew that would maximise the chances of a strong collective sense of commitment and engagement in the team. Very early on, Chris was able, as he tells us, to secure a 'collective agreement'– a great example of the mental skill of *contracting*.

This story has a winning ending. In 2015, Chris's first year as head coach and mine as mental skills coach, the Hurricanes ended the season top of the table, qualifying for a home final. Although they didn't win that time, the following year they reached the finals again in their best

'Contracting' means putting an agreement in place. Contracts are very useful in helping to delineate boundaries and responsibilities (especially when allocating work), and in avoiding confusion. The clearer the contract, the easier it will be to identify individual responsibilities and to recognise when the agreement has been fulfilled.

Contracts need to specify the desired outcomes and the actions required to achieve these.

An example of a very simple contract someone could enter into with themselves might be a 'hold off' agreement – i.e. 'I will not do X (e.g. watch my favourite soap on TV; eat a bar of chocolate; go out for a coffee, etc.), until I have completed Y (e.g. make a phone call I've been putting off; finish answering the morning's emails; cleaned the bathroom, etc.) A simple contract with another person might be around the issue of giving feedback on something they have done or said, or on an ongoing basis. This would involve first asking them if it is OK to provide some constructive feedback, pointers or advice. If they say yes and you explain your motivations – the reasons you want to do this – then there is a contract in place between the two of you. Giving feedback without asking, or without having such a mutual agreement in place, is not conducive to good communication, and risks the other person being closed off to what you have to say, or even offended.

season to date and won the 2016 championship – for the first time in the club's history! The satisfying 'icing on the cake'.

While of course every team is not playing at the level of the Hurricanes, and does not have the resources or professional expertise such elite teams have access to, they can use the basic principles of coach Chris Boyd's approach and adapt them to their own specific circumstances.

We can see how, with the Hurricanes, Chris created a process for his team to adopt success and certain winning messages, breaking these down into what the winning behaviours are – i.e. the small goals that need to be consistently achieved to ensure the big goal is within reach. So, using Chris's template, we can see a formula for success and winning which any team, sporting or otherwise, can follow when trying to establish a successful culture:

- Specify at the outset what is to be achieved, what is desirable.
- Be clear about the fact that this is achievable (as long as it is!) and that anything less is undesirable.
- Be bold in saying what is expected of each person.
- Name the behaviours and actions needed going forward to achieve the big, long-term goal.

Let's hear more about *goal-setting* in teams, and the positive impact it can have. Alan Quinlan spoke to Brent about what he learned at Munster about the importance for a team of having something specific to aim for:

> At Munster, [goal-setting] gave us real targets and it started helping the confidence of the group when we would say, 'We want to be the best team in Ireland' or 'We want to win the European Cup'.
>
> . . . I found goal-setting very helpful to me, and very helpful as a team to say, 'Well, we want to be the best team in Europe!' If we at least set [a] target, then we can start making small steps towards that – it might take a bit of time . . . But you can then measure your success!
>
> *Alan Quinlan – former professional rugby player; 27 caps for Ireland, 212 appearances for Munster; rugby analyst*

Once again, Alan highlights the value of having a goal, and, once this has been identified, the importance of creating a detailed road map to get there – working out what needs to be done to enable us to achieve our aim, and the practical processes we can put in place to bring it within reach.

However, you have more than likely spotted the potential flaw in this approach or mindset, and you might be thinking something along these lines: 'Yes, but there is no guarantee that doing all this work will lead to the goal being achieved; winning is never guaranteed, no matter what you do.' Here we come back to what we talked about in the previous chapter – what the true definition of winning is, and what represents success for each of us as individuals and as teams.

We saw that winning can be a subjective concept, and that it can be much more than, for example, getting the highest score in a competition, or more than simply 'not losing'. Just like individual athletes, teams need to work out collectively and uniquely what success looks like for them. As a team, you might like to look again at Chapter Three, and decide what winning in this more general way might mean for you. Winning could also be the sense of achievement you get in setting a target and working very hard as a group to get there, supporting one another and bringing out the best in everyone in the team. As we saw in the last chapter, winning is a far more powerful and useful concept when opened up to a broader definition – one which has a more personal and meaningful resonance for us as individuals.

'CULTURE EATS STRATEGY FOR BREAKFAST!'

As a final word on the importance of culture, the above quote, from Professor Peter F. Drucker – a famous American business consultant and author, known by some as 'the man who invented modern management' – is very illuminating. Your team can have all the strategies, all the mental skills and other resources in the world, but if you don't have a committed and cohesive *will* on the part of everyone to really want to make things work together, these will not help you when the going gets tough. We can all think of times when, within teams, strategy suddenly went out the window. When the fear of losing, anxiety about the scoreboard and other negative pressures generated by the team spread confusion and disarray. Or in business when so much time and effort was put into planning and strategy meetings, only for it all to fizzle out further down the track, with the project frustratingly getting shelved. Or times in life generally when there was an unexpected burst of creative energy, a sudden will to accomplish something, only for the whole thing to lose momentum and simply fade away. Having a strong team culture in place will safeguard against such scenarios.

Working with Your Team - Basic Structures To Put in Place: Vision. Mission. Values.

You have determined your team's overall high level goal, its common purpose - the vision for the team - and set down the practical steps to be taken to ensure you get there - the mission for the team. With collective 'buy-in' from all members, you have now established two of the three most important tenets of your team culture. Now it is time to set down another simple structure. Research shows that there are some basic behaviours that need to be in place and reinforced for high-performing teams to be consistently successful: group values supporting the **vision** and **mission** of the team. These **values** will determine what sets of behaviours, or rules of conduct, a team will adopt and follow in order to guide and maintain a culture. In sports, these are very often laid out by the coaches, in agreement with senior players or the leadership team. However, they are more likely to be respected and adhered to when they are team-created and team-managed - once again, getting the 'buy-in' of the whole team is key. This will ensure that these rules of conduct - also known as the team's 'norms' - are kept alive and remain part of a healthy 'team mindset', an all-for-one and one-for-all outcome focus, 'we are in this together' respect and mentality. Team members can volunteer or be elected by their fellow teammates to be the guardians or enforcers of certain rules and regulations - e.g. someone to write the agenda or take the minutes, someone to keep an eye on punctuality and flow of meetings, and so on.

ESSENTIAL RULES OF CONDUCT

Basic team norms usually include things like consequences for lateness or for repeatedly delaying team processes. Keeping common spaces, like the locker room or office space, tidy and in good order, serving to promote professional standards. Of benefit too will be a procedure for members contributing to meetings, which ensures that as many people as possible will have a say, and that less outspoken team members get used to sharing with their colleagues in a team setting, building confidence in themselves and generally building assertiveness skills. Good strategies like having regular sessions of small group work or designating different members each time to present to the group on a specific subject will also help here. Assigning mentors to new teammates or groups ensures values are trained, understood and kept alive. Of course rules around mobile phones, laptops or iPad usage in meetings will be helpful too.

In sports settings, guidelines around maintaining curfews and the use of alcohol, drugs, gambling, social media while on tour and in general, etc., will be very important. It's crucial to note that, for these codes of behaviour to be effective, coaches and managers need to make sure they adhere to them also, or else they risk promoting unhelpful behaviours through their own actions! Leaders and managers model the behaviour they get back.

REASONABLE CONSEQUENCES

All of these rules of conduct, these values, need to help underpin and clearly promote the overall vision and mission of the team. They should be designed to encourage behaviours that will produce and reinforce results, and put a stop to behaviours that will undermine team progress. For this reason, it's also important to work out, at an early stage, consequences for breaching team etiquette. Consequences could include measures such as straightforward fines or paying for a team lunch or dinner. In sports, a physical 'punishment' might be appropriate, like having to do extra laps or push-ups, or putting away everyone's gear. Or chores like locker room cleaning, laundry or being responsible for organising drinks all week during training sessions, and so on. Imagination can help here, within reason of course.

For consequences to be effective, members need to feel some 'pain'. More serious breaches and misconduct should have more serious consequences. In this area, as in others, *equality* of treatment is a key attribute of successful teams – favouritism is never a good idea. These norms and consequences build a high level of team trust and shore up weak links in team processes.

When putting these kinds of structures in place, along with a clear vision and set of directions, having the best people in the most effective roles is a key factor. A good approach to define and set down these codes of behaviour is a group process, where everyone is involved in drawing up a *team charter*: something that every member agrees to and signs – literally putting their name to it. A road map of sorts, of where they are, where they want to go and what will best help get them there – including what happens if they go off track.

Having all of these measures in place will help guide teams towards working well together and achieving their goals, and they are well-known winning behaviours!

OUR LIFE TEAMS

All of the above measures can be invaluable in life too. When it comes down to it, in whatever context – sport, business, home life – we are all part of a team – or a number of teams, in fact. As part of the human race, none of us is ever truly alone in any endeavour. Although it might not feel like that at times, we are never single entities living and working in isolation. We are always part of a group system. In this general way, our group might be our family, relations, friends and work colleagues, or our neighbours in the communities in which we live. This is important to always keep in mind. It means we have access to a wealth of experiences, learning, creativity and skills beyond our own.

In life, we can all set clear values and aims for ourselves and within our various groups. At home, within our family, we can determine the most constructive and enriching ways to live together, incorporating values that we can strive to maintain and rules that we do our best to live by. Straightforward stuff, like sharing the household chores and responsibilities, acknowledging and celebrating achievements, being more conscious of the language we use with each other and guarding against undermining words and disrespectful behaviour. If we can establish our own culture of encouragement and positivity at the heart of our everyday lives, in our homes, then this will radiate out into all the activities we undertake in the outside world.

TRUSTING THE PROCESS

For any team, teammates will work together more effectively when they know what to expect from each other on the field or in the boardroom. Just like the long-term goals and values of the team culture, for a process to work properly, it needs to have the 'buy-in' and be lived by everyone.

As with so many situations in sport, having trust and confidence in each other or a process will keep the team focused during tough times in performance and ensure that things do not fall apart when times become challenging. Here is what Conor O'Shea, currently head coach of the Italian national rugby team, had to say about the importance of these processes:

> The way I coach is that we work on not compounding errors with other errors. In the past, Italian teams may have made a mistake in a game, and then compounded it straight away by making another one. So, I tell players to stay focused, don't panic, concentrate

and trust in what we have worked on – stay true to the game plan and your processes.

I remember the Munster team years ago. They would be being beaten up and down the field sometimes, but when you looked at the scoreboard, they were actually never that far behind. They never strayed or got sucked into what the other team was doing, just kept doing what they knew they were good at. [In] so many games, they came back from the dead. No fluke – they just never panicked, never layered error after error. They believed in what they were about, and they were resilient.

Conor O'Shea – former professional rugby player; 35 caps for Ireland, 127 appearances for London Irish; head coach of the Italian national rugby team

RELATIONSHIPS: HAVING EACH OTHER'S BACKS

One of the most important factors in any relationship between teammates is trust. In fact, if we go back to Patrick Lencioni and his seminal book *The Five Dysfunctions of a Team*, we will see that 'absence of trust' is identified as the first and biggest dysfunction in teams. (The other four are: fear of conflict, lack of commitment, avoidance of accountability and inattention to results – i.e. focusing more on personal success as opposed to success for the team.)

In our conversations with top sportspeople, it is notable that trusting and having confidence in each other was a key feature in the successful teams they played for, as was a sense of pride in their teammates' confidence *in them* to play their part.

> In sport, you come to trust everybody because they are there, every training [session] and every Saturday for the game. Our environment was about everyone wanting to win the game. Every single one of us – players, coach, physio, team manager. Everyone wanted to win the match . . . In team sports, if you don't trust the guy beside you, you've lost the game.
>
> *Victor Costello – former professional rugby player; 39 caps for Ireland, 121 appearances for Leinster; airline pilot*

> The best thing about what I do is that I have been given a role and responsibility, and I work hard at my physical and mental skills to perform that role to the best of my ability – to help the team win. Sharing the success of everyone performing their roles is very satisfying, when we have reached the common goal and we're content with our process.
>
> *Suzie Bates – captain of the New Zealand women's cricket team, the White Ferns; ODI player of the year 2013 and 2016*

> I [actually] enjoy the responsibility of being trusted to put the ball over the bar.
>
> *Dean Rock – Gaelic footballer; winner of four All-Irelands with Dublin*

In his book about dysfunctions in teams, Patrick Lencioni proposes that the antidote to the absence of trust is the forming of closer relationships and, hand-in-hand with this, good communication. In other words, being willing to put in the time to get to know your teammates better is key to the long-term success of your team. Put simply – if I know you more, I am likely to trust you more. So, for teams to function really well, not only do the people in them need to share a clear common goal (vision) and common values and common processes (mission), but they also simply need to *share.* Letting others know what is going on for us, opening up to our teammates when things are difficult, when life is challenging or when we feel low. And equally importantly, telling them when everything is going well and something is really working for us, sharing success.

All of this involves the key mental skills of *self-awareness, active reflection* and *emotional fluency* – being in touch with how we are and being able, and willing, to communicate this to others. A key indicator of trust is the willingness to say how we are feeling and thus be vulnerable with others. Former All Black Zinzan Brooke shared with Brent some invaluable insights about this, drawn from his previous experiences as a top coach:

> If a player cannot come to you and shed light on how they are feeling, then things cannot change. Through talking and listening and opening up – only then can we change things for the better. Players should never be ashamed to talk, never feel guilty for opening up. It will not only make them a better player but develop them as a better person . . . bringing you closer. That's what building relationships is about: sharing. Things will never always go well, there will be days when the underdog defeats you or your team, but it's about sharing, finding people you trust and changing the perspective. Modern players are exposed to all sorts of pressures these days . . . Never be afraid to communicate your concerns. Reduce the pressure on you, a problem halved is a problem solved.
>
> *Zinzan Brooke – former All Black flanker with 58 caps*

Another feature of teammate relationships in successful sports teams is a desire to emulate your peers, and to bring out the best in others by encouraging them to push their own performance boundaries. A sense of healthy competition between teammates for the good of the team can help drive everyone forward:

> Most people in team sports want to be better than the guys around them, or at least to have their respect. There were times when I thought I could have done better, but you keep on going. I kept on trying to get better.
>
> *Victor Costello – former professional rugby player; 39 caps for Ireland, 121 appearances for Leinster; airline pilot*

This is equally the case in other kinds of high-performing teams. There are few more impressive than the SAS (Special Air Service), whose recruitment process is so selective and so intentionally extreme that most applicants won't make the cut, ensuring that those who do are already an elite of sorts – and that is before training even begins! Only the determined and fully committed of mind and body will be able to make a career in the SAS. In the organisation's individual units – the ultimate in high-performance teams – the element of positive, healthy competition between colleagues is absolutely crucial, as Lieutenant Colonel Rian McKinstry explained to me:

> The unit culture drives performance. The people will hold each other to account. Also, the competition to be better [pursuit of excellence] becomes a self-building proficiency. The challenge is set by one and then followed by another – like in the case of

> fitness testing . . . Comrades want to better themselves; they want to emulate or better what their teammate has done because they have done it . . . It's [a] self-propelling pressure.
>
> *Lieutenant Colonel Rian McKinstry – ex-Commanding Officer, New Zealand Special Air Service; Director of Leader Development for the New Zealand Defence Force*

Elite teams in all walks of life strive to better their results and improve their output on a continuous basis. As a group, they will seek to excel every single time. As individuals, each member will always work to bring their best for the team and for their teammates. When it comes to winning teams, this is the mindset that leads to excellence. It is the important cultural value I call the ABCD of success: Always Be Continually Developing.

BEING 'AGILE'

As we have been seeking to show so far in this book, when it comes to the approaches and strategies that best foster high performance, there is a lot in sport which is equally relevant in a business context. The converse is true too, of course, and there are many things the world of sport can learn from the world of business. An approach that has been working very well in recent years in some businesses is that of an 'agile' culture.

The term 'agile' in this context was first coined in the early 2000s by software development companies looking to establish a different, more flexible approach to project management – one better suited to the very fast-moving, constantly changing, customer-oriented environment these companies found themselves operating in. A more complete agile 'philosophy' for business has evolved since then, with a number of core values and an agile 'manifesto' comprising twelve key principles for good project – and general business – management.

While some aspects of agile culture are more relevant to the very specific environment and needs of the software development industry, a number of the basic principles are proving very effective in other types of businesses too, as well as in completely different settings – all areas where high performance teams are at work – including sport, and life in general. The music company Spotify uses the application of agile processes, and some of their 'agile coaches' were able to provide me with helpful insights when I talked to them while researching this book.

One key 'agile' pillar for success, for example, recognises the value of continuous ongoing learning and improvement, continuous experimentation and creative risk-taking. Arising out of this, then, is a continual improvement in process and performance, and a culture which fosters permission to make mistakes in the process of learning. While teams are 'allowed' to make mistakes, and don't have to get everything right first time, there is however the expectation that they will make the best use of these 'failures' by learning quickly from them and implementing constructive changes the next time around – a fail fast but learn quickly attitude.

This attitude to mistakes – that they shouldn't be simply glossed over, or regarded as a source of shame or embarrassment, but rather that they are something to be openly discussed as opportunities for learning – has been found to be a very helpful and 'freeing' approach in many areas where high performance is key. A number of the top athletes we interviewed for this book emphasised their willingness to accept and learn from mistakes as a major factor in their long-term success. This is what rugby great Dan Carter, for example, said to Brent on the subject of failure and losing games:

> Losing is always difficult at first, but then it becomes a powerful tool to get you to improve . . . [following a loss] I like to learn from it, always learn from the mistakes and of course then spend time with friends and family. Also to have a good balance in life, so I am not always thinking about setbacks. Like focusing on other things other than rugby.
>
> *Dan Carter – former All Black fly-half with 112 caps; 141 appearances for the Crusaders*

Mistakes and failures are such an important aspect of the agile culture in Spotify that many teams make use of a *failure wall*. This is a wall where team members display what went wrong – clearly and for all to see, helping to ensure others do not make the same mistake but also to learn from the process of what led to the mistake. One coach shared with me how he has carried this into his everyday interactions, with what he calls a 'failure bow' – standing up and bowing if he made a mistake or an obvious assumption.

Many other aspects of agile culture are equally helpful in other contexts and include a strong emphasis on team goals rather than the success of any individual team member; the importance of ongoing feedback sessions involving the whole team (these are referred to as 'retrospectives'), with a proactive quest for new knowledge and techniques; and most noticeably a willingness to be flexible and respond to circumstances openly, with a positive, forward-looking, improvement-focused attitude. Could some of this help in your team? How could you bring it in?

We have seen that, when it comes to putting together and maintaining winning team behaviours, there are many elements to be considered. Establishing a common goal and purpose, setting ground rules and working out basic values and priorities, knowing where you want to go and drawing up a simple, practical roadmap of how to get there, getting every single member of the team on board and signed up to what you are doing, fostering a sense of connection and great relationships between teammates – all of these things will help you on the way to winning more often. Let's leave a final word about what helps to make a good team to Eddie O'Sullivan, former rugby union head coach in the USA and Ireland:

> Focus on the positives; as a collective, let them motivate themselves. Sometimes it is hard, but it's always fixable. Put in measures, quantify things, measure the collective and personal, set performance goals as a team and as a player. [Always] turn negatives into positives.
>
> *Eddie O'Sullivan – former head coach of the USA and Ireland national rugby teams*

PART 2

Managing Roadblocks

FIVE
Dealing with Mental Blocks

'Players need to feel OK about coming forward'

Zinzan Brooke

In the early years, from ages nine to fifteen, my success came from a desire to please, and I was seeking approval from those that mattered to me. Wanting to please everyone around me including my parents and my coach. My achievements had little to do with an innate confidence. When it was difficult, it had nothing to do with my own self-belief that I could come through it. I didn't have that inherent, absolute belief in myself. If someone said something positive, I would think, 'Oh God, I'd better do that again; make them see that again.' That kept me going until I realised, 'Actually, I'm not bad at this!' Then I went on to have great success in swimming.

Things went asunder in the 1990s, prior to the Barcelona Olympics in 1992. I had a crisis of confidence. Going into the Olympics, I was in the top 10 in the world. I panicked! I felt that I had to be doing things better. I had to be training harder; I just had to be doing more! I became obsessive. I became absolutely and completely driven by the goal of the Olympic Games. Which was mentally and physically the wrong thing . . .

When I went to the Barcelona Olympic Games I was exhausted. Muscle fatigue. I finished 17th – it was a disaster! Personally, it really affected me . . . It's so important to have a release valve – and I just didn't have [one]. Mentally, I was too busy trying to please.

Gary O'Toole – former Olympic swimmer (represented Ireland at Seoul and Barcelona); swimming analyst; practising orthopaedic surgeon

Gary O'Toole is being very open and honest in his interview with Brent, opposite. In fact, he did eventually work with a psychologist, who helped him gain some key insights, (some of which he is clearly alluding to here). After he retired from world championship swimming, he went on to forge a very successful career in another highly pressurised field – medicine – as a practising surgeon. Gary's personal insights highlight the importance of self-belief and self-esteem in achieving workable success – and show how being a very high achiever can work to undermine us if key aspects of our motivation to succeed are not aligned with a sense of our intrinsic value as a person.

In the early chapters of this book we looked at how to work out our own definitions of success and winning, and the importance of delineating our own value system. Now we can look at some of the key psychological factors that can hold us back, and get in the way of us fulfilling our true potential. Sometimes these hidden 'hold-backs' only really emerge once we have achieved a certain degree of success – partly, as we

Kahler's Five Drivers

In 1975, the US clinical psychologist Taibi Kahler identified five common drivers that motivate all of us, and which can at times lead to dysfunctional behaviours. These are commonly known as the Transactional Analysis drivers, although they can also be understood as a standalone model.

They are:

- Try Hard
- Please Others
- Hurry Up
- Be Strong
- Be Perfect

All of these drivers have origins in early discipline, education and early messages from teachers and parents, who are seeking to help and guide the child but perhaps do not offer enough praise at the time, or inadvertently scare the child into acting a certain way, thus leaving the child overdoing things.

Taken onboard in a reasonable fashion, with reasonable limits, these drivers are effective in creating well-functioning and successful adult behaviours. However, when people do not know when to stop or see the limits in their behaviours, the dysfunction can set in, causing stress and consequent underachievement or poor performance.

shall see, because it is in the pursuit of high achievements that certain tendencies can quickly go off balance.

In what Gary said earlier, we can clearly identify two underlying tendencies that at one point in his career ultimately led to a major blockage of energy and talent: wanting to please others; and trying too hard. These are two of the five common 'drivers' – or motivating behaviours – we all exhibit to some degree in all aspects of our lives. How much they influence what we do and the way we are varies very much from person to person, depending on our individual upbringing and early experiences.

Although all of these behaviours can be traced back to our early disciplining, observations and feedback provided by parents, teachers, coaches and other role models, these behaviours are not all bad by any means

– in fact, the associated energy arising from any of them can be extremely valuable when we *consciously* set our minds to using it. Take the 'Try Hard' impulse. In sport and business, and indeed many other areas of life, it is essential not to simply give up at the first hurdle. Trying harder – as in, putting more energy into something – is often the way to go. However, if we get thrown off balance – and particularly when we are under pressure, we can lose our sense of reasonable limits – one or two of these key 'drivers' can begin to dominate our behaviour, which in turn can lead to unwanted, negative outcomes. Anyone who is constantly pushing themselves towards better performance, and very high achievers in particular, need to be careful about not overdoing any of these behaviours, since in some ways they will be more vulnerable to being thrown off balance – given that they are more often operating at the limits of their capacities. The forceful energy we experience when one or two of the five drivers really kick in can initially feel very energising and appealing – but can sometimes lead us to take things too far.

For example: trying too hard and not being able to relax; trying to please too many people; attempting to be perfect in every situation; always wanting to appear strong and with our emotions under strict control; tripping over ourselves taking on too much and trying to get everything completed in the shortest time possible. Do you recognise any of these behaviours in yourself? Here are some questions to think about:

- What are the types of behaviours you engage in when you are really stressed; what do you do or say?
- Which of the five drivers do these behaviours fit with?

- Who were the people from your early years who influenced you most here?
- What would they do or say when *they* were really stressed?

Driver behaviour when over-used leads to demotivation and underachieving. Even crashing and bottoming out. What's the way forward when these behaviours are starting to take over? Let's have a closer look at each of these, and at things we can do to ensure that we keep them in balance. For each driver, I'm going to suggest an antidote – an equivalent behaviour or set of actions that will help to 'deactivate' it.

'TRY HARD' — OR TRYING *TOO* HARD — DRIVER

In a sporting context, this can show itself in an athlete trying too hard to learn a technique – repeating it over and over, but not making any progress because they're not in the right frame of mind. Getting more and more frustrated at themselves, when actually, they need to take a break and stop forcing it. Or, as in Gary O'Toole's case, the 'try hard' compulsion can take over when a sportsperson over-trains and ends up becoming obsessive about 'getting it right' in other people's eyes.

Many of us fall down here, becoming so exasperated at not being able to complete a task that we simply quit or lose sight of the learning we could be achieving. We become afraid of losing face and worried about being publicly embarrassed, so we opt out. In this kind of scenario, we are so completely fixated on the outcome, we forget to focus on the *process* and the satisfaction to be had in the intrinsic experience.

When this driver gets out of balance, it causes energy to get stuck. We get bound up in doing things over and over again, when it clearly isn't working. Trying harder and harder isn't the solution; it is just compounding the problem. Just like whenever we're trying to put a nail in the wall to hang a picture, but we don't hit the nail properly on the first few strikes – and, instead of stopping and getting the nail positioned properly again, we just keep whacking it, over and over, until it's totally bent out of shape and is now almost impossible to get out again! Or remember *that* point you were trying to get across to someone – a partner, colleague, teammate – and you just kept banging on and on, getting more and more insistent, regardless of their reaction? Believing that, like a nail, you'd eventually bang your opinion into their skull, if you just kept at it long enough. But the pushing and pushing got you nowhere, because the other person just was not open in that moment to hearing what you were saying. Nor were you open to letting it go. Again, this is another example of when trying too hard just becomes counterproductive.

'TRY HARD' DRIVER ANTIDOTE

Try to relax more. When something isn't working, simply take a break before you get too entrenched.

Yes, work hard at what you are doing, but if you're not getting anywhere, stop trying. *It's not working!* Instead, do something else for a while. If you force yourself to take a break, your mind may find another way of approaching the task or the problem. When you come back to it, you're likely to have a different perspective, a different kind of energy and be more open to taking some new learning on board. Many people have slept on something only to realise a solution the next day.

'PLEASE OTHERS' DRIVER

In general, it is a good thing to want to please and seek recognition from others. Back in school, for example, it was the kids who did their homework and pleased Mum, Dad and their teachers who got the good grades. However, when the need to please others is too active, the result can be excess worry, fear, frustration and a preoccupation with the judgements of others: 'What will they think?'; 'What will they say?', and so on. This can become an entrenched way of thinking – a 'fixed mindset' – which can hamper a person's growth and personal happiness. Wanting to please others may come from a caring place – for a young person who really wants to please and show others that he/she is 'good', this may be their way of expressing their love for their parents and other mentors. However, it can also just be a way of coping, and surviving a difficult early environment where there were harsh consequences if we didn't keep others happy at all costs.

The kids who aren't really affected by negative *perfectionism* or the impossible standards of others are the ones who are more so pleasing themselves. They may also like to please the people they care about, but, crucially, they have a drive to want to do something, or get something 'right', on their own terms and for their own reasons. They may simply enjoy the intrinsic satisfaction of doing that thing, without taking into account too much to what extent this will keep others happy.

PLEASING OTHERS ANTIDOTE

Try to care less about what others think. Do what you are doing mostly for yourself, not just for someone else. Spend more time gaining *self-awareness*/getting to know yourself and finding out what makes you feel happier and more fulfilled; put care into clearly defining and planning how to achieve the results *you* want – because *you* want them. Satisfaction from you, for you. In the long run, it is way more rewarding and enjoyable, and far less anxiety-provoking. We spent some time in the early chapters of this book looking at the importance of each of us developing a personal understanding of what is best for us as individuals – reading these chapters again and reflecting on the key points being made will be a good place to begin the journey to greater self-knowledge. And ironically, what you will find is that when you focus more on your own sense of fulfilment in life, you will be more capable of bringing happiness to others too.

'HURRY UP' DRIVER

This is a very commonly activated response when stress and pressure set in. All of a sudden, it seems speed is of the essence, or that time itself is just disappearing. Or we end up pushing ourselves too far, too fast and get too much ahead of ourselves. And of course the opposite can happen too – we impose the 'hurry up' imperative on other people, or on events. We feel that something is not happening fast enough for us, or that other people aren't 'getting us' as quickly as they should, so then we just abandon the activity or lash out at the person. Do you recognise any of these scenarios?

'HURRY UP' ANTIDOTE

Take some time; take *your* time.

Often there is more time at our disposal than we imagine. Certainly, in business, not everything is as urgent as it might initially seem. We've all seen how a deadline can come and go without anyone actually dying! Often there is more time available if we ask for it. As well as this, there are other ways of completing tasks – slowing down and allowing some time for *active reflection* can help us come up with 'outside-the-box' solutions.

Take some time; make some space; connect with others. Get up and change the scene; go to a different office if you can, or go outside and get some head-clearing oxygen. And in a sporting context, even in the heat of competition, there is often time to take a moment and just breathe. To reset yourself, refocus and connect differently.

'BE STRONG' DRIVER

This for many years was perhaps one of the most commonly experienced pressures in professional sport, particularly for male players. It was part of a general culture, that men should not express their feelings; that they should not feel, or show, emotions like fear or sadness. Such feelings were seen as risky, weak – dangerous, even. Particularly in very physical, combative sports, such as rugby, boxing, soccer, hockey, and so on, this 'macho' culture was very much to the fore. Phrases like 'men don't cry', 'man up', 'just get over it', 'get on with it' were common currency – as if taking the time to feel or, even worse, express your feelings was some kind of last taboo. Rugby great Zinzan Brooke summed up this attitude well when speaking to Brent for this book:

> Players need to feel OK about coming forward, talking to other players, friends, family and coaches about what is going on off the field as well. In my era, that was hard – you would be seen as weak if you expressed emotions.
>
> *Zinzan Brooke – former All Black flanker with 58 caps*

Brent himself talks very movingly about how the pressure of such expectations actually intensified his sense of distress at times when he was feeling very low:

> I think a problem for many of us, especially men, is that we have these situations happening with us, and we feel ashamed. We feel we can't discuss it with anyone and we become stuck in a circle of self-doubt and fear, and eventually, depression can set in . . .
>
> I had lost hope, I had nothing left to give . . . I felt I had no one to talk to, no one to confide in. All my life I had lived by the code – 'real men don't cry', 'harden up', 'toughen up', and 'just go to the gym'. I saw myself as weak, as less of a man. A failure again.

The additional expectation of always needing to appear to be strong and in control just adds another layer of pressure and a heightened sense of isolation which can make things so much worse for someone in emotional pain.

Fortunately, although really just relatively recently, people in sport, business and the world in general today are much more educated about the power of our feelings and the importance of being able to express them openly. What we know now about emotions is that there is an energy attached to them, and that this energy will find a way out, no matter what.

Where being strong was once about hiding our feelings, now we can see the real strength is in being able to share our thoughts and emotions. Especially if we can do this in a self-aware and considered way. The mental skill of *emotional fluency* is now much more widely acknowledged as being important, and is increasingly regarded as an actively respected quality in men as well as women. *Emotional fluency* involves being able to identify and *label* your emotions and express them verbally to others. The way to develop this skill is by consistently checking in with ourselves, and acknowledging how we are feeling. To make this easier to do, we can narrow our feelings down to four primary ones, and then identify which of the four is being felt and making the effort to name the emotion that is rising within us – is it happiness, sadness, anger or fear? When we are able to name it, we are able then to say it. Of course feelings can sometimes come in pairs and being able to express both of the basic feelings really adds to the level of communication, helping yourself and others understand what is going on.

'BE STRONG' ANTIDOTE

Express your feelings and be yourself as much as possible. As with the 'please others' antidote above, invest some time in getting to know yourself better, in acknowledging and accepting your feelings as they happen, and work on your *emotional fluency* in expressing them. All Blacks mental skills coach Gilbert Enoka highlighted the importance of a culture of sharing and communication in successful teams in a recent interview for Adidas's online journal, gameplan-a.com: 'As a team, you can sit down and allow yourself to be vulnerable. It's a powerful strategy; once I'm prepared to share my vulnerability, and everyone else is too, we create an environment that becomes a culture of acceptance.'[1]

'BE PERFECT' DRIVER

Most of us probably know instinctively that the concept of perfection itself is a misleading one. We can see, for example, from looking at the world around us that nothing in nature is perfect. Even the most supposedly 'perfect' diamond, when magnified enough, will be seen to have flaws. And we know, from observing ourselves and other people, that there is no such thing as the perfect person – either physically or psychologically. Ideally, we also recognise that, just like diamonds, we humans are unique, precious and flawed.

However, because of our psychological make-up, we find the idea of perfection a very appealing one. Brent and I talked about this at the very beginning of this book – the fact that all human beings have within them the innate desire to grow and to realise their full potential. This is down to an energy in all living things called 'physis' – an energy not only to survive, but also to actively flourish. We humans have been given a big dose of physis, and one way our minds connect with this energy is through the concept of 'perfection' – giving us something to strive for, to grow towards, to be continually developing ourselves. In sport, this might be the perfect pass, the perfect shot, the perfect game; in business, the perfect presentation, the perfect sales pitch; in our personal lives, the perfect relationship or the perfect partner.

Athletes such as US basketball legend Michael Jordan talk about the 'perfect game' as being a motivating factor, something every athlete should aim for, and in a video interview for MVP.com he says the following: 'Mentally I like to challenge myself to go out there and play a perfect basketball game, although I know you can't do that – it's practically impossible to play a perfect game – but that doesn't mean you can't challenge yourself to do that.'[2] Here Jordan talks of actively using the mental skills of *goal-setting*, *self-determination* and an *optimistic mindset* as a means of consistently playing one's best, each and every time. This aspiration is to always want to bring a better game and never be satisfied with anything less. Such an ambitious mindset is similar to the SAS goal of 'the pursuit of excellence'.

Michael Jordan is speaking as someone with a high degree of awareness and self-knowledge, and he is very conscious of what he is saying here – he knows that there is no such thing as a 'perfect game', that the concept of perfection is a fallacy. However, because not everyone has such highly developed *self-awareness*, the idea of 'perfection' can be a very risky one. Many people, in all areas of life, get overly frustrated with trying to be perfect and can actively damage themselves in the process – berating themselves for not being able to meet an impossible standard, for not having done something perfectly. Anything else feels like an emotionally devastating failure.

While for some, the aim of perfection and, closely related to this, the tendency to compare their performance with that of peers or fellow competitors can help them connect with the more powerful idea of *bringing their best*, for others, especially children, this kind of thinking only serves to hold them back. In Chapter Three, we looked at how coaches and parents can help ensure that children and young people frame comparison and competition in the most constructive way.

In its most intense form, perfectionism and negative comparison undermines people psychologically, leading them to conclude: 'If I can't do it perfectly, then I won't do it at all!' and it means that so many miss out on so much. The saddest part for those who simply opt out – who don't try something, for fear of not getting it 'right' or not being perfect – is that eventually it leads to what they are actually trying to avoid: disappointment. Not trying is a trap, just as expecting perfection, worrying about disappointment and negatively comparing oneself to others is trapped thinking. All roads lead to disappointment. Left to dwell on loss and perceived 'failure', a person leaves themselves vulnerable. Not only do they miss out on many great experiences life has to offer, but ultimately they are 'driving a losing game', which can lead to depression and anxiety. We will look in more depth at the links between depression and an unrealistic, perfectionist mindset in Chapter Fifteen.

'BE PERFECT' ANTIDOTE

Remind yourself that the idea of perfection is a myth, a mental construct that we invented and put onto nature. It isn't real, and it doesn't exist. Don't try and be perfect, just try to do your best. Again, not just for others, for yourself, on your own terms. Track how well you can do and what you can achieve by doing your best over time. Stretch yourself in a realistic and measured way, and enjoy the experience of discovering what you can really achieve.

BEST VS PERFECT

The concept of perfection is not as useful as the idea of 'best'. Wanting to do or try one's best is a healthy idea. Deciding to strive for and bring one's best is a very constructive mental process, which can be developed by using *encouraging self-talk* and *clear decision-making*. Beating one's best can be very rewarding, as it is generally the result of a combination of hard work, practice and tenacity over time. It is satisfying seeing our efforts paying off. In the later chapters of this book, we will look at how to rewrite unhelpful mental scripts about the need to be perfect, and guard against the depression and anxiety which these often lead to.

Whatever area we are trying to achieve in, whether it is in our professional lives or personal lives, all of us are able to recognise the influence of the five key drivers on how we live on a daily basis. It's important to be able to recognise them in our behaviour, and when things might be getting out of balance.

Here are some questions to ask yourself which will help you actively reflect on where you might be holding yourself back:

- What are the top two drivers that you recognise in yourself?
- When do they get triggered – can you think of any frequent scenarios in your life where this happens?

- What are the antidotes to these drivers?
- What are the mental skill techniques you could use to activate these antidotes?

SIX
What to Do with Fear

'If I prepare really well, and do all the things around my game plan, knowing my part in the game and trusting my prep, I won't get nervous . . . I visualise a lot'

Conrad Smith

I remember just before the European indoor championships, 2005, for the whole week beforehand, I was riddled with nerves. I couldn't eat. Sitting on the plane, inundated with anxiety, nerves, negative thoughts, doubts. When I got to Madrid, all I wanted to do was stay in my hotel room. Not interact with people, just lie on the bed. I was so nervous, and every time I got down to the food hall, I had to have water to force the food down.

I did that for the whole weekend, and still managed to win and come back with a gold medal. To be honest though, I look back now – and the whole weekend, I just didn't enjoy it. It's a shame to say that, but at the time it was all about the nerves and [the feeling] that I didn't want to go through that again. This was my mindset.

Then the next season, of course, I dreaded it. I dreaded all the expectations that people now had of me, [about] what I was going to go on and do – expectations to beat some of the world's best in the outdoor championships.

So in 2007, there was a lot more pressure – I had never experienced [anything like] it before. My face all over the papers. I didn't want to leave the house and have to talk to anyone.

Only later in my career did I get an understanding of mental skills [and how they could help me] to deal with how I felt. Before, I always thought that the feelings I had were part of the way you were meant to feel.

David Gillick, Irish track and field athlete; two-time European Indoor Championships gold medal winner (2005 and 2007)

Fear is one of our oldest and most basic human feelings, and was originally employed as a natural defence reaction connected with our early warning and survival system. It is exceptionally important in alerting us to the presence of danger and keeping us safe from physical threat. The chemical reactions triggered in our bodies by fear help us gear into action and are connected with our fight/flight/freeze responses. It's very useful when danger is present – but not so useful when it is not, such as when we are only imagining that we are under threat.

In the modern world, we are rarely faced with situations where our physical safety is in immediate danger – we are certainly not confronted with life-threatening dangers on a daily, or even more frequent, basis the way our Stone Age ancestors were. Yet the fear response is still part of our autonomic make-up, and so we modern humans tend to transpose our feelings of fear onto non-threatening situations which nonetheless challenge our sense of security. Performance situations commonly trigger fearful feelings –

or at least the kind of adrenalin response we associate with fight, flight or freeze. So, an upcoming significant event, an event that has personal importance to us, can generate anxiety and nervous anticipation. This might be a big game, a test, a presentation, an interview or even a date.

Each of us feels fear in different ways and to different degrees, depending on the level of importance we've attributed to the upcoming event or performance opportunity. Just as we are all unique as individuals, so the way we perceive the situation and the way we react to it is also unique. For one person, a test or a big game or an appearance on live TV may be a thrilling prospect, an eagerly anticipated event. For someone else, it might conjure up feelings of *dread*! Highly successful professional sportspeople are not immune to such feelings. Richie Sadlier gave Brent this very candid insight into his own feelings about playing professional football at the height of his career:

> I would be unavailable for certain matches due to injury and, in some regards, be glad of it. In fact, my first cap for Ireland came when I had an injury worry, and in some ways that made it easier – I had an excuse, should it go wrong; I could focus my worries elsewhere. On the morning of some matches, [I would] be dreading kick-off because my mindset on that particular day was, 'Well, you don't belong here'; 'No one thinks you should be on the team'; 'The senior lads on the team don't know why you've been picked'; 'No one in the crowd respects you, and as soon as three o'clock comes, all of this will become obvious and it will prove to everyone why that is the case'; 'I will be what I told myself I was – a faker'.
>
> *Richie Sadlier, former professional footballer; 145 appearances for Millwall, capped for Ireland; football pundit*

Hardly what you'd imagine a professional footballer with a very successful eight years with Millwall under his belt, and who also represented his home country, Republic of Ireland, at international level might be thinking before he stepped on the pitch. Here Richie is showing great integrity and courage in being willing to speak out so honestly.

The point here is that no one – even the most apparently successful or confident among us – is immune to the feeling of fear. So, when it comes, we need to be prepared. When do you feel afraid? How do you deal with such feelings?

The energy at the heart of all feelings is useful and helps us understand who we are and what we need to do to help produce better results – and fear is no different in this regard. However, another fairly natural human reaction is to try avoid anything that feels uncomfortable – and fear and anxiety are not enjoyable feelings. Consequently, we don't want to dwell too much on them. Fear is something we'd frequently prefer to side-step and are loath to feel or admit to. Not only do we not like the effects of it, we tend to regard it as a sign of weakness and as an unhelpful and unwanted experience. When it comes to performance and improving our wellbeing, however, this is a mistake.

Trying to ignore, deny or repress fear and feelings of anxiety is what could be called the 'low performance' way: rather than leading to better results and greater mental and physical wellbeing, it takes us in the opposite direction and can be actively detrimental to us. There is a natural energy connected to all feelings, and ignoring our emotions means that energy has no healthy outlet. But it has to go somewhere – so it goes underground. If not acknowledged and usefully channelled, the energy of fear will transform into worry, 'dis-stress', anxiety and, ultimately, panic – which we will look at more closely in the next chapter.

There is a direct correlation between stress and productivity. The more a person can manage themselves emotionally and psychologically, the better they can perform in many stressful situations. And the more stress we can manage, the higher our productivity can be. But all of us can reach a limit, a breaking point where additional stress leads to a reduction in productivity – in a very dramatic way. Our performance crashes, productivity goes out the window. This is our 'dis-stress' level. If stress is productive, then dis-stress is unproductive.

At this tipping point, our systems become overloaded by competing demands, like a computer crashing due to a 'too many commands' error – and this can be very upsetting and damaging.

A 'high-performance' approach, one leading to wellness, involves *acknowledging*, *reframing*, *reducing* and *redirecting* the nervous energy generated by fear and anxiety. We can learn to use the extra adrenalin to actively improve our performance and bring better results; in time, we may even be able to transform our feelings of dread at the prospect of upcoming challenges into a sense of excitement and positive anticipation. Which in turn can enable us to actually enjoy the moment of performance itself!

So, what's the 'high-performance' way to deal with fear? I find the following three-step approach, which involves the mental skills of *active reflection* and *self-awareness*, to be a very good place to start.

Step One: Acknowledge how you are feeling and the physical symptoms of fear

Checking in with your body, where are the 'fight, flight or freeze' chemicals making themselves felt the most? *Where* do you feel fear? Common sensations include an overactive or painful stomach or upper gut, chest tightness, neck tension and jaw-clenching, tight facial muscles, a dry mouth, sweaty palms, increased heart rate, flushing of the face or chest. In a more general, ongoing way, unsettled sleep can be a strong indicator of fear and anxiety in our system. This of course makes sense. The mind is overactive and agitated, filled with anxious thoughts – why would we go to sleep if there was an external threat in the room – like a fire, or a burglar wielding a knife?

Step Two: Measure and assess

On a scale of one to ten, where does your level of anxiety sit? Once you've put a number on its intensity, it's time to examine the feeling, to take a closer look at what thoughts could be activating these chemicals in your body. Rather than trying to deny or ignore fear or anxiety, assessing it in this way helps you to get a greater sense of control over it, and gives you some distance too. Ask yourself some questions, such as: 'What am I worrying about?' 'What am I afraid will happen?' 'Is it about right now or something coming up?' 'Or am I afraid that something which happened in the past will happen again?', and so on.

In performance situations, immediately before an event, we can sometimes project old fears into the future ('This happened the last time; it's going to happen again now'). Past fear response is *not* helpful – not just as regards performance, but generally too, most of the time. Past events are over and done with and cannot be altered. Their time is gone. In the most practical sense, they cannot hurt us, since this time no longer exists. This type of fear is *archaic* (outdated) and the best way of dealing with it, after acknowledging it, is to simply use some basic calming techniques – such as the mental skills of *grounding, meditation* and *talking to someone* – to reduce the intensity of the feelings.

Present or *future* (anticipatory) fear – such as the nerves we feel before a big event/performance – is useful, however, if we approach it in the right way. The associated chemicals which flood our body can have a galvanising effect, providing us with the extra energy to do something. The trick is learning how to manage this energy properly.

Step Three: Make the energy of fear work for you

Decide that you want to express and exercise this energy in a productive way. There are several key mental skills which will help you here.

One of these is *goal-setting*, which we looked at in Chapters Two and Four. Get a pen and paper, and write down what you will do with the extra energy generated by nerves. How will you translate it directly into action – by, for example, training or preparing more often or with greater focus; by repeatedly practising and honing a skill, especially if the worry is about that particular skill.

In a business context, this might mean doing more preparation for an important meeting, or practising a presentation out loud in front of others which will provide constructive and supportive feedback. In personal relationships, where there is a difficult conversation to be had, or a challenging issue that needs addressing, this might involve using the energy of nervous anticipation to get your thoughts clearer and work out the most constructive language to use when you're expressing them to the other person. The mental skills of *active reflection, thought writing* and *clear decision-making* will be most useful here. *Visualisation* is another good technique to use and we will look at this in more detail later in this chapter.

As a kid I actually enjoyed exams. Not always in all subjects, admittedly – but the experience of exams generally was something I liked. Exams didn't happen that often, so I liked the sense of taking part in an important event. Each time, I'd be curious about the challenge: how I'd be able to stay really focused; how I'd manage my feelings and if I would be able to actually enjoy them, so that the nervous excitement wouldn't tip over into anxiousness. As I said earlier, different people react differently to the same circumstances – different strokes for different folks, as they say.

While exams didn't frighten me, other school experiences did, however. For example, I hated the prospect of reading out loud in class. I was not a fast reader, largely due to having a mild form of dyslexia. I struggled to read at the same pace as my classmates. Particularly when trying to read quickly and under pressure, I'd see the letters of the words on the page back to front and stumble over certain words. I was fine in a more relaxed situation, at my own pace – reading in a library or at home – but once I was expected to read in public, and in front of all my classmates, I would find it so much more difficult.

So, each time the teacher decided to go around the room and randomly choose students to read aloud, I'd feel my upper gut start to tighten – the fear was in me! Churning stomach, dry mouth, heart rate up, sweaty brow and hands, blurry eyes – the stress hormones would surge throughout my body. At the same time, my thoughts would be racing, panicked: 'Oh no! He's going to call my name. I'll have to speak out. I'm trapped! I'll have to run the gauntlet of ridicule, the risk of being seen as a fool.'

This fear of ridicule or to be seen as stupid didn't go away after my schooldays were over. It sat, unacknowledged, in the recesses of my mind. Unbeknownst to me, it would grow over time in an upsetting way. It reappeared in my twenties, in a very specific context. Each time I found myself in the situation of being asked to introduce myself in a large group setting – a frequent occurrence at that time in my life, as a student and academic – the stress hormones would kick in and start to hijack my brain in anticipation. My brain felt fuzzy, like cotton wool. My heart rate again increased. I would be sitting there, waiting and squirming, until it was my turn to say something. Even something as simple as 'Hello, I'm Jason . . .' seemed so difficult; almost insurmountable.

Years later, I picked up an expression that beautifully described the sensations I would go through at these times – sitting there, waiting and watching as the energy of the room moved around the circle of people and the focus switched to next in line, slowly and gradually coming for *me*. I called it 'creeping death'!

I can laugh at it now, and at this melodramatic term – but at the time it was very discombobulating and distressing. I know I am not alone. Many others I've worked with and spoken with have described having very similar experiences. Individuals who in small groups are confident, outspoken and eloquent, but who, when faced with a larger room and a bigger audience, suddenly find themselves dumbstruck, fearful and embarrassed when they are asked to say something. When our systems are on high alert, adrenalin, cortisol and other stress chemicals are released in our bodies, and make for a powerful cocktail that can befuddle our brains.

So, to the conclusion of my personal story. Although it never really went away and I just got used to it with more practise, some years later, when I was in my thirties, this lurking fear of speaking in public situations began to unexpectedly increase at the beginning of workshop presentations I was giving. Even though by this stage in my life I had done hundreds of presentations and a lot of work-related public speaking, all of a sudden at the opening of workshops I would start to feel the familiar unpleasant sensations in my body. As I stood up at the front of the room, with all the attention focused on me, to introduce myself to an audience of 60–200 people, the sense of pressure was enough to re-trigger all those feelings in my body, from the time in my schooldays when I was asked to read out in front of my classmates.

Fear is not logical or reasonable – it is an instinctive response, a hangover, if you like, from our earliest days as humans but still hugely important. Although the risks involved in reading out in front of the class are light years away from being faced with the very real physical threat of being gored by a wild animal, at the moment the fear sets in, our bodies do not make these kinds of distinctions.

So, how did I overcome this distressing, or at least highly unpleasant, problem? To start off with, as well as practising and knowing my opening lines, I began using an *anchoring* technique to help me get through these sensations when they were happening. I held something smooth but with a sharpish edge or point in the palm of my hand – like a white board marker or highlighter lid, or even a stone I picked up from outside on my way into the venue. Each time I felt the feelings of excessive nervousness rising, I would gently press the sharp edge or tip into my hand. The mild discomfort this caused was instantly picked up and responded to by my brain, which, registering the sensation, immediately sent attention and energy to its source, in order to find out what was happening to my hand – presenting my body with the possibility of a real, physical threat, as opposed to a false, imagined psychological one (the fear of freezing up and ridicule). Breaking my mind's intense focus on my unconscious imagined fears by means of this mild physical sensation was enough to halt the nervous energy in its tracks, allowing me to speak freely and open the workshop as I had practised and planned for. Strange as it may sound, this tactic really worked and enabled me to break the cycle of anticipation and dread my body would feel when faced with initiating public speaking. It goes without saying of course (although I will say it anyway) that I am talking about inducing just a mild feeling of physical discomfort, not encouraging anyone to hurt themselves more seriously, or self-harm. And there are many *anchoring* techniques to choose from, this is just one that worked for me.

EXERCISE

When it comes to dealing with fear and nervous energy prior to performance, *centring* is another very useful mental skills technique. It is a breathing technique that focuses on our breathing muscle, our diaphragm – located at the centre of our torso.

Begin by saying in your mind, 'I am breathing in; I am breathing out,' as you feel your breath going in and out of your body. Now give the act of breathing your full, undivided focus. As you breathe in, feel the sensation of air entering your nostrils. Notice how the nose feels a bit cold with each in-breath; how the outgoing air feels warmer.

Then move the focus of your energy to your diaphragm – just below your ribs. Feel this large muscle in the centre of your body as it controls the inhalation and exhalation of each breath. As you breathe in, your belly should expand outwards like your belly is filling with air, then push back with this muscle, towards your spine, like you are emptying the air from your belly. When you are comfortable with this motion, try holding the muscle and your breath as you breathe fully in or fully out – like the belly is either full of air or empty of air. This technique is about gaining greater control and mastery over your breathing and, consequently, over the physical symptoms of nerves. Long, slow breathing in particular brings a greater sense of calm throughout our nervous system and more oxygen into the body will clear the head and help to disperse stress chemicals. When finished, just let go and breathe naturally again.

Practised often and regularly, *centring* is a really effective technique for focusing the mind, calming the body and absorbing pressure. Other mental skills such as *visualisation* and *strength-based thinking* (a technique described later in the Glossary section) are very useful too as ways of redirecting the mind and channelling the energy of nervous anticipation. Let's hear again from All Black great Conrad Smith about how such techniques have helped him:

> I know if I prepare really well, and do all the things around my game plan, knowing my part in the game and trusting my prep, that I won't get nervous or not know a call or something like that. I visualise a lot. I visualise what happens in a game; I visualise making mistakes and how I am going to react to them. Visualising myself being under pressure and feeling nervous, and then [thinking about] how I am going to breathe and deal with it.
>
> *Conrad Smith – professional rugby player, former All Black centre with 94 caps; 126 games for the Hurricanes; qualified lawyer*

Using *visualisation* just prior to an event, we can also imagine and picture exactly how we want our performance to go at each stage – and how we will retrieve the situation if things don't go quite as planned. We can also spend some time thinking about how satisfying it will feel when we are able to see these plans through; about the sense of fulfilment excellence in execution will bring. Research shows that our bodies react in a very similar way to visualised (imagined) stimulation as they do to the real thing.

If we find that our bodies are still generating too much nervous energy, we can call on techniques like *flicking*, in which physical gestures are used to expel the excess energy. We will look at this technique in more detail in Chapters Nine and Ten, where we'll explore the most effective mental skills tools and strategies to use during performance.

SEVEN
When Fear Becomes Panic

'I was too young to be having a heart attack but that's how it felt'

Brent Pope

Brent

I remember the first time I had a major panic attack. It was out of the blue. I was about 13 or 14, and having a bath on a Sunday night. I was sitting there in the bath, thinking about school and life, and all the normal sorts of things you think about at that age, when suddenly heaps of negative thoughts started to roll in like a dark cloud in my head. I know people with depression often talk about the 'black dog' or the fog, and I understand what they mean. I suddenly felt afraid of everything. I was terrified and crippled with panic. I was so scared that I started to hyperventilate: my breath came in short gasps, and I had pains in my chest. I was too young to be having a heart attack, but that's how I felt as I sat there, shaking and cowering with fear. I sat in that bath until the water was cold. Crying like a scared little boy. I had no idea what was wrong with me – but I knew also from that moment on that it was not normal, that not every teenager was going through this. This was not just worry or anxiety, it was a terrifying, panic-driven fear of failure.

Over time, and if there is no safe outlet for them, continual worry and feelings of pressure can accumulate, building up a physical response in our system. The chemicals released in our bodies as a result – namely, adrenalin, cortisol, norepinephrine – lead in turn to our brains being flooded with more anxiety-provoking thoughts. This eventually triggers a simulated external threat reaction, whereby our system believes that a very real danger is imminent – one which threatens our very survival – but does not know what, where or how to tackle it. This is a panic attack.

Our internal alarm has been triggered, alerting our bodies to real and present danger, when in fact there isn't any. Panic attacks are very upsetting, leaving our bodies and minds very distressed and confused. It is as if our system is glitching – in a very dramatic and disempowering way. This is where the IT analogy ends, however, because unlike a computer, we cannot simply reboot. Which is why we feel powerless.

But we are not powerless!

We *can* help the system figure out what is happening and provide an avenue for this energy to go. When fear has developed into panic or anxiety, mental skills such as *grounding* and *centring* are very useful, to begin with. As are *talking, encouraging self-talk* and *progressive thinking.* Let's hear more from Brent on how he managed his own experiences of panic attacks.

I have learnt from my experiences, and today I know I can do a lot of things if I feel a panic attack coming on. Even being able to recognise when one is about to happen helps, making it less of a sudden shock. I know that it starts with a series of negative thoughts that are becoming more irrational – and they keep on coming. That's how it starts. Maybe following a minor incident, but sometimes out of the blue, when my normal thinking might develop into a negative, persistent and crippling thought pattern.

So, the first thing I do is try to calm myself down by visualisation. I don't call it meditating – it is more like, 'OK, this is happening right now, what can I do right now?' I picture myself in a calm place as best I can. I'm not the world's best person at creating pictures and images in my head, but I try – I have to. I picture myself in the ocean, for example – I am sitting down, waist-deep; the water is warm, and it feels soothing. I am always facing the shore; tropical palms are swaying, beyond the turquoise water. The waves break gently against my body in a nice slow, soothing rhythm: in and out, in and out. I try to replicate that in my breathing – in and out, calming and soothing, as the waves just roll over my body. This helps me, even when I'm curled up in a ball, wondering when I will feel OK, wondering if I am having a heart attack. After a while, the panic slowly starts to dissipate, meaning that the physical symptoms – the shortness of breath, sweating and rigid state – start to ease off. This allows me to go to 'stage two', which involves changing my thought processes.

VISUALISATION

We can see here how Brent uses the very useful mental skill of *visualisation* to very powerful effect as a means of managing the peak moments of a panic attack. In an earlier chapter we looked at how *visualisation* can be used as a technique for enhancing future performance, by creating a mental story ahead of the event which helps our bodies 'see' success – acting it out in imagination activates the same neural pathways and chemical responses as actually playing it out in real time. The principle when using this technique to cope with panic and anxiety is the same – your body (and mind) will respond best if all the senses are activated in the *visualisation*. Choose an image or create a scene which you associate with a feeling of deep relaxation, safety and comfort. If you are afraid of water, for example, you won't recreate a scene like Brent's, where you're lying in the ocean with the waves washing over you. Only you will know what place or activity will work for you. Some people imagine being in a very large and very soft and comfortable chair or bed, for example. Imagine what your body will feel like, what the smells and sounds around you are, what you see close by, painting in the detail as you continue to take deep, slow, regular breaths. Imagery works best from the first person, so always start with yourself – seeing through your own eyes and from your own perspective. As with *meditation*, regular practice of a particular *visualisation* will make it easier for you to enter into it, and relax, more quickly. So don't wait for the moment when a panic attack strikes to bring your calming *visualisation* into play for the first time – try practising it whenever you are reasonably calm and relaxed, and make it a regular part of your mental skills routine.

'PROGRESSIVE' THINKING (FOR PANIC)

So, what else helps in dealing with panic and panic attacks? Above, Brent mentions being able to move on to 'stage two', once he has managed to get the most pressing physical symptoms of panic to subside. Let's hear more from him on this:

As I try to time my breathing with the waves in my visualisation, the feeling of panic dissipates enough for me to start working on the overall process of tackling – and changing – my thought patterns.

When I get the negative thoughts, I start by working backwards. I know this sounds weird, but I need to tell myself that these thoughts are not real, that they are only thoughts. So I ask myself, 'What's the worst that can happen? And is that really likely?' If I'm worried about work, I'll reason with myself like this: 'OK, so I lose the job I love in RTÉ and I'm no longer wanted as a pundit in the sports industry. What's the worst that can happen? Maybe I'll get another TV job, one that allows me to make documentaries, or something else that I would love to do. And that in turn might open up some other new avenues.' Or, if I start thinking about my partner leaving me, I'll talk myself down in the same kind of way: 'OK, it would be hard and hurt like hell, as relationship break-ups do, but maybe I might meet another special person in time, or even be OK on my own.' And so on. I'll challenge myself, asking if my thoughts and fear have any reality or foundation, or if they are just that – thoughts. Am I really going to be homeless, living in a shelter somewhere, alone and isolated? Really?

For me, the secret to surviving mental health difficulties is – in that moment of panic or depression – to work on simply getting over that initial hump. And I think that is vital for people to know – that small steps to recovery are the way forward. Sometimes just being able to reassure somebody in a dark place that it will get better is enough to give them something to hang on to. Try and look at what you are most worried about, and ask yourself what is the worst that can happen. I start there, and I always look at other scenarios, other options – and that starts calming me down. I also focus on the highlights of what I have achieved so far, and start to find the positivity in the situation. I think about just taking small steps. Nobody's life runs completely smoothly, we all face ups and downs. Just like any athlete, we have peaks and troughs and moments of greatness and pride. Moments of weakness too, mistakes, disappointments and regrets – it's what makes us all human. It's what we learn from these experiences that helps us win.

Here Brent is using the mental skill *progressive thinking*, which is invaluable when we are trying to deal with feelings of fear and the overwhelming barrage of negative thoughts that so often accompany them. When feeling afraid or panicky, just follow through to the other side of the scary images or thoughts. Work through the imagined scenario. Where does it actually go? How bad is it really? Play it out fully, until the thoughts and images get to a place of less intensity, like asking yourself 'and then what might happen . . . and then what might happen'. In doing so, you will find your thinking becoming more rational and reasonable – maybe even enough to recognise the overblown nature of the fears generated by your sense of panic. Then you could make a plan of action, if appropriate – or write down the other, more positive options and alternative scenarios that could equally happen. Instead of feeding the negative by replaying negative scenarios in our minds, start to feed the positive too.

As Brent's example shows, it doesn't matter who we are or what we have achieved (or the level of confidence we present to the outside world); we can all be affected by anxiety and panic attacks. We will look in more detail at the problems of anxiety and depression, some of their deeper causes and how to tackle them, in Chapter Fifteen.

MEDITATION MINDSET

One of the most effective mental skills techniques for calming the body and mind, and settling the brain chemicals generated by stress, is *meditation*. The 'peacefulness' of this simple practice defuses the internal strife that negative, worrying thoughts can create. Regular *meditation* sends a message to the body that there is no immediate external threat. To use the lingo of the US military, this enables our body's autonomic defence responses – our fight or flight instincts – to stand down from 'DEFCON' level 1 (high alert, imminent threat of global attack) to level 5 (normal peacetime status quo)!

Meditation has been around for thousands of years but is only now having a wider impact in the western world. Recent scientific and medical research has endorsed the beneficial effects of regular *meditation*, which include: 'significantly increased practical intelligence, field independence, creativity, and speed of information processing, as well as significantly decreased anxiety'.[1] Regular practice also helps with pain management, a healthier immune system and increased focus and self-discipline.

Many people first experience *meditation* in a free class or a weekend workshop, where an instructor may say things like: 'slow your breathing'; 'clear your mind'; 'be at peace'. Instructions like this can be very frustrating, however, and can quickly put people off meditating or going back for another session. Clearing your mind or being at peace is not easy to do, especially when our minds are very active, and we find ourselves plagued by the many thoughts that randomly bombard us. Slowing breathing is also not that straightforward when stress chemicals are present, or the person feels very self-conscious, sitting quietly in a group. So people can quickly give up on *meditation*, believing that it's not for them or that they just can't do it properly.

If this is you, don't worry – you are not alone. And ironically, the fact is that we all know how to meditate naturally and don't need a classroom setting to do it. We just need to bring some awareness and structure to it for greater beneficiary effects. An obvious example of *meditation* is simply experiencing weather – appreciating the quietness of snow, the sound of rain or the smell of a breeze. The simple act of sunbathing can be an act of *meditation* – sitting or lying, and just listening, feeling the heat on your body and being semi-conscious of the noises that are going on around you. Listening to music is another good example of informal *meditation* – being so absorbed in the music that time means nothing; we are simply immersed in the moment and the sound. Many of us find people-watching to be an effective form of relaxation – the act of just observing others passing by, busy with their own lives and preoccupations, without the need for us to engage or intervene.

Remember being at school on a hot summer's day and letting your mind drift off into the sunlight, to what was happening just outside the window; hearing kids playing in the sports fields and imagining being out there too, perhaps lying on the grass, away from the lesson going on in the classroom? Remember the sense of rest that you felt, that sense of ease? Daydreaming can be another type of *meditation*!

So, there are lots of different ways to meditate.

A VERY OLD PRACTICE

Perhaps the reason that *meditation* can have such a profound effect on us is that its roots go back a very long way in human history. There is a theory that back in ancient times we would sit around for long stretches of our day, in a world free from all the excessive noise and stimulation we have to contend with today. Once sustenance-gathering had been done, we just sat around, being very present, relaxed, connected and at ease. No chores to do: no vacuuming, no laundry, no dish-washing. No worrying about money or things, no social media to constantly demand our attention. Just lots of time to simply sit and connect with our environment, ourselves and our tribe. There is evidence for this in one of the oldest living races on the planet, the Aboriginal people of Australia who have been around for 40,000–60,000 years. These people do not have a word for chores. Traditionally, they simply carried with them all they needed, finding food each day. It would probably be fair to say however that they experienced more moments of deep peace and connection than most of us living in modern western society ever do. What does this say about advancement?

Meditation is the ability to be either very present and at ease or very focused on something, such as a thought, a concept, a feeling, a word, a physical sensation, an external noise or an object. So, it can be a process of going in (internal focus) or going out (external focus), or a combination of both. For most of us living in our society today, the most successful type of *meditation*, especially when starting out, is a structured *meditation*. Apart from anything else, it involves a defined period of time, which can be booked in to a hectic diary. Experience tells us that actively scheduling something makes it happen – not deliberately setting time aside usually results in it being 'deprioritised' and forgotten about.

Initially, you should aim to practise for just a few minutes daily – setting an alarm on a phone or a watch will help you define in advance the exact time you want to spend on each session. To get started, you might like to read up on the subject. Joseph Goldstein's *Mindfulness: A Practical Guide to Awakening* or *The Art of Happiness* by Howard C. Cutler and the Dalai Lama are good jumping-off points and I've included some helpful apps and websites at the end of this book. Most meditations start with a focus on breathing, but what is often missed is the simple but important phrase, 'I am . . .' These words allow the mind and body to feel more connected in terms of time and place. So, actually saying, 'I am breathing in . . . I am breathing out' in your mind as you inhale and exhale will anchor you more strongly to the present moment and to reality. Regularly thinking this phrase with each breath helps to bring the mind back when it starts to go elsewhere (which it inevitably will, especially when you begin). Repeating this simple practice on a daily basis, increasing the length of time you spend in *meditation* very gradually, will help to build discipline of the mind – a key factor in high-performance situations and when trying to calm nerves and fearful feelings immediately prior to an important event. (We touch on this again in Chapter Seventeen.)

DISCIPLINED MINDSET

This exercise is similar to the earlier daily discipline exercise in Chapter Two which combines the key qualities of focus and discipline through *meditation*, but with an additional challenging distraction to really embed the results. Use a stopwatch to set the length of time you wish to do this discipline meditation. Begin as usual with the phrase 'I am breathing in, I am breathing out' and repeat this for a number of minutes.

Then begin to repeat the word 'discipline' in your mind. If the mind begins to wander, keep bringing it back to the word 'discipline'.

With practice, the mind will make the connection between this word and the state of focused attention that is *meditation*. The word 'discipline' will become *anchored* to this physical and mental state, meaning that each time it is repeated, the mind will automatically become more focused. When external distractions or noises occur, bring back this sense of focus by simply bringing to mind the word 'discipline'.

To help with filtering out distracting noise, this technique should be practised with loud music playing. This can prove invaluable for a sportsperson trying to maintain their focus at a critical point in a game while an excited crowd is screaming encouragement (or the opposite of encouragement!). Crank up the sounds and, for the time you have set the meditation, see how calm and focused you can be with the disciplined meditation mindset.

ENGINE OIL FOR THE MIND: MEDITATION

As far as mental skills techniques go, there are few more powerful than *meditation*.

Meditation can be as important for an athlete as engine oil is for a high-performance engine.

With regard to engine oil:

1. It lubricates moving parts, preventing them from rubbing together and creating friction, therefore protecting them from excessive wear. *Meditation protects the mind by reducing negative, conflictive thinking.*

2. By reducing friction, it allows the moving parts to work more smoothly and efficiently together. *Meditation helps develop psychological awareness and clearer skills-based decision-making.*

3. The higher the grade of oil, the better the performance. *With meditation, the more regular the practice, the higher the performance.*

When introducing *meditation* to athletes or teams, it's important to understand that there are different ways to meditate, not just one way. The key element, though, is that it helps develop awareness and it is better to have structure to it.

THE HABIT PROCESS

A key to consistent performance success is the ability to form habits, and this is the same with *meditation* – initially, daily for just a few minutes, which can easily be achieved by setting a daily phone or watch alarm.

Another of the beauties of meditation is that it helps build mindful focus. Both discipline and focus are highly sought after for sporting success. (Focus, or concentration, is covered as part of The Four C's of Performance, in Chapter Ten). A variation of the above meditation is with an externally focused mindful exercise. To do this, begin as always with the phrase 'I am breathing in . . . I am breathing out' and repeat this for a number of minutes.

Then begin to quietly repeat the word 'focus' in your mind. If the mind begins to wander, bring it back to the word 'focus' and breathe in and breathe out as usual. Close your eyes. When your body feels relaxed, allow yourself to calmly listen to and pick up the various noises that are happening in your environment. Use the ears to focus on the various sounds, acknowledging them but not having to do anything with them, not having to react to them but simply acknowledging that they are happening, that they exist.

See if you can name the various noises without holding onto the thought, just let it pass by like thinking 'I hear air blowing, I hear a car horn, I hear an elevator, I hear a child's laughter' – listening without reaction, just pleasantly enjoying the *in the now* experience.

Over time and with practice, the mind again will attach the habit connected to this word, *anchoring* it to this physical state and focusing the mind whenever the eyes are closed and the word 'focus' is repeated.

This is particularly good when a person is feeling the sensations related to excess nerves, anxiety or panic. Simply remind yourself of the word 'focus' in combination with the other mental skill of *grounding*:

Step 1: Recognise if you and your body feel anxiety rising.

Step 2: Lower the tension in your body by *grounding* yourself. To do this, send attention to your feet. Your big toe first, on either foot, is the best place to start. Send energy there and start feeling into your big toes, listening to them and seeing what messages come back – hot, cold, sweaty, tingly, painful, etc. Then gradually feel into your other toes, wiggling them, and then to your whole foot.

Step 3: Start to feel yourself breathing in and breathing out as above. Start to slow your process of breathing, gradually longer breaths and slower and slower.

Step 4: In your mind focus on your breathing more and more by repeating the word 'focus' quietly over and over to activate the familiar sense of relaxedness. Allow any external noise to just come and go, to pass through you but not affect your relaxed mindful state.

When you are ready to go and do what you wanted to do, tell yourself 'I am ready now' and come out of the meditation.

When Fear Becomes Panic

As a mental skill, *meditation* is exceptional. It is free, and available 24 hours a day and for any length of time – from 20 seconds to multiple hours. It is especially valuable when dealing with overwhelming feelings of anxiety, or with nervousness.

EIGHT
Rethinking Fear

'Nerves are a good thing. I came to embrace them'

David Gillick

A panic attack is a very extreme form of anxiety – a culmination of ongoing stress and pressure on the system, which eventually goes into overload, causing critical chemical imbalances in the body which in turn disrupt our normal functioning. As Brent's example clearly shows, anxiety and panic attacks can affect anyone. So how can we manage ongoing, long-term fears which hamper our performance and our freedom to do the things we most want to in life – in sport, in business or in any other area of endeavour?

In the following interview with Brent, Irish rugby great Victor Costello provides an astonishing insight into the power of confronting head-on the things we fear the most:

Brent: Victor, you originally had a fear of flying but you went on to become a pilot. You must have stepped right out of your comfort zone doing this! When did you first experience your fear of flying?

Victor: What happened . . . was that, since I was 15 years of age,

I'd been sent places I didn't really want to be. Being in the Irish athletics team [a five-times Irish shot put champion, Victor also represented Ireland internationally, including at the 1992 Olympics in Barcelona] . . . meant that during the summer period I was away in other countries. It was great, but at times I was forced to not be with my mates at the weekends. On one of the flights coming back from Dubai, we hit an air pocket. It was a very disturbing experience. As a young guy, every time I got on a plane [after that], my fear became: 'Is that going to happen again?' It became a real anxiety thing: 'What might happen this time?'

Later, with rugby, we were also travelling a lot. I knew about the 'fear of flight' courses, but I didn't want to spend the money on them – so I decided instead to go and do a flying lesson! Early on during the lessons I would be saying to the instructor, 'Jez, avoid that cloud' or 'Don't go up too high!' or 'Don't go down too fast!'

Coming to the end of my career, I then realised I needed another career and decided to follow the flying through. In the theoretical part, I learned what keeps a plane up in the air; what makes it drop; what makes turbulence or clears out turbulence; what's dangerous for a plane and what's not. I realised it's [all about] Mother Nature. Like, if you go out to sea in a kayak, you are trusting the sea. It can still turn at any stage, but if you go down this way in a kayak, it's fine, or if you go down that way, it's not.

Victor Costello – former professional rugby player; 39 caps for Ireland, 121 appearances for Leinster; airline pilot

Victor's story is incredible in many ways, an example of what we can achieve if, instead of ignoring or denying the things we are most afraid of, we engage with them directly. Instead of giving in to his fear of flying and spending the rest of his life avoiding air travel, and perhaps turning down many important opportunities and experiences because of this, he became a professional airline pilot, making a living from engaging every day with what was once one of his greatest fears. What is interesting also about his account is that gaining knowledge and practical understanding about flying and the physical principles behind it helped him get a handle on how realistic and unrealistic his fears actually were, making it possible for him to challenge the irrational and illogical aspects of his thinking. (In the same way that Brent's understanding of the physiology behind panic attacks – the physical reasons why they happen – helps him to handle them better when they occur.) The *what* of what is happening, and the *how* to influence it.

Later in the same interview, talking about the real-life challenges of being a pilot, Victor tells Brent about a difficult situation he once had to deal with, which anyone would have found terrifying (let alone someone who had a fear of flying!):

> I was in severe turbulence once flying over the Alps. We had gone in twice and there was a jetstream getting worse each time. On the way back out the last time that night, the turbulence was ferocious. We slowed down and, because we had already been through it that day, we knew how to get out of it; where to climb to, and so on. I could hear on the radio that other flights were nervous going through it. When we got to where it smoothed

> out, we got on the radio to tell these flights, 'If you pass through it, you will be fine.' Even with all of the adrenaline, when you are in that position, you are dealing with it. But then I spent the rest of the flight worrying in case we hit it again. So, the fear of it happening is worse than it actually happening! I learned a lot in sport that has helped me manage this.

Here, Victor highlights something very important – that imagined fear often feels far worse than going through a real-life challenge. All of us have experienced this – where the anticipatory fear far outweighs the actual event. This is the fear associated with negative expectations: as we think about an important upcoming performance or event, we create fear around all the possible things that could go wrong: 'What if I don't play well?' 'What if I get sent off?' 'What if I don't speak well?' 'What if I faint or forget my words?' These are the dreaded 'what if's!

THE 'WHAT IF' GAME

Especially just prior to an important event, many a person's mind has been hijacked by the very damaging 'what if' game. Where we torture ourselves by imagining all the ways in which something could go wrong. Where something we've been hoping for and working towards – the opportunity to showcase our skills and fulfil a long-held dream – becomes something we dread and would do anything to avoid if we could. It's a horrible, self-destructive game many of us can't help playing with ourselves, and which always ends in an image of us losing.

'What if's are all about the *potential* for certain negative things to happen in the future. Initially, they might seem reasonable enough – 'what if' implies that something is plausible, that it could happen. So it might seem that we are just covering all our bases, considering all the options, when we follow this line of thinking. However, what is striking about 'what if' or negative speculative thinking is that the outcomes envisaged are invariably pessimistic and self-defeating.

These 'what if's are nothing more than negative thoughts gone wild. The best way to deal with them is to simply refuse to engage with them, to just say, 'No, sorry, I don't want to play that game today, thank you.'

Here's what to do.

EXERCISE

Step 1: Recognise them for what they are: negative, unhelpful thoughts. Make a conscious decision to give them less mental energy.

Step 2: Balance the spreadsheet, and challenge them. If you are going to imagine a negative possibility, then the proper thing to do is to also imagine an equally positive possibility. This is only fair. Otherwise, don't get involved in negative speculative thinking either way – simply stick to your prep and wait to see what unfolds.

Step 3: Manage the energy behind these thoughts by letting them play themselves out. Allow yourself to follow the 'what if' scenario through to its conclusion. Imagine what might happen next, and after that, and after that, and so on. Also, then have a useful plan already formulated for the eventuality that something does go wrong, like Conrad Smith spoke about earlier. This is reassuring in itself – and can also help us distinguish truly ridiculous 'what if' thinking from more reasonable consideration and planning. But what we also find with *progressive thinking* is that there is always a next, and a next, and a next . . . Eventually, we'll simply get bored with the train of thought, the negative energy around it dissipates and soon a more reasonable train of thought filters through. Reality based on experience is much plainer and more straightforward than we often like to admit to ourselves.

NATS ARE THE PITS!

The vast majority of the fear-generating thoughts we have ahead of performance are unconscious – we're not aware of them – and for that reason, psychologists refer to them as negative automatic thoughts (or NATs). They work away beneath the surface, undermining our confidence and, ultimately, interfering with our performance and our ability to put energy into action. Here are some of the most common types of mental blockers or negative automatic thinking:

- trying to predict the future
- downgrading and degrading one's abilities
- devaluing oneself – name-calling
- negatively imagining what others will think/do/say

Do you recognise any of these? NATs usually come in clusters of about three to five, which feed off each other, generating fear, anxiety and even dread. As I have said, all negative automatic thoughts interfere with our ability to perform – so all NATs are also PITs (performance interfering thoughts). The trick is to become aware of these kinds of thoughts when you are having them and a good tell-tale sign is excess fear in the body, feeling afraid and very uncomfortable. Once we realise we are having these type of thoughts, we can use some key mental skills to challenge and stop them in their tracks.

FUTURE FEARS AND FEAR OF FAILURE

Negative 'future-predicting' is perhaps one of the most common types of negative automatic thinking when it comes to anticipating an upcoming performance or event. It is closely related to a fear of making mistakes and, ultimately, fear of failure. A little different from 'what-if' thinking, all these are variations on the same theme – an assumption that we know what a future outcome will be. To counter this kind of thinking, just begin with a basic fact: we cannot predict the future! We are terrible at it! For example, even with all our advanced meteorological technology, we can't fully predict the weather – there are just too many variables in the mix. If we really could predict the future, surely we would all be lotto winners – right?

EXERCISE

So, when you find yourself bombarded with undermining thoughts about a future performance, which are all built around a prediction that you are certain to make some terrible mistake, or fail miserably, or reveal what a loser you really are, try going through these simple steps:

Step 1: Remind yourself that we cannot predict the future. Catching these NATs early will enable you to challenge them quickly and reduce the mental energy you give to them.

Step 2: Talk yourself through them by telling yourself, well if this was to happen I would then do this . . . or this . . . and create a next step plan of action.

Step 3: Check in with yourself to see if there is any basis to some of these negative thoughts. Not *all* negative future predicting is completely baseless (although most of it is) – sometimes these vague fears can be pointing towards areas in your abilities or skills where you instinctively know there is a weakness or vulnerability.

Is there something behind the thought that you *do* want to work on? Is there a specific aspect of your performance that you don't feel as confident about? Are you worried about the competition? If yes, then this is useful information you can act on as soon as possible, by improving your preparation and spending more time working on a specific skill or area.

If, however, there is nothing behind the NAT, then not only is it simply unfounded and therefore a waste of energy, but it is ungrounded and has nothing positive to bring to you.

The other types of NATs mentioned above – downgrading and degrading one's abilities, devaluing oneself by name-calling and negatively imagining what others will think, do or say – are all bound up with our self-esteem and self-confidence and many mental skills like *self-awareness, encouraging self-talk* and *assertiveness* skills help most here.

REFRAMING FEAR

In these chapters, we have looked at various ways of dealing with fear, especially the kinds of fears that we can experience in the period just prior to a performance situation or an important event. We have seen how lots of mental skills like *active reflection, self-awareness, goal-setting, grounding* and *anchoring, visualisation, centring, meditation, progressive thinking* and challenging negative thought patterns (NATs and PITs) can be used to handle feelings of fear, anxiety and even panic, and to develop new, more helpful ways of thinking. Another mental skill that can be invaluable, and even transformative, when it comes to facing down fear is that of *reframing*.

THE BULL JUMPER

When covering the topic of fear in my workshops with individual athletes and sports teams, I sometimes show a video about an 18-year-old Spanish 'bull jumper'. That's right – a person whose occupation involves jumping over a charging bull. The bull has only one goal and focus – to try to impale him on its horns. Quite a job to have! Every jump is potentially harmful – perhaps even fatal – so the bull jumper is well accustomed to facing fear.

In the short clip, when asked about how he deals with such regular risk-taking, this young man talks about the importance of not ignoring the fear or pretending it isn't there. For him, it is quite the opposite, in fact. He fully knows that he could get hurt and die – and he acknowledges and embraces this fact. He explains that he sees fear as something that keeps him 'safe', giving him a sensation of power and control. He talks of how he feels bigger than the bull, and of how his heart fills with joy because he is dancing with the bull. Beyond the fear, each encounter he has with the bull is fun; something which actually makes him happy!

This young bull jumper has managed to transform one primal feeling – fear – into another – happiness. Unlike the other types of fearful thinking we have been looking at, it should be noted that, in this case, his fears are not imagined or unfounded. They are based on the very real possibility that he risks injury or even death each time he 'dances' with the bull. And yet he has been able to *reframe* what many people would see as a terrifying and very dangerous situation as an exciting challenge, a thrilling situation to prepare for and to be enjoyed. Where almost all of us would feel terror, he feels exhilaration.

This is of course a pretty extreme example! However, many successful athletes and sportspeople are able to use the same strategy of transforming feelings of nervous anticipation into a positive, a source of huge psychological strength.

Very much in the public eye lately, cage-fighter and boxer Conor McGregor is a very good example of someone who is able to *reframe* the pressure he faces in performance. MMA (mixed martial arts) is perhaps one of the most demanding sports to be involved in these days. Set in a cage, surrounded on all sides by a screaming audience, it is hand-to-hand combat and the pressure is intense, to say the least. And yet, by his own admission, there is nowhere McGregor would rather be than in the octagon, fighting or sparring – as he puts it himself, 'Combat is my escape.'

In a recent documentary, McGregor discussed how he evolved this mindset:

'[In the early days] I had nerves in my stomach. I used to celebrate these nerves . . . The more I felt these nerves, the more I would be comfortable in the actual fight. It's been the exact same ever since . . . a comfortable feeling: a mix of excitement, and a mix of energy and nervousness.'[1]

Like McGregor, many high achievers thrive on pressure, *reframing* it as a healthy challenge, seeing the excitement, the risk and the reward that the chance to perform offers. They allow themselves to get excited about the experience, to look forward to it. By seeing it in these terms, they turn it into a more *potentialising* experience.

Reframing simply means looking at a situation through a different lens, like putting a different frame around a picture to make it show up differently, seeing something from a different perspective to our usual, initial take on it. We can frame an opportunity – an upcoming performance, an important event in our lives – using a positive lens, a rational lens, an enhancing lens, and so on. Reframing is an excellent mental skills technique to get the most out of any situation. It moderates an overly emotional reaction and invites us to engage our capacities for problem-solving, balance and understanding. By enabling us to break away from familiar, emotive thinking, reframing actually opens up and builds new neural pathways in our brains.

EXERCISE

Here's a simple exercise in reframing:

1. Pick a situation that is worrying or frustrating you, something that you are thinking negatively about.

2. Score the intensity of this feeling out of 10 (with 1 being the least intense and 10 the greatest intensity).

3. Next ask yourself: 'How can I look at this situation in a different light and from a different perspective?'

4. To help with this, some of these further questions will guide you:

    - How could I learn from this situation? What am I finding out about myself? What is good about what I am about to do?

    - What's the opportunity being presented to me here? How could I make the *best* of it?

    - How might this experience help me in the future?

5. Now, rate the intensity of your feelings about the situation again. What you will often find, now that you've allowed yourself to think about it in a different way, is that you will feel less intense and a good deal less emotional, as well as less negative.

As we have seen over the last few chapters, fear and the nervous energy it generates can be a very difficult challenge for high performers to overcome – for some of us, it can even be debilitating and risk undermining our ability to perform at all. The good news is that it's a problem that can in time be overcome, by practising the mental skills techniques we have been looking at and having a determination to confront things head on. Let's hear again from track athlete David Gillick, whose moving testimony about managing his nerves we read about at the beginning of Chapter Six.

> I eventually got my head around the fact that nerves are a good thing. I came to embrace them . . . I began to visualise, seeing myself winning. Going through the races, the different scenarios. Embracing them a little bit more. I went onto YouTube and looked at all my old races. Something I never would do, I previously could not do it – I just couldn't go back and look at myself. One day I did – I looked at them all and downloaded them, and made a 50-second video that I put on my phone. A video of my best races. All the positive races, not just of me winning. Times when I raced against some of the best. Reminding myself of all those real things I had done . . .
>
> *David Gillick, Irish track and field athlete; two-time European Indoor Championships gold medal winner (2005 and 2007)*

PART THREE

Building for Success

NINE
The Big Day

'The most important thing is to be decisive. Then the mind and body will fall into line and will co-operate.'

Sonia O'Sullivan

The period immediately prior to a big performance, match, game, race or presentation is when our sense of nervous anticipation – or our expectant excitement, if we have managed to reframe it that way – peaks. We all know that the moment before you step out on a stage to give a speech or the moment *just* before some other kind of performance is usually when our nerves reach their height – once we actually begin to speak, or sing, or play, most of us feel the tension subside, as our energy and focus shift to the immediate task at hand. What we have been working for.

In the interviews Brent and I carried out for this book, we were keen to find out what some of the world's most successful professional sportspeople do in the time leading up to an important performance. One key common thread was the value of having a set routine or ritual on 'game day'. The familiarity of routine and sense of security created by a ritual can have a *calming, anchoring* effect which helps to keep intense emotions in balance.

The morning of a race, we usually have a fairly busy schedule. We spend 20 or 30 minutes doing a light paddle to sweat out. Following this, we have to hydrate, and [we] eat something light for energy. Gary will have the music playing in the team tent to keep us entertained. Then we change into our racing gear and start the warm-up. Do some pieces at different intensities so that we are prepared. The busy schedule means we don't have time for our minds to wander. Sometimes the mind strays and you end up thinking about other things, but you have to bring it back to the job at hand.

Paul and Gary O'Donovan – Irish rowers; European gold (2016) and Olympic silver (2016) medal winners

I was very strict in my routine, as that gave me confidence and helped relax me. Pack my bag, go for a walk, watch a movie. There were times I used to write down all my doubts, as I would still get these thoughts that came into my head. I'd write them on a piece of paper. I would either rip them up and chuck them in the bin or I would go into my garden and burn them. I had to get them out of my head; I had to get them out.

. . . I might then note down my good training sessions; the good races that I ran; the good times. I would look at [what I'd written], and tell myself, 'Well, that actually happened.' I then got a lot of confidence.

David Gillick, Ireland track and field athlete; two-time European championships gold medal winner (2005 and 2007)

It's always easy to overcome the self-doubt when things are going well and feedback from training and racing is positive. When it is not going so well, the self-doubt appears and this is when I would have some great tools that I could then recall and reuse

> when I find myself back in a negative thought drama again. I used to always write in my training diary so that later I could reflect on work I had completed and fitness I had gained to reassure myself that I could race at the level that I wanted to. Confidence and self-belief are essential for success. You have to know what gives you confidence and belief so that you can go back and reset yourself when things start to get out of control and you're not where you want to be. I always find that once you make a decision to do something, the uncertainties disappear and the focus narrows. The most important thing is to be decisive, then the body and mind will fall into line and co-operate.
>
> *Sonia O'Sullivan – Irish track and field Olympic silver medal winner; world record holder*

Knowing that we have practised and prepared sufficiently in advance is key, and connecting with this knowledge can be a great source of confidence just prior to performance. Practising some familiar moves before a match or game reminds us of all the hard work that has led to this point, and again, this can help combat last-minute nerves. This is what some other top athletes had to say on the subject:

> **Jason:** Suzie, how do you like to prepare mentally on game day?
>
> **Suzie:** I want to be the best I can be on the day. Not by focusing on the outcome, but focusing on the process of what is needed. To [be able to] make a decision in any given situation. Outside of the games, I keep focusing on my processes to be better.
>
> *Suzie Bates – captain of the New Zealand women's cricket team, the White Ferns; ODI player of the year 2013 and 2016*

> Later, playing for the All Blacks, I had such confidence. I had done it [practised this move] on the farm day in day out, it didn't matter that [now] it was on a world stage. I was just rolling out a skill I knew I could do.
>
> *Zinzan Brooke – former All Black flanker with 58 caps*

> A big key for me is . . . making sure I am well prepared. Focusing on what needs to be delivered. On the day, it's not actually about me, it's about the players, and as soon as I start finding myself wanting to control things, I know that then I need to pull back because it doesn't help the players in their performance. When I'm feeling under pressure it is because I usually haven't done some of the basic things that I know need to be done.
>
> *Haidee Tiffen, head coach of the New Zealand women's cricket team, the White Ferns; holder of New Zealand Order of Merit*

> With the mental side of the game, if you're not right upstairs in terms of how you are approaching the game or in how you are preparing for these games you're already on the back foot. In terms of professional rugby the pressure just mounts, and how prepared you are for events determines how far you will go in the game. It's just something you have to work on.
>
> *Victor Vito – former All Black flanker with 33 caps; 100 games for the Hurricanes*

These athletes and coaches are again highlighting the importance of practice and process, of having already developed and repeatedly practised a process that works – that is reliable, time and again. For all of us, this can be the case, if we are actively putting energy into creating a process that will help us achieve on a consistent basis. In sport, business and life there are times we simply need to knuckle down and really focus on what we are doing. We need to close out the noise and stimulation that is coming at us, putting our energy instead into getting done what needs to get done. Either way, having a process will help us focus and achieve when pressure is at its most intense. The same is true in so many areas of life – including, for example, the military. When I spoke with Lieutenant Colonel Rian McKinstry, ex-Commanding Officer of the New Zealand SAS, this is what he had to say about the importance of process and practice in critical, 'performance' situations:

> When I think of dealing with pressure, I start thinking about preparation. I think about what's gone in beforehand from a basis of experience.
>
> With drills, the idea is that when you are put under pressure and you are in your fast-thinking brain, you're reverting to drills. You're reverting to your basics, you're not thinking about it and you have the edge – which might be the difference between split-second results. Breaking it down to drills and muscle memory, so that performance under pressure looks like almost referring to the known and basic levels of training . . . so that when someone says go left, you know everyone will go left, every time.
>
> *Lieutenant Colonel Rian McKinstry – ex-Commanding Officer, New Zealand Special Air Service; Director of Leader Development for the New Zealand Defence Force*

MANAGING FELT PRESSURE ON 'GAME DAY'

As we have said, the pressure to perform reaches its peak just before the event in question, usually in the hours preceding the match, presentation or live TV interview, etc. Here are some useful mental skills techniques to help you manage this 'felt pressure' and defuse nerves immediately prior to performance.

'SHAKE IT OFF'

Too much pressure coming at a person causes a charge in their body that needs somewhere to go. This technique is a way of discharging this kind of excess nervous energy.

Have you ever noticed what a dog does right after it has had a fight? It shakes itself from head to tail, literally channelling the energy out of its body, and then expelling the excess charge through a flick of its tail. Afterwards, the dog is calm and in control, as if nothing had happened.

We can do this too, with a little conscious focus. Imagine that you are gathering the energy you don't want up from your ankles and legs, through your hips, your chest. Channel it through your shoulders and neck, then down your arms and finally out through your fingertips, in a wrist-flicking motion. It really works!

In private, you can practise this in as animated a fashion as you like. In public, you can simply do a 'flicking' gesture through your fingertips to expel the charge. If you have ever observed soccer players shaking their arms/hands or bouncing on the spot in the tunnel on their way out to play, now you know why!

TRIGGER WORDS

The benefits of the above 'flicking' technique can be enhanced by using a psychological trigger word. *Trigger words* help train the mind. In this scenario, we can use a single word like 'free', 'gone' or 'flick' to easily reinforce the effect of the gesture.

Another means of combining a gesture with a trigger word to help expel unwanted energy is to simply stamp your foot and focus energy there, while simultaneously thinking of a word like 'strong', 'smash', 'solid'. This is a good *grounding technique* also.

In a business setting – say, before an important meeting or presentation – a helpful gesture might be to plant your feet firmly on the ground, while internally repeating the word 'solid' or 'confident'. Having this word to go to in your mind will bring a sense of calm, focus, openness and confidence, while bringing your attention to the sensation of your feet firmly on the ground will help make you feel more secure and more anchored, both literally and metaphorically. Practise this technique a number of times before an important presentation, at home or in your office, so that it becomes something of a ritual – until the desired effect is felt in the mind and experienced in the body.

TRANSFERRING PRESSURE

A final technique for dealing with pressure, to be used principally in sporting contexts, involves psychologically harnessing and transferring as much energy onto the opposition as possible. Whenever (overwhelming) physical or psychological tension is experienced, a player can convert this energy into an image of defeating one of the opposition players – say, their counterpart on the other team – along with a word or phrase that helps them connect with how much they want to beat their opponents. This redirected or projected energy can be built upon and strengthened by connecting the words and/or gestures any time prior to the game – the month before, the week before, the day before, even an hour before.

For example, in preparing for a game it is useful to watch footage of your opponents playing, especially watching the individual opponent player you will be facing. In training, then, practise seeing the player you want to out-tackle, out-run, out-smart. Actively visualise this as part of your preparation, seeing yourself actually doing these things on the field, or in your mind in the gym, or when you are writing out your goals for the week, and just before the game.

Think of a word or phrase you could use when visualising these things – maybe something like 'quick and smart', 'fast and fluid', 'nimble and agile', etc. See the opponent being out-tackled, being out-run, being out-smarted. See them looking disappointed and deflated with your doing this. Whenever you feel worried or anxious, remember in your mind's eye this image of them being disheartened; by doing this you will be using more wisely the energy connected to the feelings.

In business a similar technique can be used when worrying about a big presentation. In practice and preparation beforehand, write out how you want your audience to receive you and your information. If you are using some humour in your presentation, picture them laughing at your jokes, looking really energised and interested in what you are telling them or showing them. Think of some words to describe how you want them to be, for example 'open and curious', 'generous and willing', 'confident and connecting' etc.

Then, whenever you feel worried about the presentation while you are preparing, go to this image of the audience and their receiving you well; connect with the energy of doing a good job.

CREATING THE RIGHT KIND OF INTERNAL PRESSURE

So far, we've been focusing on managing the intense *external* pressure – from one's teammates, from coaches, from friends and family, from supporters, from the media, from the public in general – which can make itself felt ahead of an important performance, especially just prior to the event in question. It's important too, however, to make sure you as an individual are generating, and regulating, the most helpful kind of *internal* pressure at this crucial time – by this, we mean the psychological drive someone puts on themselves to perform to the best of their ability, and to win. We spoke in earlier chapters about creating and sustaining the drive to win, and wanting to do one's best, as opposed to simply playing well or just doing enough, and how important this drive is for high performance. It's good to check in with this key, self-generated sense of motivation just prior to an important performance. None of us operates from a peak level of motivation at all times – if we put constant and intense pressure on ourselves, what we can find instead is that our drive to succeed fades at certain times and picks up again at others. So sometimes it's a case of needing to generate adequate *internal* pressure in order to perform well – consistently.

A helpful way of thinking, when approaching an upcoming challenge, is to concentrate on what is specifically needed to succeed in that particular situation from a first-person perspective, i.e. 'what do I need to do, to be most successful here?' What are the actual tasks we need to complete, the actions we need to take to be successful? This creates an internal energy keenly focused on exactly what is required in order to be successful in that situation, as determined through knowledge, research and clear decisions taken in training and already practised and prepared for.

The mental skills of *strength-based thinking*, *thought writing* plus *visualisation* helps greatly here, enabling us to envisage successful execution in advance; knowing and seeing the actions in our imagination first helps the actual action happen more easily in practice. Especially just prior to performance, repeating the imagined scenario over and over in our minds in real time from a first-person perspective, until it feels good to go, creates an intensity of focus in the mind and body.

We can also prepare in this way for when the pressure comes on during the game, imagining specific challenges and how we will deal with them, including recovering from making mistakes, and reinforcing our confidence in our ability to handle whatever happens. This act of repeated imagination builds a sense of self-created expectation – as opposed to an externally imposed pressure – that will seek its own fulfilment, which in turn makes it more likely that on game day we will release and act on this energy. Executing one's role really well feels very satisfying, regardless of how a game turns out.

For this reason, many successful athletes routinely do this as a way of imprinting the image of success on their minds in the last few moments before performance begins, as former All Black Victor Vito reveals here:

> Visualisation is one big thing I like to use [before] a game. Generally I do it a little bit early in the week, but more so on the day of the game. I wake up and imagine myself being really energised. I visualise things I want to achieve in the game. Like from during the training week, seeing a number of moves we have practised. Seeing myself pulling them off really well. Seeing myself making a break or having a good run or a good tackle. Also balancing the visualisation by taking myself away from the game and just chilling and relaxing.
>
> *Victor Vito – former All Black flanker with 33 caps; 100 games for the Hurricanes*

AVATAR VISUALISATION

This technique is a more specific form of *visualisation*, which can be used to great effect in very physical sports when an athlete is seeking to refine and improve on a particular skill. (I can assure you, it has nothing to do with the remotely controlled, genetically engineered human creatures that appear in the sci-fi movie *Avatar*!) It can be used during training, and also just before and during performance, to activate higher levels of energy and motivation as well as a greater sense of confidence and self-belief. It will galvanise the release of certain key body chemicals that work to improve our performance – most importantly, adrenalin. Like all the mental skills we have been looking at so far, this is a technique that can be drawn upon in other settings and for other challenging situations. The principle behind it is that our minds respond not just to pictures and images (as in *visualisation* more generally), but also to metaphor and symbols. The two most common physical qualities that *avatar visualisations* are used to enhance are speed and strength – however, they can be effective for improving the execution of almost any physical action, such as jumping, punching, throwing, kicking, and so on.

EXERCISE

The first step is to decide which action you want to get better at, or which quality you want to enhance. Now think about which animal or object you think best represents this action and quality. If it's speed, strength or stamina you want to work on, think of the fastest or the strongest or most resilient animal – a cheetah or a tiger, say, or a rhino or a gorilla, etc. Or you may prefer to conjure up an image of the toughest or most agile person or character – whether real, mythical or fictional – you can think of, such as, for example, a well-known action hero. You could also think of an object that for you typifies the quality you want to develop – like a tank or a hammer or a bulldozer. It's important for each person to choose their own, personal 'avatar'. Selecting the image that speaks most powerfully to you as an individual will be all the more effective in generating the necessary adrenalin to produce that extra burst of speed, strength and confidence.

Once you have chosen your image, spend some time seeing the animal (or person or object) in your mind. If an animal, what does it look like? What is it doing? While imagining this, try and breathe into the experience, as you picture it running to pursue its prey, or, for strength, as you watch it locked in deadly combat with a rival. If you are immersed in the experience enough, you should start feeling more adrenaline in your system – an increase in your heart rate, faster breathing, a sensation of heat and muscle tightness – even if you are only sitting down. Now repeat the name of the animal (or person or object) to yourself. The physical experiences your body is registering should then *anchor* to the word you are repeating.

In training, call up this image in your mind and say the associated name or word just before doing an exercise, or when you need to summon an extra burst of energy. Allow your body to flow with the image of the animal as it runs or fights or pursues its prey. A helpful way of measuring the effectiveness of this *visualisation* technique is to monitor your normal speed or strength, etc., and then use the *avatar imagery* to see if you go faster, achieve greater strength and so on.

Historically, more often than not an animal was used on a shield or a coat of arms, for example, to represent strength, courage, valour or bravery, and some tribes still exist today that believe in the power of the energy associated with certain animals and the powerful link with this side of our physical selves.

MOOD-ENHANCING MUSIC

Listening to music, or singing, can be used very effectively as a mental skills technique. Playing music helps us enter more of a 'flow state' by turning down the activity of our self-conscious, analytical and self-critical mind. Listening to music can help increase the production of key performance chemicals, like norepinephrine and anandamide, which will make us feel more 'pumped' and active; depending on the choice of music, it can also help to raise our levels of feel-good chemicals like dopamine, serotonin and endorphins. This in turn creates a greater sense of wellbeing and a more relaxed state.

It is very useful to create a playlist with songs to get active to or relax to. Songs, for example, from inspiring movies or from other sources that we know lift us. Such *MEM – mood enhancing music* – can provide a boost in gym training or on long runs, and can also be very effective just prior to performance in helping to generate the right kind of motivational energy. Listening to podcasts or an inspirational speech from a movie can also help you to get into gear – think for example of Al Pacino's 'inch by inch' speech in *Any Given Sunday*. However, the chemical changes that music effects in our minds and bodies tend to be even more powerful and immediate.

It's worth noting again that, in general, pressure is a good thing, a great driver of performance. Most people understand the value of a deadline or exam in helping to focus the mind. The majority of us need timeframes and other markers to work towards and get energised by, in order to be really productive and achieve results. High achievers in particular respond to such motivating factors. To help us continue to develop our abilities and processes, and remain curious and open to new challenges, we need to always be working towards something, as opposed to nothing.

TEN
Handling Pressure During Performance

'I just try and control what I can control'

Dane Coles

Brent

When I was in New Zealand last year, I watched the State of Origin rugby league decider between Queensland and New South Wales – this annual event between the country's two major sporting states showcases one of the biggest rivalries in Australian sport. Johnathan Thurston, one of the greats of the Australian rugby league, had a last-minute kick to win Queensland the match and take the series into a decider – which, as it turned out, the Queensland Reds would go on to win against all the odds.

Thurston had suffered a shoulder injury earlier in the match, and had continued to play regardless – but as he lined up to take the kick, there was some concern that this might go against him at the critical moment. The conversion – from wide out on the pitch – was not an easy one.

The team medics monitoring his heart rate courtesy of trackers (they have to monitor everything these days) noted that it rose significantly when Thurston realised that he had the responsibility to win the match, that all the pressure was now on his shoulders. But here's the interesting thing –

even though Thurston's beats per minute stayed high as he placed the ball and walked back, he was then somehow able to reduce it. So that by the time he ran in to kick the ball, he was composed – ice-cool in the veins, as the All Blacks like to call it. Like a lot of athletes in this book, he'd calmed himself down by going through his usual ritual, knowing that he had made this kick in his mind thousands of times – so that, to him, it became just another kick on another day. His heart rate dropped, his breathing went back to normal and he made the game-changing kick perfectly. Of course it was Thurston himself who made the successful kick – but he did so by drawing on the mental skills at his disposal, in the right place and at just the right time. He changed the 'in' to change the 'out', as they say – creating the best internal processes, mentally and physically, to deliver the optimum result.

PRESSURE DURING A PERFORMANCE

Among the many performance situations we can imagine, up there among the most stressful must be trying to score a winning penalty, in front of thousands of people and a TV audience of millions, when there are just minutes to go.

Being able to handle this kind of high-performance pressure is a key component of success, whether in sport or other areas of life. Our ability to do so can be worked on and enhanced, like so many other aspects of performance. There are many mental skills techniques that will help with managing and controlling how we deal with high-pressure situations, and we will look at some of these in this chapter.

In Chapter Eight we heard the remarkable story of Victor Costello, the former rugby pro, who overcame his fear of flying by booking a flying lesson, and eventually went on to establish a second successful career as a commercial airline pilot. So we thought Victor would be a good person to ask about how to handle pressure in a critical situation – whether a key moment in an international rugby match, or when encountering turbulence at 30,000 feet. This is what he told Brent:

> **Victor:** As [an airline] captain, it's just like in rugby. Making split-second decisions – it's what you do. In rugby, you are surrounded by players who can handle pressure in front of 50,000 people, like I did. So when I get into a difficult position in a plane, I manage my way out of it. I can do this because I have the knowledge to do it. I paint a mental picture of what to do to get out of this thunderstorm; what it's going to take. All my cognitive resources go to solving that problem. Just like I did defending the five-yard line.

THE FOUR C'S OF PERFORMANCE

Sports psychology often refers to the four C's of performance, which are:

1. Commitment

2. Concentration

3. Control/Composure

4. Confidence

The four C's address the key qualities we need to bring into play to help us manage critical moments during performance. First and foremost, we need to commit to the challenge in the first place and to doing our best in that moment (potentialising). We need the ability to focus our full effort and concentration on the immediate task at hand. We need to be able to control our thinking and compose our emotions during that critical time, and, lastly, we need to be able to confidently draw on our experience and resources in order to complete the challenge.

Let's look at how some more highly successful sportspeople handle these 'big' moments in performance:

> Back in the day, as a hooker, if I missed a throw I would start thinking, 'S**t – I have to get this [next] one!' I was putting pressure on myself and became outcome-focused.
>
> [Now] I've got a process . . . a bone-deep process to bring me back into the moment. I look around into the crowd to connect with my surroundings. I connect with the ball boy and say, 'Thank you' when he hands me the ball, which helps me feel nice and calm. Rugby can be pretty fast, and doing those few things and taking a deep breath brings me back into the moment, and I feel like I am engaged in my next task. I just try and control what I can control. When things go wrong, I know I have a process to deal with them.
>
> *Dane Coles – All Black hooker with 56 caps;*
> *plays club rugby with the Hurricanes*

As a youngster, you naturally shrivel up and go into your shell, for example when you hear the word 'pressure'. Now, when pressure comes on, I like to encourage it. Confidence in myself comes through my prep and having a new mindset of embracing it. The challenge is to stay in the moment when the pressure is on.

. . . Pressure moments in a game for me could be a shot at goal. Or making a decision for the team, as to whether we go for points or we go for a line-out. Or calling set moves. I have to make a lot of those decisions out on the field, but [now] I don't really see them as high pressure. I have a good gauge of my team around me. When the spotlight is on, there is leadership pressure and skills pressure. Being able to perform when it's your turn.

[What helps during these times is] trusting the process and not getting busy mentally – being light, bright and clear. I play best when I am in this headspace. Light, bright and clear-headed. It's about being consistent with this.

Beauden Barrett – All Black fly-half with 62 caps; plays club rugby with Hurricanes

Although Gaelic is a team sport, I immediately shift to an individual mindset once the free has been awarded. My kicking is built on purposeful practice and going through my routine, time after time. I am very much process-driven, with the outcome of a score looking after itself once I execute my process. I get great confidence in being in control of the free-taking situation with a well-rehearsed routine.

Dean Rock – Gaelic footballer; winner of four All-Irelands with Dublin

Time and again, top athletes highlight the importance of practice and process, as do Dane, Beauden and Dean. At critical moments, it is the knowledge that we have developed and worked on a process that delivers consistency in training. Dane Coles talks of having a 'bone-deep process', which gives him the confidence he needs to execute a successful line-out throw when the pressure is really on, like in the final moments of a game to retain the ball on the opposition's try line. The word 'bone-deep' conveys very well the extent to which he has practised and perfected the moves he will make. For all of us, this can be the case, if we are actively putting enough energy and time into creating a process that works for us, and then practising it until it becomes second nature when we are in difficult situations.

Being in the right place mentally is also crucial. Beauden Barrett sums this up beautifully when he talks about the ideal 'headspace' for him: 'light, bright and clear-headed . . . not getting mentally busy'. This is the kind of relaxed but highly focused mindset that enables us to perform at our absolute best.

There are key times in sport, and in all areas of life, when we need to simply close out the noise and stimulation that is coming at us and put all our focus onto the task at hand – super-energising it, in fact, if we can, so that we complete it to the best of our ability. *Potentialising* each moment by moment with deliberate focus and execution. In sport, today more than ever, there is so much to distract players from performance. Often there is overwhelming stimulation from so many external sources – from their own fans or the opposition's fans, the opposition team players, from over-eager coaches and teammates, over-excited family members or friends; also from media crews, who are desperate to secure the best possible coverage for their viewers and readers.

Noise and excess stimulation can also come from within. An overactive mind, too many 'low-quality' negative or distracting thoughts, excesses of emotion – all of these taking us away from what we are trying to do and detracting from the quality of our focus and concentration. During a game, our minds may be clouded by negative thinking about our abilities and whether we are going to be able to play our part without letting our teammates down.

We saw in Chapter Six how ex-pro footballer Richie Sadlier, at the start of his career, would find his mind being taken over by fears that no one – neither his coaches nor anyone in the crowd – really believed he had the talent to be there, that he was an imposter of sorts on the pitch, and so on. Such internal stories create their own distracting inner monologue, and heap yet another layer of pressure onto the person who is trying to perform at their best. Reacting excessively to mistakes or missed opportunities can also make us lose our focus. Worrying about the scoreboard or about our place on the table or ranking, our place on the team; worrying about the time; thinking too far ahead – for example, envisaging getting into the locker room at half-time, or fretting about the next two plays, while there is one going on right here, right now . . . All of these things indicate that we have lost focus and are moving away from our processes, and the impact on our performance can become disastrous.

FOCUSING TECHNIQUES

Let's look at some practical mental skills tactics that can be used in sports performance situations, and others, to help maintain focus.

HAND-CLAPPING

One technique that can help players refocus after an error, or to drown out the noise of the crowd (who may be booing as a result of a mistake), is to simply clap their hands hard a couple of times. Then they take a moment to focus on the resulting stinging sensation on the palms of their hands. The harder you clap, the better, in this context, as the mild pain will last longer. This is similar to the example I gave earlier of inducing mild pain just prior to a presentation as a way of combatting extreme nerves around public speaking. In both cases, the brain will quickly direct its attention to the immediate physical sensation, sidelining any negative or unhelpful thoughts about having made – or making – a mistake. And in this instance, clapping will also have the secondary benefit of encouraging your teammates!

BEARD-PULLING (!)

In a variation on this technique, some sportsmen actually grow beards to help with this pain/presence focus. During a game, when they want to slow down their thoughts and bring themselves back into the here and now, they simply pull on their beard and focus on the minor pain this produces. Other examples of these kinds of 'displacement' gestures that we looked at in Chapter Nine are flicking, stamping, bouncing and shaking.

For some sportspeople – such as golfers and snooker players – these particular techniques may not be so appropriate, as they may prove too distracting for the audience or the other players. *Grounding* and finding one's feet is a more appropriate strategy here.

DIVE REFLEX: 'ICE BLUE'

In intensely physical sports like soccer, rugby and GAA, another very useful strategy for regaining focus is tapping into our 'Dive Reflex'. This is a natural physical reaction that is triggered when our face hits a surface of water. As part of this response, stress chemicals in the body are instantaneously reduced and our system goes into a different mode, designed to conserve energy. Our breathing slows, as we take longer breaths, and our heart rate lowers by up to 30 per cent.

We can recreate this experience by splashing cold water onto the face. The colder the water, the better the effect. So, in a game situation, players can ensure that they have a bottle of icy cold water handy, or quickly available, which they can squeeze onto their face. The sudden shock this produces helps the brain to become very immediately present. This can in fact be practised in training, to the point where even imagining the sudden sensation of cold water on the face will bring about a similar stress chemical reduction in the body. Then, in a game, all we have to do is bring to mind a trigger word or phrase – 'ice blue' is the phrase sometimes used for this exercise – as we imagine icy water splashing into our face, being poured over our head or even being poured directly onto the brain. The imagined coldness will instantly slow us down – including the rate of our breathing.

'ZONING OUT . . . ZONING IN'

Another technique that is very effective in helping to sharpen mental focus involves fixing the gaze on a point far off in the distance – usually slightly higher than where our normal eye level would be. You could, for example, pick a point or face in the crowd above you and lift your gaze there. Then for a short time, you alternate between focusing hard on that point or object and letting your eyes go slightly out of focus again – a kind of 'zone-out' or 'zone-in' action, during which you also take some deep, slow breaths.

Like the 'ice blue' technique, this one will help our system – body and mind – to slow down and slightly detach from what is going on in front of us. Then, with a few hard, deep breaths, we can refocus and come back to the present moment with sharper, renewed attention.

BUSINESS PRESENTATIONS

This last technique can be helpful in a business context too. When doing a presentation, picking a spot at the back of the room, slightly higher than the heads of the audience, will help the speaker as a point of focus to project one's voice towards – especially when addressing a large room of people.

In an important and perhaps tense business meeting, another helpful strategy for heading off too much nervous energy or agitation is the very simple action of slowly taking apart a ballpoint pen. Still listening to what is going on, a person can gradually dismantle the pen – taking off the lid and placing it down quietly, unscrewing the top, taking out the ink cartridge and spring (if there is one) and so on. Then putting the component parts on the table close by, before putting the pen together again slowly – making sure all the while to continue breathing deeply and listening.

This simple exercise serves to preoccupy the body and mind enough to allow any tension to come down a few notches and any stress chemicals to disperse a little. It is especially useful in situations where you feel there is a risk of 'firing off' and losing your composure. Focusing on such a basic task helps us to slow things down a bit, giving us time to gather our thoughts enough before responding in a difficult exchange with others. It can of course be repeated as many times as necessary – as long as it doesn't drive the other people in the meeting to distraction! Of course *grounding* is also a great option here, just sending the energy to your big toe, starting to feel the sensations there and then throughout your feet and taking the time to relax and slow your breathing (some people even take off their shoes to crunch their toes and feel the carpet). As your feet are under the table they are out of view and only you will know that you are sending your energy there.

As well as these tactics, there are a number of other mental skills that can be brought into play in a performance situation and that will help with focus. We have looked at some of these in previous chapters – for example, *centring*, *grounding* and rehearsed or preconditioned *trigger words*, such as 'focus', 'discipline' or 'spot' (as in, a spot on the ball) all work well. What is known as 'pro-line' *visualising* is also a key skill to develop – in sport situations such as golf, soccer, snooker: looking first, and then seeing the strike or line of the shot in our mind's eye prior to kicking or hitting the ball. Practising it in our mind a few times, imagining the shot executed precisely and then lowering the head and actually kicking or striking the ball. There is no need to raise the head to look at the target again at this point.

With all of these different strategies, it's up to each of us as individuals to discover which will work best for us and adapt them according to our own requirements. Then it's a matter of continual practice and repetition until we have a 'bone-deep' process that we know will consistently serve us well.

Let's see how some of our greatest sportspeople have developed and adapted such techniques as part of their own repertoire of mental skills.

> Before kicking, I would use visualisation and imagery, picking a point, and the main thing for me was telling myself: 'Stay tall'; 'Follow through'; 'Finish the kick'. These were my trigger words. For a while I was missing the goals, and I realised I was dipping, but of course if you tell yourself, 'Don't dip', what's the first thing you do? You dip! By talking negatively, it just comes into your actions. So always create positive affirmations. Thinking the opposite of 'Don't dip' is 'Stand tall', and this worked for me.
>
> *Ronan O'Gara – former professional rugby player; rugby coach; 128 caps for Ireland*

> [To focus] I assess the wind conditions by picking up a piece of grass and tossing it in the air. I choose my 'pro-line' (seeing where I want the ball to go), and then I step directly back in the line of where I want the kick to go. I compose myself with two deep breaths and reduce my heart rate. I then firmly pick a 'sweet

spot' on the ball where I want to strike it. I stay upright and tall as I approach the ball and commit to the strike.

Having this routine and structure with my kicks allows me to assess what went right, or wrong, with each kick. Allowing me to be more in control. I can make slight tweaks or alterations based on best practice. I have the utmost belief in myself when it comes to kicking free kicks and I block out the crowd, with sheer focus on my process.

Dean Rock – Gaelic footballer; winner of four All-Irelands with Dublin

People always asked me, how did I block out the pressure of 50,000 or 60,000 spectators in a big match, in the sense of winning or losing a game. For me, it was nothing to do with that, it was all about the technique. To go through the very same technique that I used every week at training or for my club, Old Belvedere. It was my way of taking away all the outside influences – just to go through my technique as usual. If that was right, then the result would be the same.

I was always visualising the technique. I remember hearing years ago, when Welsh centre Scott Gibbs broke through in the last seconds to potentially deny England what looked like a probable Grand Slam title, and Welsh out-half Neil Jenkins had the conversion to win the game. While it was kickable, under such pressure it was also quite missable. Jenkins said that he just pictured himself back on the training pitch taking his usual kicks. He removed all the pressure from becoming tight or nervous and just went to a place he was comfortable and calm with. It was great to hear [this], because I had been doing that all my life!

Ollie Campbell – former professional rugby player; 22 caps for Ireland; 217 test points

Of course, performance doesn't always require us to be actively in the driving seat. Depending on the individual sport and the circumstances, being in the spotlight can also involve waiting – sitting back until it is your turn to act – while you are still very much under the public gaze. Waiting on the sideline, needing to come on and to perform to a high level at any moment. In some ways these passive, waiting moments can be just as tough – or even tougher – as you are still performing in yourself psychologically and emotionally. Having the emotional control and mental resilience to ride out these times and quickly kick into gear is key – and again, these are qualities that can be learned, practised and improved upon all the time. Ken Doherty, ex-professional snooker player and 1997 World Snooker Champion, gave Brent some fascinating insights into how he dealt with these challenging situations. Snooker of all sports requires having the mental toughness to wait things out.

> The most frustrating thing about snooker is that, when [my] opponent is at the table, there is bugger all I can do about it. I can't do anything until he misses. So, I'm relying on his mistakes. I can't tackle him; I can't hit a forehand back to him; I can't give him an ol' elbow. I've just got to sit there and be patient, and when I'm sitting in that chair, I've got to tell myself, 'OK, when I get my chance, I'm going to take it.' [I've got to] think positively, sit up in the chair straight, don't look like I'm not interested, keep my eyes on him, watching what he is doing. Always keeping a positive frame of mind. 'Remember, I'm playing well, I've practised hard for this.' This is what I am telling myself. 'He might win this frame, but I'll get in.' Talking to myself constantly.
>
> *Ken Doherty – ex-professional snooker player; snooker commentator; 1997 world snooker champion*

Here, Ken is calling on a number of key mental skills – *positive attitude, encouraging self-talk* and, perhaps most importantly of all, the ability to remain *calm and composed,* keeping his impatience in check and not concerning himself about his opponent's performance, or about the real possibility of not even getting the chance to play again – if, say, the other player wins the frame in one break. He remains focused, self-assured and ready to prove what he is capable of when given the chance. *Visualisation, meditation, grounding* and *centring* will all help with such mental and emotional control. In a later chapter we will look in more detail at how to specifically manage our emotions at times of key and ongoing pressure.

BUSINESS WORLD DISTRACTIONS

In business, there can be as many – if not sometimes more – external distractions as in a sports context, although these will take very different forms. For example, most athletes spend a lot of time training or competing, and at these times they generally leave their mobile phones and other electronic devices in the locker room, meaning that they get a break from checking emails or texts, and aren't necessarily expected to respond immediately. In that sense, at least they get regular time away from technology and social media, and don't have this huge source of distraction to contend with during performance itself.

This is not the case for business folk, of course. It is not uncommon for a business person to check their phone or computer for messages on average anything from 43 to 150 times a day. Think about that for a moment. Not that long ago, there were no computers or mobile devices at all; we are the first generation to have to manage this additional aspect of daily life. Now, vast chunks of our day are taken up hooking into electronic devices, each time downloading a constant stream of new information of all sorts into our brains. Much of this stimulus – like emails, voice messages, texts and social media alerts – is demanding something of us: a meeting to be scheduled, a deadline to be negotiated or agreed to, an opinion to be given, an article to be read or some kind of other task to be done.

In our lives generally, for those of us who have to fit family time around work and other responsibilities, the daily tasks we set ourselves can pile up quickly. Washing, cooking, vacuuming, exercise, organising all the aspects of our children's lives – even the 'task' of eating – all of these must be done regularly for us to just keep on top of things. With all that is going on in our lives, it is not surprising that at times we can feel overwhelmed, and that we find it hard to focus, prioritise and allocate time to the people and activities that are most important to us.

While handling this kind of pressure on a daily basis is of course not the same as a high-performance sports situation, it is becoming increasingly demanding, and we have a greater need than ever to have some easy 'go-to's and practised techniques to help us focus or refocus our energy at certain times. Using and adapting the mental skills we have looked at in this chapter will help us achieve more focus and the structure needed to ensure that we achieve what we want to in our everyday lives, and stay well in the process.

As well as the techniques we have mentioned earlier, *meditation* is again a key mental skill when we need to heighten the focus of our mental and physical energy. For this purpose, we can practise by consciously choosing just *one thing* as the focal point of all our attention for a defined short period of time. This could be an object we are looking at intensely, it could be an action like a slow intentional walking exercise, it could be the experience of listening intently or even laughing or it could be a repetitive sound like humming or mantra – a single word or phrase repeated over and over again. Whatever you choose to focus on, the aim is to intentionally slow down and shut all other distractions out of your mind for a pre-defined period of time. Recharge the mental batteries, as it were.

The more we practise focusing all our attention on our chosen object, or sensation, action or word, the quicker we will find ourselves being able to achieve a relaxed focus each time.

Here is one such technique I devised to help people who struggle with a fear of flying, especially at key times such as take-off and turbulence. (You will need to have some chewing gum handy for this one.)

CHEWING GUM MEDITATION

Step One: Pop some chewing gum into your mouth and chew until soft.

Step Two: When you are feeling nervous (take-off, landing, sudden turbulence), chew pretty vigorously and focus completely on the act of chewing. Really think about the gum moving around in your mouth. Focus on the flavour and the sensation of saliva being produced. Notice the placement of the chewing gum – which side of your mouth is it in right now, and under which tooth? Notice what it feels like in your inner cheek or being moved by your tongue.

Step Three: When you feel you have chewed for a while, now stop. Move the chewing gum to the very front of your teeth and place it in the middle of your front teeth. Do this gently. Hold it in place there with your teeth, but very gently.

Step Four: Now the *meditation* really begins. The challenge is, as you continue to hold the chewing gum in place, begin to bring your two rows of teeth together, upper and lower, at the front, as if you are closing your jaw to join them. The key, and most difficult part, is to do this *as slowly as possible.*

The urge will be to do it quickly. You need to fight this urge – resist it! You need to hold yourself back from going quickly. Slowly, ever so slowly, focus on the very small movements of your closing jaw on the soft chewing gum. If you go too fast, start over again.

Step Five: If you continue to feel excess energy in your body, as if you are nervous, excited or on edge, try the following. While you are intently focusing on the chewing gum – send this extra energy to your feet. Start to wiggle your toes, or move your feet back and forth in a rocking motion. To further help you shut out any external stimulus, close your eyes.

Your primary job is to focus on very, very slowly chewing the gum. It's not easy to do and the longer you take, the better. When you are feeling calmer and are ready to stop, simply stop. Repeat again if you feel the nervous energy returning at any point.

REFRAMING THE RISK

Once again, in any performance situation, or indeed faced with any stressful situation, the mental skill of *reframing* will help you develop an attitude of positivity. Rather than seeing the task of taking a free or penalty as a huge and overwhelming responsibility – one you might gladly hand over to someone else – you can think about it in an entirely different way. Gaelic football star Dean Rock and rugby great Beauden Barrett shared with us their own ways of turning things around mentally:

> As I prepare for a game, I know there will be certain times in that game where there will be more pressure than other moments. For me, it's good. It challenges me to overcome my fears and embrace what challenges me; embrace those pressures . . . I like to embrace it and walk towards it. I have always been encouraged to stand up more when the pressure comes on.
>
> *Beauden Barrett – All Black fly-half with 62 caps; plays club rugby with Hurricanes*

> When it comes to handling the focus of needing to score in big games, I [actually] enjoy the responsibility of being trusted to put the ball over the bar.
>
> *Dean Rock – Gaelic footballer; winner of four All-Irelands with Dublin*

> When I felt pressure, I would realise that pressure is a test of my character and it will make me stronger. I try and thrive on the pressure rather than succumb to it. Control the pressure, not let the pressure control me.
>
> *Eamonn Coghlan – Irish track and field Olympian; gold medallist in World Championships (Outdoor) and European Championships (Indoor); former senator*

We have seen in this chapter how investing time and effort in preparation and in creating a reliable process, and having a range of mental skills to draw upon, are all really important elements in helping us perform to the utmost of our abilities when the pressure is really on. A final point to bear in mind however is that no one can ever predict exactly what will happen on 'game day' itself – what the weather conditions will be like, what the form of the other team will be, when and how injury or mishap might strike, how the other members of our own team will perform. And so what sets the really versatile and consistent player apart from the rest is the key ability to adapt to what happens in the moment and to trust their own instincts. Again, having the right attitude and mindset is crucial in this regard too – we need the self-belief to know that we can adapt and be flexible when the situation calls for it; we need the ability to accept that some things are out of our control; we need the positivity to trust our own reactions.

We will leave the final word on this to Irish rugby legend Ronan O'Gara, who made these very points when he spoke to me about how to handle 'big' performances:

> I think it is hugely important [to trust and listen to yourself as a player], especially as this might be missing in the modern game. Nowadays many players want to be fed all the information, but something I am a massive fan of is trusting your instincts and what's playing out right in front of you. Have a general plan, yes – but I think the great players have the capacity to change the plan on the run. There's a big difference between that and breaking away from the game. Trusting and believing in the game plan, but at the same time putting your individual stamp on it.

. . . You cannot plan in training for every eventuality of the game – [each time] will always be different, no matter how much you recreate in training scenarios. The game is different; the picture in front of you is different. You need that capacity to adapt – adapt on the run, as opposed to just taking in information from the coaches' box. And I think that's what very good players are able to do.

Ronan O'Gara – former professional rugby player; rugby coach; 128 caps for Ireland

ELEVEN
Managing Pain and Fatigue

'Usually it would get most difficult about halfway through the race. Negative thoughts would enter my head . . . I'd switch my thought process immediately to one of positivity and remind myself, "This is what you trained your ass off for and it's supposed to hurt – especially if you want to succeed!"'

Eamonn Coghlan

Brent

I remember how, as a keen cross-country runner in my teenage years, I would write on my hand before going for a run, to remind myself that when I felt tired, I simply had to push myself further – as this would be the very moment that the next guy would give up. When I felt like throwing in the towel myself, I would simply look at what I'd written on my hand – which would usually be something like 'Don't give up before he does' ('he' being the competitor in the race I most wanted to beat) – and I'd keep going, driving myself out of my comfort zone and further through the barrier of physical pain. In my own way, I had discovered – and understood the power of – the mental skill of *positive self-talk* in building resilience and pushing the boundaries of performance.

Pain is an inevitable aspect of physical exertion. The more we physically exert ourselves, the more pain we are likely to experience, as we work, stretch and demand sustained effort from our muscles. As we up our levels of activity and push ourselves beyond our normal limits, physical discomfort is an inevitable consequence. Even those of us who are not athletes have experienced the 'burn' that happens if we push our bodies beyond what they are used to. When our body has used up its normal energy stores, but we continue to demand more effort and more energy from it, lactic acid is released into our muscles. Small amounts of this natural compound will operate as a temporary, 'emergency' energy source to help our system avoid fatigue during intense physical exertion. However, if the exertion continues beyond a certain point, a build-up of lactic acid will soon create a burning sensation in the muscles that makes continued activity more difficult. Athletes who push their physical boundaries will routinely experience this type of pain. During practice and performance, there are of course other factors that will cause physical pain and discomfort – collisions with other players, injuries as a result of a badly executed move and other general aches and pains which go with the territory of intense physical exertion.

All physical pain has a job to do in sending us messages. The pain receptors have been activated to indicate that that part of the body has been affected and has changed in some way, been stretched, strained, bruised, otherwise damaged or even broken. The 'burn' in our muscles is our body's way of indicating that we're pushing beyond our limits, reminding us that our energy supplies are finite and that we should slow down if possible; the more intense pain of, for example, a broken ankle is a warning that damage has been done, that we should not put our weight on it and that it needs urgent attention.

As human beings we can of course feel other types of pain too, beyond the purely physical. We also experience emotional and psychological suffering, and in relation to these our physical pain is undoubtedly the most straightforward to deal with, since it's generally easy to identify its source and treat it accordingly. Emotional and psychological pain are a bit trickier, as we know, as getting to the heart of them can be a complex process, one we are not always willing to engage in and can consequently choose to avoid. We will be looking at how to manage emotional and psychological suffering in the next chapter.

In this chapter, however, we will focus primarily on the issue of physical pain and discomfort, and look at some helpful ways of dealing with these in sport, in other types of physical exertion and in daily life. This is not to ignore the fact that body and mind are of course intimately interconnected – 'fully wired' – and that emotional pain can manifest itself physically and give rise to physical pain, and vice versa. Physical ailments such as headaches, extreme muscle tension, teeth-grinding, ulcers and irritable bowel syndrome are just some of the common ways in which psychological distress can manifest itself in the body. We are complex creatures.

As we can see from Brent's example at the start of the chapter, pushing ourselves to achieve our best as sportspeople means we sometimes need to confront and manage physical discomfort. In sport and exercise, pain and fatigue are part and parcel of taking part, and, as with many other aspects of performance, how we manage them can be greatly enhanced by drawing on a range of mental skills. As a teenage runner,

Brent developed his own version of *positive self-talk*, in the form of written messages on the back of his hand. This is a very common technique for top athletes today who also write words and messages on wrist strapping and even tattoo them on their skin. Let's hear from some other top athletes about their ways of coping when the 'burn' sets in.

> Usually it would get most difficult about halfway through the race. Negative thoughts would enter my head and I'd wish it was all over . . .
>
> I'd switch my thought process immediately to [one of] positivity and remind myself, 'This is what you trained your ass off for and it's supposed to hurt – especially if you want to succeed!' Then I'd convince myself the other competitors in the race must be hurting too, and I'd welcome the pain!
>
> *Eamonn Coghlan – Irish track and field Olympian; gold medallist in World Championships (Outdoor) and European Championships (Indoor); former senator*

Irish Olympic rowers Paul and Gary O'Donovan have also talked about dealing with this kind of pain. They have a few strategies that help them keep going, especially in training. One is the mantra 'pull like dogs', which, for them, brings to mind a pack of sledge dogs working and pulling hard together and helps them really focus on the job at hand. Another tactic is to keep shifting their attention and energy between the 'push–pull' effort of rowing, as they push with their legs and pull with their arms. Shifting the focus like this means that they are regularly moving their attention away from the place where the 'burn' is most intense – which tends to be in their legs. The brothers have also described how they use imagery to go to a more pleasant place in their minds. The burn for them is *reframed* into the celebratory bonfire that the local community puts on every time they return home from competition. A fun time, when everyone gets together and there is the chance to huddle around with friends and family, enjoying the heat from the burning fire. In their chat with Brent, it's clear that humour helps them too:

> **Brent:** When the rowing gets tough, what helps? What do you tell yourselves?
>
> **Gary:** With the racing being reasonably short, we don't have much time to think but we always tend to go back to Dory's advice in *Finding Nemo* – 'just keep swimming'. Though, of course, we think about rowing and try to avoid the swimming at all costs if possible!

'WIM THE ICEMAN'

As a mental skills coach, I have done a lot of work with high-achieving athletes around how physical pain can be reduced and even turned off, using psychological techniques. Two athletes in particular, whom I worked with separately in the same season, stand out in my mind as great examples of how successful these techniques can be, and showed me once again just how strong the mind–body connection really is.

These two players – Tim Bateman, Maori All Black and New Zealand rugby professional, and Motu 'Mots' Matu'u, the Samoan internationally capped hooker now playing with Gloucester Rugby – had attended a presentation I did that season on the power of the mind in countering pain receptor messages. In this workshop, I showed a video of Wim Hof – otherwise known as 'Wim the Iceman'. This 58-year-old Dutchman has built an international reputation, and a very successful career, on his ability to withstand extreme cold using a combination of *meditation* and *breathing techniques* and he has set 26 Guinness World Records for his feats in this field – but of course this type of extreme training is not for everyone.

In the video, we see Wim swimming on camera for a full fifteen minutes in the iceberg-infested waters of a glacial lake – wearing nothing but a small pair of swimming trunks. Most people on average would suffer from hypothermia after five to ten minutes. Yet in the film, Dutchman Wim is in no way struggling. In fact, he is reframing the risk and actually enjoying the experience, describing his surroundings in a relaxed, upbeat way. Following his swim, he does not gingerly struggle out of the water, in any obvious distress. In fact, immediately after getting out of the water, he goes for a run. Yep, a run, in his trunks, in his bare feet and over rocky and very icy terrain.

Of course, Wim has trained for this extensively and if you or I were to try this, the outcome would be very different. So what is 'The Iceman's secret? It's simple, really – a combination of *meditation*, repetitive exposure to cold and psychological *pain management*. Basically, mind over matter.

After watching the video with the group, I talked with them about psychological messages and several techniques we can use to control pain. Tim Bateman in particular had had recent issues with pain, having just returned from a serious shoulder injury, and was now facing into the prospect of playing in one of the most significant, 'turning-point' games of the season for his team. As a big, solid hooker, Motu 'Mots' Matu'u came up against pain on a regular basis while playing, and was interested in some tips and strategies for how to handle it during matches. As it turned out, the next game both Tim and Motu would play proved significant for these two players.

For the purposes of this book, Tim told me more about what happened in the 'big' game he played not long after our session. He told me how, just 20 minutes in, he injured his shoulder yet again. When that happened, his first thought was immediately about coming off. He tells us here what happened next:

> It was just following the session we had on pain management. I channelled the mentality I learned in that session. In that moment when I got injured, I told myself, 'I am stronger than the pain.' I knew that I had the control to react the way I chose to. So I chose to ignore the pain and play on. I focused on my breathing in the stoppage times and told myself that I was strong; I was OK; that I had an important part to play.
>
> *Tim Bateman – Maori All Black inside centre; 78 Super Rugby appearances*

In fact, Tim went on to play a significant role in winning that game. I asked him what advice he would give about managing pain following his experience:

> I would say, understand that we can choose to react how we want to. Not just how our body is telling us to. Pain is like an opinion, you can put it aside through various techniques, for me it was breathing and self-talk.

What this shows clearly is that, following a pain receptor activation, we have more than one option open to us. Tim knew that his body was hurt, but he also knew he could choose how he wanted to respond to this pain – and he chose to work through it. He decided not to allow himself to be overly affected, not to let it get in the way of what he wanted to achieve that day. So he was able to turn off the thoughts connected to it, like a tap, and, instead, simply breathe through the pain. There was something greater than the pain for him in that moment – the drive to continue to play for his team – and he made the decision to look beyond the immediate pain to a bigger picture using *perspective thinking*. Later it was shown that the injury was only minor.

A cautionary note here is around gauging the level of pain each time. You can do this by putting a number on it, to ensure the pain is understood correctly. For example, 100 is the pain limit or incapacitation – where it is not possible or wise to go on, for example a broken ankle – and 10 is, for example, a bruise. Knowing your own body, listening and gauging the pain level in this way ensures that serious injury is recognised. The scale itself can also be used to reduce non serious pain, using mental skills to bring it down from 60 to 40, and so on. This is vital to remember. You can do serious injury to yourself and cause long-term damage if you do not learn to recognise when you are in serious pain.

For Motu 'Mots' Matu'u, his next game after the *pain management* session was a smash hit at home against an avid rival. 'Mots' made a very big impact on the field in more ways than one – many impacts, in fact! So much so that he got 'man of the match'. He came off the pitch looking like he had been hit repeatedly by a freight train.

In the dressing room, he was hobbling around, wincing, with an eye swollen and a cheek bleeding. Every so often he doubled over, due to the pain from a number of big blows to his ribs. He saw me standing in the corner and gingerly came over to give me a shoulder bump. Just before he walked away again he turned and said, 'All in the mind, right!' – and in an instant his whole posture changed. His body suddenly relaxed, and he stood upright, and he began to dance! He actually danced! As he went back over to his locker, he was dancing all the way. Others joined him in his 'body boogie'. Incredibly, for the rest of the evening, 'Mots' showed little sign of being in much pain. Instead, he spent the whole time smiling and laughing, just really pleased with his performance for the team. 'All in the mind, right!'

Of course professional and high-level rugby is a rough-and-tumble sport like American football, hurling or Gaelic football and each team usually has a doctor and a medical team on hand after games to check each player's injury status and get them recuperating straight away – ice baths, physio treatment, concussion checks. A simple rule of thumb in sport is always: *if in doubt, get checked out!*

As we said earlier, the job of physical pain is clear – to alert us to the fact that we have received an injury or that some part of our body is otherwise under duress, that we should be aware of it and that it will need attention at some stage. In some cases, as with Tim, above, we have a choice as to whether to continue to dwell on this pain or temporarily postpone putting our full focus on it. The power of mental training to help turn off, or at least turn down, the pain receptor sensations has been proven many times – for example, in scenarios where medical procedures have been performed without traditional forms of pain relief, instead using meditation or hypnotism. In order to find out more about this phenomenon, scientists today are investigating the power of *meditation*, with experiments such as monitoring the brain waves of Buddhist monks, long-term practitioners of *meditation* and mindfulness.

SNOWWORLD

A remarkable illustration of our mind's potential to distance itself from even very high levels of physical pain can be seen in the use of relatively recently developed software in some hospitals to help burns patients better manage particularly painful aspects of their care. Severe burns are one of the most painful injuries a person can endure. The treatment of such injuries can be excruciating – often involving daily bandage changes, the cleaning of wounds and the removal of dead tissue in order to stave off infection and prevent scar tissue from forming.

To help burns victims psychologically cope, these hospitals have been using a virtual reality video game – *SnowWorld* – which patients are encouraged to play during wound care and physical therapy. The *SnowWorld* software was designed by Drs Hoffman and Patterson, research scientists in Seattle. Once the system is turned on, the patient enters a virtual world of snowmen, penguins and polar bears that are perched on icy ledges or are floating in a frigid river. The snowmen use their spindly arms and hands to throw snowballs at the patient, who can, with a click of the mouse, deflect the incoming ball of ice with a snowball of their own. Further clicks can unleash a torrent of snowballs that on contact cause the snowmen and igloos to explode in powdery puffs in the cold icy blue world.

The virtual-reality system eases the pain of treatment by completely immersing burns patients in a wintry, computer-generated environment. Its interactive, multi-sensory features put patients into a 'deep freeze' of distraction, displacing their attention from the incoming pain signals. To a patient recovering from severe burns, no place would be more soothing than an ice-cool landscape of gently falling snowflakes, with snowmen, penguins and igloos. An intense level of focus on the game during the ordeal of bandage-changing has been proven to raise patients' pain thresholds by up to 50 per cent. In a recent interview, Dr Richard Gamelli, director of Loyola University Hospital's Burns Centre in Maywood, Illinois, where the software is used regularly, simplified the principle behind the system as follows: 'The theory is solid. Think of a toothache . . . During the day, it's less painful because you have more demands on your attention. However, when night comes and things quieten down, your pain can flare up because you have far less to focus on.' In many dentists' surgeries, this distraction technique is also being used by placing a TV or changing landscape picture on the ceiling above the dentist's chair.

MANAGING PAIN EXERCISE

Here's one of the simple exercises I use with athletes in my sessions on *pain management* – which anyone can apply in any situation where they need to temporarily phase out or reduce painful sensations. You will see that the *visualisation* sequence works along the same lines as *SnowWorld*, above, in calling upon images of cold and ice, as well as the colour blue, to cool the body and reduce the sensation of heat and painful inflammation.

DISTRACTION

A key way to reduce pain is to cease to allow it to preoccupy our minds. Our minds can be engaged and diverted by many things, and since pain is not a useful preoccupation or narrative to dwell upon, we can simply choose to focus on something else.

Once you have received the pain message, and acknowledged it, you can move on. You do not need to keep thinking or talking about it to yourself internally. You simply tell your body, 'Message received', even thanking it if you wish, and then move to what you were planning to do with your time before the pain made itself felt.

Pain causes our body to tense up. So, part of the first phase in managing it is to relax the other parts of your body, where no pain is felt. To do this, start with a few deep breaths and focus your mind on releasing tension. Again, focus on the areas free from the pain – for example, freeing up your head and neck, dropping and rolling your shoulders, freeing up your hips, using *self-talk* to tell yourself to 'Relax'; 'Let go'; 'Just breathe'. Doing just this part of the exercise might be enough to reduce the pain enough to no longer be paying much attention to it, and allow you to focus on what you would be doing otherwise. If not, just continue to the next step below.

ENGAGE

Now, engage directly with the pain, and with your mind, start to actively reduce it. A good technique to use here is *imagery*. Like unwanted noise, pain can disturb and upset our minds, but we are not helpless and need not be passive victims at the mercy of either internal or external noise. Remember that we can influence our minds and bodies at any time.

Try imagining that the pain is like a sound wave coming from a radio. Picture the radio. Imagine the 'pain noise' as being very loud – loud enough to be actually hurting your ears. A very uncomfortable noise, and one you want to shut off.

Picture going to the radio and reaching for the volume control button. Imagine repeatedly pushing the button to turn down the horrible noise. Notice how the noise starts to lower, bit by bit. Notice how the feeling of pain is less and less intense, as the body relaxes more and more and the unpleasant noise gets softer and softer. Keep on gradually reducing the noise until it is nice and quiet. Then start enjoying the quietness and the good feelings. The nice sensations of being more relaxed, quieter and free from the painful noise.

RISE ABOVE

This phase draws on a combination of *self-talk* and *imagery*. When pain is interrupting our flow of energy, it is hampering and holding us back. We can choose to rise above it by giving ourselves powerful messages to release greater stores of energy. Messages like, 'I am bigger than the pain'; 'I am stronger than my body'; 'I can go away from the pain; I can rise above it'.

These mental messages can be helped by adding strong images and images of strength in your mind.

Or by creating a numbing image to help 'cool down' your mind, which will counteract the sense of inflammation we tend to associate with pain. For this one, start by picturing a bottle of icy water being poured directly onto your brain. Not the skull, but directly onto the pink and yellow, jelly-like stuff that our brains are made up of. Slowly, allow the water to roll down over your brain, covering it. Take a few deep breaths.

Next, begin to mentally picture an icy blue world all around you. Imagine yourself standing in a wide, open expanse, covered with snow and ice. Feel the freshness of the air as you breathe in; see the icy steam of your breath as it leaves your body. See the icy brightness of the sunlight being reflected, as it hits the snow and ice all around you; focus on the sparkling, twinkling white light. The more time you spend in this landscape, the more your body will cool down. This mental imagery has the power to numb the area in your body where you feel pain and inflammation, just as cold can freeze any body part. You can imagine putting ice on the painful area and the physical pain will recede as the numbing effect takes hold.

Mental skills such as *meditation*, repeated *psychological exposure*, *centring* and *anchoring words* all help with physical pain resistance training.

FATIGUE

Pushing through the barrier of physical fatigue is also something all top-level athletes must practise at some stage. Some of the mental skills and techniques we have looked at already for overcoming physical pain can be useful here too, though there are also specific strategies which help when managing physical tiredness or burnout.

One of the keys to managing physical fatigue in performance is regular *fatigue training* in conjunction with specific mental skills techniques. This works by habituating the body and mind to what it feels like when we repeatedly push ourselves to our physical limits, and experiencing how practising mental skills techniques can help at these times, so that we experience over and over again, in a very real way, the positive effects the skills have. Doing this repeatedly when feeling physically tired, exhausted or fatigued will anchor the experience to the skill, which will reinforce its benefits even more in helping at a later stage with actual performance. Trusting the skill.

Much of what we consider to be fatigue is actually generated by the mind – a tired mind will produce symptoms of fatigue in the body. None of us knows what our bodies are really capable of; our minds determine a lot of this for us, in that they have the power to hold us back or drive us forward. Once more, the skills of *self-awareness* and *assertiveness* are important in this context in helping us spot and shut down the negative self-talk of fatigue, which will kick in when we are feeling tired. Practices like yoga, and especially Bikram (or 'hot') yoga, really help train the mind in making the shift from physical stress and strain to mental rest and replenishment in a smooth, practised and easy transition.

Below are a few 'anti-fatigue' techniques you can start practising in training.

CLAP, HOLD, FOCUS, REPLENISH

Whenever we feel ourselves fatigued or low in energy, a good technique is to drum up some 'fast' energy in the form of an easily executed action.

Try one loud, effortful and sharp clap. Then keep your hands together and just focus your attention on the sting of your hands. Next, begin pushing your hands together with as much strength as you can muster. Focusing intently on your hands, start to take some long breaths in and out. Imagine the oxygen going in and out of your body and the energy starting to gather in your chest as you push your hands together.

When you feel stronger and more energised, just let the hands release and shake them and your shoulders a little. In this way, you are dispersing the energy around your body. If you feel like jumping up and down on the spot to help with this process, do this, all the while continuing to breathe in and out.

After this exercise, you should feel more energised, focused, clear-headed and replenished.

'FLOW' MINDSET

Another technique is to release some energy using the mind – this can be used during the activity, whether in training or performance. Instead of thinking or feeling or telling yourself that you are tired, try to enter more of a 'flow' state. This is where we focus mindful energy on the pleasant aspects of what we are doing in the moment. Yes, you might feel tired, but remind yourself that you are feeling this way because you are doing something that you really want to do, and enjoy doing. Remember that there are lots of other things you could be doing, but that you choose to do this activity – so just allow yourself to enjoy it a little more!

One way to help yourself with this is to draw in the energy of the moment; the energy of the universe as it is right now. Remember that there is energy all around us at all times.

Everything in nature and in our immediate environment gives off energy, and we can tap into this simply by being open to it and bringing it in to us. Simply lift your head, open your mind to the process and breathe this energy into your body through your nose and mouth. Clear the cobwebs, as they say. Imagine that your skin is like one big receptor. Since our skin is the largest organ of the body, it makes sense to use it to receive this energy.

Stand upright, straighten the spine, head up and arms down to the side with palms turned facing out to receive the energy like you are scooping it up.

When you feel the energy beginning to flow more, you can help the process by keeping your mind as clear as possible. Let yourself zone out a bit and try not to think. Just stay quiet, allowing yourself to simply breathe and feel and smile. As the transfer of energy gradually takes place, whatever activity you are doing will start to feel easier.

HUMOUR

This final technique is really quick and simple! When we feel happy, and that what we are doing is fun, energy flows and is replenished more easily and things don't feel like such hard work. When we smile and laugh, we release lots of feel-good chemicals into our body. These make us feel nourished, relaxed and more energised. To tap into this, all we need to do is think of something we find funny, that makes us laugh.

A good strategy is to have a few jokes or funny images ready to go. Telling them to ourselves or sharing them with others or picturing the image will instantly give a much-needed energy boost to the system. The key is to get smiling – the body will do the rest.

EMOTIONAL AND MENTAL FATIGUE

As we have mentioned, feelings of fatigue may have causes other than intense physical exertion, and this is something we should be vigilant about. In Chapter Five we heard former Olympic swimmer Gary O'Toole talk about the overwhelming exhaustion he felt just prior to the Barcelona games, due to over-training compulsively in the immediate run-up. What is certain is that the physical fatigue he felt was also due to the fact that he wasn't giving himself proper breaks mentally – he tells us that he had become obsessive about his sport and increasingly unable to switch off. So, Gary's physical tiredness undoubtedly also reflected his mental and emotional state, and the fact that this was leading him to getting close to burnout.

As stated previously, the fact is that when we feel emotionally and psychologically fatigued, we can often perceive this as physical fatigue – and we tell ourselves so. Due to the bombardment of excessive stimulation that is coming at us from all sides these days, the stress-related chemicals in our bodies are active more often and have no obvious outlet. Telling ourselves we are too tired, when actually we are not, we can find ourselves deciding not to exercise, or to give up our regular hobbies, and so on. We may even begin to avoid social gatherings because we feel our energy is too low. All of this is risky, because the fatigue we feel is the result of the build-up of stress, and the activities we opt out of are precisely the things that would help combat this stress and provide an outlet for the associated chemicals and give us more energy.

Over time, this stockpiling of stress chemicals will take us closer to our 'dis-stress' tipping point. If we breach it, we crash – emotionally, mentally and physically. Today, more people are experiencing this more frequently than ever before, which is why anxiety and depression are becoming so common in our society. In Chapter Fifteen we will look in some detail at how to combat this stress and what to do once you feel you are reaching that tipping point.

TWELVE
Supporting Your Team During Performance

'The less focus I put onto myself and the more I focused on the team as a whole and how I might help the team, the better I became . . .'

Lar Corbett

The less focus I put onto myself and the more I focused on the team as a whole and how I might help the team, the better I became on and off the field. Thinking about how I might help a teammate [who] was struggling with confidence and remove the pressure of scoring myself. This freed my mind up. I'm not putting pressure on myself but focusing on helping others. It's a win–win, for yourself and your team.

Lar Corbett – hurler; two All-Ireland titles with Tipperary; three All Stars

When I began working as a mental skills coach with the New Zealand cricket team, the White Ferns, I spent an initial period simply observing some of their matches, to get a feel for how the team was functioning as a whole, and a sense of what areas of their play might need mental support techniques. Something I noticed very quickly was how a number of key batters would visibly express disappointment or frustration as they left the field during matches – regardless of whether they had had a good innings or not. When I discussed this with the head coach, we decided that it was something that should be raised in the mental skills sessions.

At the next session, we spoke directly to the players about these behaviours – what this looked like from the outside, to both the spectators and teammates or wider team members, and what effect it might be having on the oncoming players within our own team. Everyone took on board our point that such negative displays of dissatisfaction were potentially damaging for team morale, and risked giving a competitive advantage to the other side by projecting a pessimistic, under-confident view of our chances of winning.

Our next step in that session was to talk about oxytocin – otherwise known as 'the bonding hormone' – a chemical released by our bodies which builds trust and attunement with others, and promotes a sense of team bonding and common purpose within a group. We explained that many of the routines and exercises the coaches took them through during pre-game warm-ups were devised to help raise oxytocin levels, but that this negative behaviour from some members of the team during play would have the effect of depleting the oxytocin. We then suggested, and everyone agreed to try, a strategy whereby individual players would hold off on showing disappointment while on the field. Instead, they would try to adopt body language which looked confident and upbeat, so as to encourage the incoming batter. By doing this, they would be sending a positive message to the rest of the team, the on-looking opposition team and the crowd, including their own supporters. As they walked off the pitch, they would keep their heads up, their eyes forward and focused, their backs straight, making sure to connect briefly with the batter who was next up as they passed each other – keeping the oxytocin levels up, maybe with a simple glove touch.

It worked – morale increased for the players sitting down at the side of the field, as energy levels stayed higher with calls and positive comments being shared amongst players. Younger players especially enjoyed this change and this type of connecting, making them feel more relaxed, engaged and part of the team and less intimidated by senior players looking dejected. There was a noticeable increase in the younger players' confidence and on-field performance with this lowering of pressure about making a mistake.

Being able to postpone strong emotional responses during any performance is a key way of ensuring that we maintain our focus on what is happening in the immediate presence of a game – particularly in a long game like cricket, where there will be a number of opportunities for a player to refocus their mind in order to keep playing well – and postponing responses in this way can help us take full advantage of these opportunities when they arise. This is equally effective in individual sports, like tennis – getting into the habit of quickly acknowledging the feeling of disappointment, frustration, irritation etc. to oneself, and then moving on to focusing on the next shot. Brushing it off, as it were.

In this way, we release some of the energy of the emotion in the moment, but re-engage as soon as possible with the bigger goal of playing well, executing the plan and winning. There will always be time later, after the game, to reconnect with disappointment and share it with others, such as a coach, another player or a close friend or family member. Holding off on negative feelings can also have an added benefit, in that later there may be little need to feel the full extent of the emotion, or even to feel it at all, since the game may have ultimately been won. In this way we get to influence our emotions and not just 'feel' at the mercy of them.

This ability to *self-regulate* our emotions is a key mental skill that can be worked on, and improved upon at every opportunity, until we are practised enough to be able to manage what is going on and navigate our way through it, experiencing and managing feelings while not getting stuck in them. This is all part of the more general, but also incredibly useful, mental skill of being able to maintain *balance* in our emotions – not allowing ourselves to get too high or too low about what is happening in the moment. We will look in more detail at the importance of balance, as a sporting skill and as a general life skill, in the final chapters of this book.

We can use the technique of *encouraging self-talk* to help us get through such emotionally challenging moments. This involves training ourselves to use key phrases to help us push through a difficult point in a game and propel ourselves forward – language such as: 'come on; get up; get going; keep moving; you are able to do this; focus on the next task; lift yourself; head up, eyes forward; keep talking, keep connecting, push on through'. These phrases are used often in team sports, especially when a team is falling behind. As players repeat them to teammates and to themselves, a new energy can be generated – a bit like feeding the furnace of a steam train. This energy will carry the team forward and build renewed momentum. As we have seen previously, releasing and refocusing energy will always help to take us forward.

This *connecting* technique can be invaluable, not just at times in a game when someone has played badly or is visibly struggling, or when the team as a whole is flagging, but also to help individual players to simply refocus and stay in the game. All athletes can drift at times – suddenly finding their mind is miles away and not focused on what is going on in the here and now. In team sports, teammates can help by calling out a few select catchphrases that they have practised in training. One team I worked with used the call, 'Next task' to help players focus their attention on going forward. Another team I worked with used a simple Maori chant to raise focus, intent and commitment in the team. This was a similar device to the All Blacks haka, but was used during the game, rather than just prior to kick off.

SUPPORTING YOUR TEAM DURING PERFORMANCE

We looked in Chapter Twelve at how to work with your team, including how to build a successful team culture that would help everyone within the group, and the group as a whole, to maximise their potential and perform at their best on every possible occasion. During performance itself, a lot of the same key principles apply in terms of supporting your teammates, playing to your own full potential and ensuring that things go as well as possible in the match.

As we discussed earlier, the currency of sporting relationship success – and indeed success in any kind of relationship – is communication and a commitment to sharing the load. In sport, during a game, this can mean taking the initiative and activating a big play that lifts the energy of the team. But it can also take the form of simply noticing when the team's energy is low and helping to lift it by encouraging individual players who are flagging. Speaking out and asserting with your teammates what you think will help the flow of play and create a more positive momentum. Talking to Brent for this book, Irish rugby great Victor Costello hits the nail on the head as regards the essence and importance of team spirit:

> The lads I played with really knew what made me tick. They would encourage me, tell me to keep it going, simple stuff like that. In a game also if things were going wrong, you'd notice your

teammates. Their heads were down. You'd try and be the catalyst to get us back into the game.

Victor Costello – former professional rugby player; 39 caps for Ireland, 121 appearances for Leinster; airline pilot

In a business context, this can mean speaking up in meetings if you feel the energy rise in you to do so – having first taken a moment to actively reflect on what you want to say and why you believe it is important to say it; what positive contribution it will make. In a more general way, it can be about bringing and sharing new ideas, encouraging and reinforcing existing team ideas, and challenging and testing these if they seem unclear or if the desired outcome is not in line with the overall goal.

With your 'team' at home, communication and commitment to sharing the load will be about taking the time to talk, and listen to the important people in your life. Helping to foster an environment where talking, asking questions, healthy challenging, open sharing and reflecting, encouragement and having fun are all part of the picture. In our closest relationships, conflict is inevitable. It needs to be there for us to be truly honest. In intimate relationships, conflict and challenge happen naturally, so we don't have to look to generate them. They happen because we care. If we didn't care, there would be no challenging – we just wouldn't bother to put the energy in.

The key here is to *speak up, and not go quiet.* Many sports teams facing into tough times during a game (and off the field as well) tend to do one of two things: they either go quiet and clam up, or get too loud and urgent – shouting, blaming and criticising others in the group. This is the opposite of communicating well and sharing the load – and will have the opposite effect, leading a team away from success and towards frustration, division and failure. The same very much applies to a business context, and in our personal relationships. Lack of communication or too much negative currency puts any team into the red.

On the other side of the coin, sports teams and athletes who know how to share energy and bring intensity during a game, a competition or a tournament are already winning. Being willing to communicate honestly with teammates is an indicator of real commitment to the group, and if it is done with enough self-reflection beforehand, in a culture where sharing in a straightforward way is encouraged, then it becomes a win–win scenario for everyone.

I remember for example how, during a workshop I did with the Wellington Lions in New Zealand, a key influential player spoke up and shared with all of us something he admitted that he 'hated'. He said that whenever he made a mistake – like a missed tackle – he hated it when his fellow teammates ran up to him and told him not to worry, saying things like, 'You'll get him next time!' He said this particular phrase would drive him crazy! He explained that he would already be angry inside for making the mistake, and so when someone assured him that he would get it right next time, well then he would get really mad. He'd be thinking things like, 'How the hell do you know that?' 'You can't possibly be sure of that, so now you are just patronising me.' (He added a few expletives here, as you can imagine!)

Many of the team had played with this guy for a number of years, but none of them knew this. How could they! After all this time he'd never told them! Thanks to his openness on this occasion, now his teammates knew what *not to say* when this situation arose. The next step in the session was for us to ask the player the very straightforward question, 'What would you like people to do or say instead?' It turned out that for this particular player, humour was the key! His advice was that his teammates should help him to distract himself from thinking about the mistake somehow. He said that helping him forget about what just happened by making him smile was by far the best way. So that's what everyone worked on, and with great success!

When I chatted recently to former Irish rugby star Ronan O'Gara for this book, he emphasised the key importance of a culture of encouragement and positivity in a team – as well as the huge impact a coach with the right attitude can have on his players:

> You can get confidence from your teammates and your coaches. I remember one particular coach – he made me feel ten feet tall. Just before a game he used to call me 'king'; he'd just whisper in my ear something like, 'Everything alright, King?' – then he'd go around the dressing room and connect with [the other] players like this. He mightn't even have meant it, but when you were receiving it, it felt like he really meant it . . . And I think his timing was great. Everyone has doubts before big games. Two minutes before you get into a huddle and before you go on the pitch. It's your time. It's a collective sport, but it all comes down to the individual getting himself right.
>
> *Ronan O'Gara – former professional rugby player; rugby coach; 128 caps for Ireland*

Operating successfully in a team means, firstly, having the *self-awareness* to know what makes us tick, what motivates and what de-motivates us, and then being open and willing to share with others, in the most constructive way possible, what is happening for us. This enables others to have our back more easily, more often, which in turn props us up and allows us greater confidence as a member of the team. It is of course a two-way, reciprocal process, and as they share more easily with us we too are able to give them more support and a greater sense of security.

EXERCISE

Have a think now about your team, and how supportive and effective you are as a teammate. These questions will be equally relevant in other contexts, such as work/business or home/personal life.

- What will help me understand myself, in terms of how I would like others to help me?
- How can I find out the best way to help others on my team?
- How can I help my teammates understand the best way to help me? How can I express what works for me, and what doesn't, in the most constructive way?
- Who else in my life might find this information about me useful?

PART 4

Try, Fail, Try, Succeed

THIRTEEN

Handling Setbacks: Injury, Illness and Downtime

'I put things into perspective and just thought there are lots of other people out there that are having it a lot tougher than I am'

Nehe Milner-Skudder

Brent

The year I aspired to make the All Black World Cup squad of 1987, I made up my mind to be the fittest rugby player in the country. People around me had their doubts as I embarked on a strenuous training ritual that only a professional athlete would truly understand. They said that I was mad to be training during the Christmas festivities, or lifting weights or getting a run in on Christmas morning. On weekday mornings before work, I pounded the steep hills of Dunedin, building up my lungs, then headed to the gym to work on my muscle strength. During lunchtimes, I went to the running track at Otago University to improve my sprint speed, and at night I swam length after length at Moana Pool – and I hated swimming.

By the time I played the first set of trial matches, of which there would be a few before the All Black World Cup squad would be named, I was not really on the map, but I knew I was ready. I was confident that I was where I wanted to be, physically and mentally, and I used the fact that I was not on the selectors' radar to spur me on – I would show them;

I would prove them all wrong. As a result, I played one of the best games of my life and after it I was named in the All Black trials a week later. Later future teammate and an All Black captain, Paul Henderson, whom I was marking in that first game in Central Otago, told me when we became friends that I was far fitter than anyone on that field. Paul had a serious rugby pedigree, much better than mine at that stage – he had been a New Zealand schools and under 21 player, and at that time was considering a move from second division Southland to Otago. Otago was a first division province and Paul felt that he would have a better chance of becoming a full All Black if he made the transition. But we were both in the same position, open-side flanker, and Paul obviously intended to take the spot that I felt I had earned. He told me though that he considered not making the move after that game, and in fact when he did, I moved to No. 8 to accommodate him. For years after, myself, Paul and another great All Black, Mike Brewer, became one of the best loose forward trios in the country.

After being named in the trials, I was on the path to making my dreams come true, and I fully believed in my ability. Mentally, I was now on track to achieve my ultimate goal – to come from the small rural township of Ashburton and play for the mighty All Blacks.

I still have one of the final All Black trial match programmes, in which it was noted that, 'Today two up-and-coming youngsters of New Zealand rugby will compete for the no. 7 jersey – Otago's Brent Pope and Auckland's Michael Jones.' Jones would later go on to become, in a lot of people's eyes, the best flanker to ever play the game.

Fast forward to the last series of warm-up games and trials, just a few days out from the start of the rugby World Cup, and the moment it was announced over the radio that I, Brent Pope, was player of the match. The sheer joy I felt at giving myself the best shot at making the final team was short-lived, however. Suddenly, I felt the most incredible, searing pain I had ever experienced. Getting my arm caught behind the post in the very last minute of the match, as I rabbited for the try line, I had dislocated my elbow and it pushed its way out through the skin of my arm, which I had also broken in multiple places.

I was immediately rushed to the hospital. There, through the excruciating pain and hurt, I had to listen to the doctor tell one of the All Black selectors who had kindly called the hospital that I was out of contention for the team, and might never actually play again. The real hurt was the sudden loss of all I had worked for. My dream – the dream I had had ever since I'd been a young boy – was shattered in one agonising moment. The dream I visualised when I would play in the back yard as a boy – Brent Pope, All Black.

The next move for the selectors was to put a call out to a young Aucklander named Zinzan Brooke, who was flown in straight away. Unlike me, as he will tell you himself, Zinzan never played a trial or warm-up game that year, but in the week I lay on the hospital bed, he was named in the first ever All Black World Cup team.

Zinzan is a good friend and one of the true greats of the game, and I am delighted for all the success and adoration he has in his life: he warrants it all. But even now, not a day goes by that I don't find myself wondering, 'What if . . ?' What if I had had the ability to be as good as him? What if it had been me, running on at no. 8 against Argentina for my debut? What if I had a World Cup medal sitting at home instead of him? What if, what if . . .?

Realistically speaking, in 1987 Zinzan was much younger than I was, and would always have been an All Black at some stage. But for me, this was my time. I was ready!

That disappointment would come to haunt me. It triggered the emergence of some mental health struggles which perhaps had always been latent in me – and missing out on my All Black dream became just another thing that would lead me to many moments of despair and depression. Of course, like a lot of people suffering in this way, I masked it well, trying to tell the media that it was just one of those things. But it wasn't, it was just another thing to tell me that this was always going to be the way for me.

Brent's personal account above shows very poignantly the devastating effect a setback such as serious injury can have on a high-achieving athlete at a crucial moment in his or her career. As he says himself, the emotional pain of seeing his dream come crashing down was far more traumatic than the – albeit very distressing – physical injury he suffered. Fortunately, as we know, Brent's journey to success and fulfilment was far from over at that stage, and he would go on to do many things he might never have had the opportunity to pursue had his sporting life taken another direction. In Chapter Fifteen we will hear more about his experiences with depression, and how he managed to overcome so much on that front.

In this chapter, however, we will look at the difficult hurdle of injury in sport, and how to cope with the psychological impact this can have. For a top athlete, physical injury will in all likelihood represent a much bigger problem than for someone who does not depend on having peak fitness for their livelihood. However, many of the strategies and approaches we will put forward here will be equally applicable in other contexts in life where we find ourselves having to deal with this kind of unexpected setback.

INJURY

In the vast majority of sporting activities, especially in very physical sports, getting injured is pretty much a given. Our body is being exercised – pushed, pulled, thrown around, struck, contorted, elevated, dropped, flung down and so on – so it is fairly predictable that at some stage injuries will happen. For most of us – but, as we have said, especially for athletes – getting physically injured is a double whammy. The first blow is the physical pain and discomfort we suffer at the time of the injury and during the recovery process until full healing has taken place. The second knockback is psychological, as we try to come to terms with the injury and to adjust to its impact on our everyday lives, which, in an athlete's case, is more radical than for the rest of us. Let's hear from a few top athletes about how injury affected them.

Rising rugby star Nehe Milner-Skudder made an exceptional debut with the All Blacks in 2015; in the same year, he was part of the ITM cup-winning team, played internationally for the Maori All Blacks and was named World Rugby Breakthrough Player of the Year. Very early in the 2016 season, however, he suffered a shoulder injury as a result of which he was out of the game for the rest of the season. When I chatted with him, he told me about this very difficult and frustrating period at a key time in his career.

> I was pretty gutted. I missed being out there with the boys the most, going out on the field with fourteen of your best mates. That was the toughest bit, knowing that I [wouldn't] be able to do that for a while. [I kept asking myself] why did it happen to me, so early in the season as well? This was a big one. To miss the whole season was tough to come to terms with.
>
> [The toughest time was] the first couple of weeks after surgery . . . A lot of us rugby players are pretty active, and we don't like sitting around doing nothing . . . I was under strict orders from the doctor to just park up at home, and make sure I got the pain under control and not move around too much – but I was getting all fidgety, wanting to go to the gym or sit on the bike . . .
>
> *Nehe Milner-Skudder, New Zealand professional rugby player*

Other athletes have a very similar story to tell about downtime due to injury, when the psychological impact was as bad as – if not, perhaps, in some ways worse than – the physical discomfort.

> Most of my dark times came when I was injured. Two reconstructed shoulders and knee surgery threw my head all over the place. It put me under a huge amount of strain, both physically and mentally. It's hard to describe the feeling – lonely, worried, and scared that this could mean the end of my sporting career. That someone might take my position. Second-guessing myself. Thoughts like, 'Will I return to the physical standard that I need to be as an international rugby player?' 'Will I be back in time?' 'Will it hold up again?'
>
> *Tania Rosser – professional rugby player, 50 caps for Ireland*

> In 2015 I had a serious back injury. What was meant to be an eight-week injury turned into 16 months out. Every time I seemed to take a step in the right direction, I would take two steps backwards. I watched my teammates train and work hard, while I was struggling with simple movements. I was frustrated and fairly miserable. I had a growing fear that I might not play again.
>
> *Jenny Murphy – professional rugby player, 28 caps for Ireland*

As we have said, injury can be part and parcel of being a sportsperson, especially in a very physical sport such as rugby, and so we were keen to hear how these athletes coped with this kind of setback, which will likely happen a number of times during a career. All three of these players – Nehe, Tania and Jenny – had their own strategies for getting through these difficult times, and we can see how each drew on various mental skills in doing so.

> I listened to the physios and doctors – they are the experts, and have dealt with all these injures thousands of times. They know the process to go through . . . [I relied] on knowing that they know what they are doing. Leaving it in their hands and [trusting] what's going to happen works better in the long run.
>
> *Nehe Milner-Skudder, New Zealand professional rugby player*

Once again here (as throughout this book), we can see the value of *process* in helping when it comes to managing a difficult situation in sport – knowing that there is an established, tried and tested way of dealing with things already in place, and realising the importance of trusting that process. Also, acknowledging that there are valuable outside resources – in this instance, the expertise of doctors and physios – that can be drawn on, and, crucially, being able to accept that help. This final point is an important one, not only in sport but in life generally – we all need to acknowledge sometimes that we can't handle every situation alone, that we need to be able to ask others to help us, and to allow ourselves to be helped.

Nehe had some other great tips to pass on, in terms of how he dealt with his understandable feelings of frustration, and times when negative thinking set in:

> I put things into perspective, and just thought, there are lots of other people out there that are [having] it a lot tougher than I am. Another thing that I would think of is comparing injuries. With the shoulder [injury], I still could run around. Six months felt like a very long time initially – but there are lots of injuries, like [damage to the] ACL [anterior cruciate ligament] that happen to the knee, that mean you are out for a whole year.
>
> Also, once I started getting back into some form of exercise and got the ball rolling, I'd tell myself I only have a bit more time off to go.
>
> Injuries happen. This was my first major injury, but I have been playing for a little while. You don't want injuries to happen, but it's part of playing the game.
>
> *Nehe Milner-Skudder, New Zealand professional rugby player*

By reflecting on the fact that there are bigger things that can happen in life, and that his situation, relative to that of other people's, was not so bad, we can see how this young player used *perspective thinking* to deal with setbacks. In this way, he avoided thinking of his injury as a disaster, something catastrophic. By considering things in a more relative way, he allowed himself to see that six months away from the game was not a year, a year was not two years and so on.

Perspective thinking means looking at a situation from a different angle – from a 'big picture' viewpoint. It involves taking an alternative standpoint on something, and seeing how it fits into a wider picture. We can challenge ourselves to do this by asking questions such as:

- In the grand scheme of things, how big is this really?
- Are there more important things happening in the world?
- Are there others worse off than I am?
- Have I experienced bigger things before?
- How does this fit into my overall picture of who I am and where I am going?

Bringing in *perspective* allows us to move out of 'mind traps' and unhelpful negative thinking, by enabling us to see things as they really are, both in the context of our own wider experience and of the rest of the world in general.

Nehe also used the technique of *reframing* to help him deal with the stages of his recovery. While he initially found the idea of being out for six months very challenging, as he began to gain more physical mobility he allowed himself to be pleased about the fact that his injury did not prevent him from doing other things to channel his energy, like running and walking – again using 'big picture' thinking by acknowledging that other types of injuries would have made such things impossible. Resilience techniques like these take the energy out of negative psychological games, like the 'what if's we looked at in Chapter Eight.

Let's hear what Tania and Jenny had to say about their ways of coping with injury:

> I was very lucky, I had great support. This has been one of the most important components in my sporting career. I surrounded myself with the best skills coach, physio, chiropractor, mentor – and of course, my biggest support [was] my partner Simon. They all played a huge role in getting me through the tough times. They always believed in what I was doing, always guiding me through on the days I wanted to give up.
>
> . . . Once my head was clearer, I was able to set new goals. Getting me through to the next phase. I decided that I needed to do something for myself each day – something that I really enjoyed and something that I did only for [me]. I called it 'My Time' – a set time to truly enjoy something that day, [even] for a small moment. It was as simple as enjoying my morning shower or a cup of tea. I would sit there and just enjoy that time to myself.
>
> *Tania Rosser – professional rugby player, 50 caps for Ireland*

> I spoke to a sports psychologist, and to my close friends and teammates. I couldn't have done it on my own. I also realised that I'm more than just a rugby player – it's something I'm good at, but it doesn't define me.
>
> *Jenny Murphy – professional rugby player, 28 caps for Ireland*

Once more, both of these athletes talk about the importance of turning to others for help and support. As well as professionals – physios, sports psychologists, a mental skills coach and so on – having personal support from those close to us – friends, family and personal mentors – is crucial in challenging times. We all need to know who our own support team consists of, or could consist of, and whom we can call upon when we need them. Not only will they be able to help us when the going gets tough, but having this kind of circle of support will also have an ongoing protective effect, insulating us from negative thinking and stress, both of which tend to thrive when we isolate ourselves from other people.

The key mental skills of *assertiveness* and *emotional fluency* are invaluable here, enabling us to connect with others more easily by helping them understand better what we are going through. (We explore these more in Chapter Sixteen).

Tania's testimony also highlights another key mental skill – that of *goal-setting* – as a helpful approach when getting through a period of altered circumstances. Goal-setting enabled her to adapt more easily to the daily reality of her injury, and helped her to keep in mind that, in time, recovery would happen, her downtime in this instance was only temporary and not a permanent state of affairs, and put a healthy psychological boundary in place. When *goal-setting* in this kind of situation, it's important to be realistic in terms of what is achievable – expecting yourself to be up and walking unassisted again within ten days of breaking your leg, for example, would not be a reasonable or helpful expectation to have. Thinking unrealistically like this would only lead to disappointment at a time when your defences are already low, whereas realistic goal-setting really helps, especially when coupled with fun, 'feel good' pastimes or moments.

A final point that these players also make is the importance of remembering that we are all whole, complex human beings, with many facets to our lives. Tania's 'My Time' is a way of reminding herself that she has a value, and an existence, outside of sport; that playing rugby professionally is only one part of her life (albeit a very important one for her).

High achievers tend to fall more easily into the trap of psychologically identifying themselves with their work – although this is something we can all be guilty of, no matter what field we're in or what type of work we are doing. Some of this is down to the way we use language, for example 'I'm a doctor', 'I'm a builder', 'I'm a footballer', 'I'm a psychotherapist' and so on. Remember how Gary O'Toole talked in an earlier chapter of how he over-trained for the Barcelona Olympics, with the result that he was too exhausted to perform properly when it mattered most. By his own admission, he had become obsessed with his sport and with constantly achieving, and he didn't have anyone in his immediate circle who was able to flag this up to him.

Seeing ourselves in this minimised and very limited way is not good for our physical or mental health in the long run. It's very important for this reason that we make a conscious effort to separate out *what we do* from *who we are*. Many professional athletes struggle with this identification, not only when injury forces them to take time out, but also later in life, as their careers wind down and they face retirement. Again, however, this is not an experience specific to sportspeople. Seeing ourselves as more than just what we do for a living, or even as a passion; taking time to develop other sides of ourselves and of our lives; realising that we have a value in and of ourselves, regardless of what we do or don't do – all of these things will stand us in very good stead, especially when injury, illness or other life-changing events strike us. We'll talk more about this key issue – keeping a sense of balance in our lives – in a later chapter.

HAVING A PLAN

In sport, as in life, things happen that we don't expect. Even when we *know* that they can happen and, in some instances, that they certainly *will* happen, when they do, we are often blindsided by them.

For sportspeople, unexpected setbacks include, as well as injury, illness, adverse weather conditions, suspension, delayed flights, substandard accommodation and food while on tour, rescheduling of competition dates and so on. In performance situations, these unforeseen circumstances can include missed tackles, handling errors, mis-runs, mis-jumps, misjudgements, bad referee calls, red/yellow cards, heckling by loud, disgruntled fans – to name but a few.

In business, unforeseen circumstances might include missed deadlines, the loss of contracts, a high level of absenteeism, resignations, restructures, market share decline, new competitors, advances in technology, changes in legislation and, more recently, recession. In life, they could include illness, bereavement, financial setbacks, accidents, unexpected pregnancies, unemployment, divorce, redundancy, natural disasters such as floods, fires or earthquakes, and so on.

In research about mental resilience and winning behaviours – i.e. those most likely to result in successful outcomes and the achieving of long-term goals – the importance of the skill of *preparation* consistently and repeatedly came up. Over and above this, one aspect of preparation more than any other really came to the fore in relation to high-performing teams and individuals. Simply put, this is preparation *for when things go wrong* – for when things don't go to plan or when unexpected events conspire to derail things. Although it might seem like a very obvious aspect of planning, it is one many of us simply ignore or put minimal time and thought into.

Remember back to Conrad Smith's psychological preparation – planning for adverse circumstances and events means not waiting until they actually happen before working out how we will react and cope. So, in this context, why wait for an injury to happen before having a strategy to help you deal with it? Have a psychological plan to hand for that time. *Actively reflect* on what it will mean if you get injured. How might this feel, what might it mean in practical terms and how might you like to respond? Consciously explore all of this when you are removed from the immediate stress of actually being injured, and work out what steps might help you if it does happen.

As part of this planning, use the mental skill of *progressive thinking* (which we looked at in Chapter Seven), envisaging the best, most constructive ways in which you could react on a stage-by-stage basis, i.e. 'Well, what if this did happen – what would I do? And then what would I do next, and after that, what would I do?' Following through the scenario as far as you can take it into the future, with an *optimistic mindset* and a sense at each step of how you would most like to respond.

Thinking about, and planning for, adverse future events in this way acts to lower the risk of our primary defences quickly being activated if such an event does actually occur, because it is less of a shock to the system if it does happen. Thus our acute stress, and panic/fight/flight/freeze responses are less likely to be triggered, as might otherwise be the case, because we can tell ourselves, 'Well, I thought this could happen and I have a plan for it'. As well as having some kind of process in place, or plan at hand, we will be less likely to respond in extreme ways, enhancing our ability for *affect regulation* and this in turn will help us to make better decisions for ourselves in adverse circumstances, or even actual survival situations.

This 'planning for not having a plan' involves several basic premises, i.e.

- realising that no plan will ever encompass every possible scenario
- accepting that, at any given time, there will always be external elements that are out of our control
- knowing that there are always internal things that are within our control, and which we can change and influence at any given time – i.e. that no matter what happens outside of us, we can always influence our own energy in response (our internal reaction).

EXERCISE IN ADVERSE PLANNING

For the simple assignment below, which is split into two stages, you should select any event that you are worried might happen in the future. Try to choose something feasible – something that you believe could really happen. If in sport, have a think about some of the scenarios mentioned earlier, and pick a common one, like injury or non-selection. If in a life or business context, choose a probable event the thought of which stirs up emotions in you.

PART ONE

- Think of something that might happen which concerns you, and which you would prefer to avoid thinking about. It could be something that has recently happened and that you are concerned could happen again, or something that will likely happen in the future.

- If a possible future event, write out all the things that you can imagine might happen in relation to this.
- What is most upsetting about this image?
- Name the feelings that arise for you, and imagine you are feeling them now.
- Now think about what might happen in the moments after the imagined event.
- Keep going – what might happen further after this, and after this, and so on . . .
- Now try to imagine a positive picture of how things look in relation to this, in the farther future.

The above exercise should have initially raised some emotion for you, relating to the concerns you have about the undesirable event. Then, as you work through the detail of the event happening, you should find that this helps the emotion to subside. This lessening in pitch happens because our mind has the ability to envisage time lapsing, and knows from experience that our feelings change, especially the intensity of our feelings. Our mind can just as easily picture life after the event as it can the event itself. Meanwhile, our body knows we cannot sustain a heightened level of emotion indefinitely, and that, regardless of how intense an emotion feels in the moment, it will eventually subside. The high initial energy that feelings generate cannot be sustained indefinitely and the body eventually invites reality. This is where the phrase 'Time heals all wounds' comes from: the body wants to heal itself. Although in the case of, say, the grief of bereavement, it might be more accurate to say that time helps to make our feelings easier to live with rather than making them disappear completely.

This – the fact that, with time, our feelings will become less intense and not all-pervasive – is a very good thing for us to remind ourselves of when we contemplate a future event going badly and how that will make us feel.

PART TWO

Using the same event as before, think about how you *would like* to react if this event were to happen.

- What would you like to do in the moments immediately following this unfavourable event?
- Write out exactly what you would like to have happen.
- Write down what you would like to be *thinking*; what you would like to *say to or tell* yourself and/or others; what you could *do* that would help most.

This simple task involves the mental skills of *goal-setting* and *planning* and is a form of self-coaching. Take making an error, for example. If you can think about it happening, you can also think about what you can do just after it happens. You can then plan for it – plan for what you will do in the moments immediately following the mistake; plan what you could do and say to help yourself regain some composure and to refocus on what it is you wanted to achieve.

Perhaps it's a scenario in life where you have to address a large audience, and you are someone who gets very nervous when speaking in public – say, you have to give the best man's speech at a wedding, or say a few words at a local community group meeting. Your worst nightmare might be that you mispronounce or stumble over the names of people you have to mention in your speech – in case this does happen, you could think beforehand of how you might get over the awkward moment and put your audience, and yourself, more at ease. Perhaps you could say something light-hearted – or even just explain that you aren't used to public speaking – which will straight away get the audience on your side, normalise and lighten up the atmosphere. Thinking in advance about how you could handle something like this will make you feel more relaxed about the possibility of it happening, and may even reduce the chances of it happening at all!

In sport, being told that you have not been selected for a team or a tour is a very common experience. Knowing this – that it is a scenario you are bound to encounter at some point in your career – can help you plan for what you will do, think and feel immediately following such an announcement. How would you most like to be able to respond?

In a business context, this adverse event planning might take the form of envisaging the best way to react to a rejection letter after an interview or the news of a deal not going through. How will you respond?

We have seen that there are many strategies and techniques that can really help us when adverse circumstances strike, all of which are equally relevant when it comes to sport, business or life in general. For some final words on setbacks, and some great pointers on dealing with them constructively, here are some insights former sprint hurdler Derval O'Rourke and Gaelic footballer Bernard Brogan shared with us:

> For me, identifying the worst-case scenario became important. Generally, the worst-case scenario isn't as bad as you might think, and knowing this helped to relax me. I then moved on to think of what the best-case scenario was, and that made me get excited – imagining all the good things that could happen was uplifting for me.
>
> *Derval O'Rourke – former Irish sprint hurdles athlete; Irish national record holder in 60 and 100 metres hurdles*

> I had a lot of setbacks early on – like picking up injuries or not making teams . . . At 20 years old, I spent nearly a year out of the game, but I turned that feeling of disappointment around. I looked for an opportunity to build my body up, [and] I put on over a stone of muscle. When I was back, people said I looked so much more powerful. It's a great lesson. When faced with adversity, you can look at it two ways – you can give up, or you can see it as an opportunity to make strides in another area.

. . . I thought about this later [in my career] also, when I tore hamstrings. I would get down for a while – that's natural – but then [I'd] decide to use my time as positively as I could. Train the areas that may have been ignored, come back better than before. Explore other avenues – build up my core with Pilates or yoga; increase or lose weight. We can always work on aspects of ourselves.

Bernard Brogan – Gaelic footballer; winner of five All-Irelands with Dublin

FOURTEEN

Handling Setbacks: Losses, Lapses and Disappointments

'There's always a pathway to overcoming tough times'

Conor O'Shea

'Nana Korobi, Ya Oki':
'Fall down seven times, stand up eight'

(Japanese proverb)

In August 2000, when we were both in our mid-20s, my wife Vanessa and I made a huge life change. Without having ever visited the country, we decided to 'up sticks', leave our native Ireland and move to the other side of the planet, to live in Wellington, New Zealand. When we told friends and family we were emigrating, they thought we were crazy. 'The two of you must be mad,' they said, 'you've never even been there before!'

In Ireland at that time, the Celtic Tiger was in full roar and the country's future, and especially Dublin's, where we were living, looked very healthy. Why were we turning our backs on such financial opportunities and potential security of employment to go a country where we had no guarantees of either? Leaving probably did seem like an absurd thing to do. Of course, little did anyone know then what the future held for Ireland and the financial hardship of a devastating recession that many would have to face.

However, Vanessa and I were determined to go on a journey, to be challenged, to learn and to experience the excitement of being out of our comfort zone. We wanted to explore a new culture and discover a new past, in a fascinating country with its own unique sporting history. There we would stay, and enjoy our lives, for the next 16 years. It wasn't a decision either of us has ever regretted.

That is not to say, however, that there weren't many very challenging periods for us along the way. One of these in particular still stands out in my memory – because it was a time when suddenly, unexpectedly, circumstances out of my control were taking hold and adversely affecting me. It was also a watershed moment for Vanessa and me in many ways, one that would ultimately lead us to a much deeper connection with each other.

Building our first house in New Zealand was another big endeavour. It was an exciting and challenging project, as the site we decided to go for, situated on the rugged south coast of Wellington, wasn't by any means an easy proposition. It would be a tough piece of land to develop – more like a cliff, really – but the location was spectacular. We knew it wasn't going to be straightforward, but we were up for the challenge. In the very early stages of the project, it came to light that the reports on the land which had been initially provided were misleading, and that the groundworks would require extensive re-engineering. Of course, this was only discovered once we had already broken ground. While we were in the process of getting the new engineering plans drawn up, we realised that the amount of money we had paid the builders to that point far exceeded the volume of work done, or the materials bought. We quickly smelt a rat – and sure enough, a rat was exactly what we found.

Around this time, we were tracked down by another family in the local area, who told us that the same builders had built their house, and that it was now subsiding in a catastrophic fashion, and they were pursuing a legal claim against the builders. This was a complete shock to us – we thought we'd done our homework on these guys! Following a number of meetings and lawyers' letters to the builders, their company ended up filing for liquidation, which meant that we had very little legal recourse in terms of getting our money back or compensation for all the time and resources wasted.

One day, shortly after getting the news about the builders going into bankruptcy, everything just hit me all at once. We were staying at a friend's house for Christmas and I remember being there, in our room, with my wife and our one-year-old baby girl, when – WALLOP! – it all came at me. All that money spent; the dig half-started on a site that looked like a gaping wound; the extensive new engineering and retaining work now needed just to get the project off the ground, with all the additional costs this would entail; the uncertainty as to whether we'd be able to afford to actually finish the build; all the money we would lose if we decided to cut our losses and try to resell the site. As well as the inescapable sense of the sheer injustice of it all, it all came down on me in one fell swoop – or, to use a building analogy, 'like a ton of bricks'!

I remember asking Vanessa to just hold me, while two physical waves of intense anxiety surged through my body. My psychotherapy training quickly alerted me to what was going on, so I just let it all come out. Fortunately for me, within just a minute it had passed. Vanessa and I were just left holding each other. We had no words, just physical closeness.

I was with my closest friend and a woman who knew me very well. When I most needed it, she simply did as I asked, with sheer openness and support and without any questions, discussion or further analysis. It was an experience I won't forget – nor do I want to. As I have said, it would be a defining experience for us as a couple, when, in a single moment, Vanessa learnt more about me as a person, and I about her.

The positive outcome to this story is that we learnt some very valuable lessons about house building and about business, and we pushed on through. Within two years, our house got built on that site with the breath-taking views, and we went on to have some great times and happy memories there – including the birth of our son. Over time the anger and hurt that both Vanessa and I felt about the injustices done to us by those builders subsided, and we were able to put the whole episode down to experience and the fact that, sometimes, life just throws curveballs at us in ways that can't be foreseen. We are both more resilient for having gone through this experience together, and for having reflected on and learned from the process about what we are able to handle. If faced with a similar situation again there are some things we would do differently, but we have the deeper assurance now of knowing that we can work through something very challenging and very upsetting together.

In this chapter we are going to look at some more instances of challenging situations when things go awry – whether this is through sheer bad luck or some misjudgement of our own –

and how we can deal with the emotional fallout. In sport, this includes losing competitions or matches, making mistakes that impact on the outcome for the whole team or being dropped or not selected for competitive events. In business, this might mean recession, the mismanagement on our part of resources and people or the loss of contracts due to poor performance. In life, this might involve such scenarios as losing out due to the errors of others, or unforeseen serious health problems, or devastating blows such as bereavement. We'll explore some further strategies and techniques for coping with these types of situations, many of which, once again, draw on some of the core mental skills we have already looked at.

So, in relation to my own story, how did I manage to get through and move beyond those moments of feeling utterly powerless? First, because of my experience and training as a psychotherapist, I was able to sense that my body, my mind, my emotions and my thoughts were out of kilter with how I normally am. Knowing that I was in a safe and secure environment, I felt comfortable enough to purge my system, as it were, of this sudden, distressing energy. In reaching out to my wife Vanessa, I was drawing on the skills of *emotional fluency, self-awareness* and *assertiveness*, telling her what I was feeling and asking for what I needed. I used the *centring* technique to allow the energy to come up and also to bring it under control once I'd fully acknowledged that it was there, simply breathing through the experience.

It was not until I reached out to my team – first of all, to Vanessa, and later to my friends and family – for support and advice that I really felt a shift in momentum, a change in my energy that would allow me to move forward. The energy of momentum, of moving forward, changes our body chemistry, and with that, our thoughts and feelings about things. For me, with this change, I was able to shift out of the narrow, circular mindscape being generated by my sense of panic and move back into reality – a reality much bigger than my own limited perspective in that moment. Once this happened, I could start to refocus my thinking on practical steps towards a solution, rather than getting stuck in anxiety, panic and anger at what had happened to us. Our friends proved our best support over the period that followed – helping us not just personally but also professionally, with their advice and guidance. In fact, the house would never have been completed without the tireless assistance of two key friends, Gareth and Chris (thanks again, guys!).

Once the feeling of crisis had passed, I was able to take a look at why I reacted in the way I did. Of course, I'm aware that many people in the same situation would have felt similarly overwhelmed, but as we have been saying throughout this book, building *self-awareness* is perhaps the most useful mental skill of all when it comes to living consistently more happily and more successfully. It is often in our most difficult moments that we are presented with the biggest opportunities for learning about ourselves. In my case, I was able to work out, with the help of some time spent in *active reflection*, that in terms of the situation with the house, I had been psychologically taking on board too much of the blame for what went wrong – I was *over-personalising* the situation. At the heart of my fear and anxiety was an old family *script* around money and security, in which I identified the safety of my family with being financially secure. Beyond this, on some level there was a core belief that my worth as a man was defined by my ability to provide security for my family. This was generating a barrage of negative self-talk, which was undermining my confidence and my self-belief with an ongoing unhealthy mental script along the lines of: 'How could I have let this happen? What kind of man am I, to have put my family in this position? How could I have been so stupid?' Because of this, I was getting stuck in the *fear* of not being able to 'dig our way out' of the financial situation we were facing into, and unable to focus on solutions once I felt overwhelmed by it all. Thankfully, Vanessa's mindset around these things was very different to mine, and so we didn't both get locked into this feeling of being overwhelmed. This type of core belief – with such focus on income and status – is a very common one nowadays.

LOSING IN SPORT

> There's always a pathway to overcoming tough times, to becoming a stronger, more resilient person. When I got my first Irish cap, Garryowen's Philip Danaher came up to me and said, 'Respect comes not just from being capped for your country – of course, that's a fantastic achievement – but also [from] how you come back after you have been dropped.' He helped me recognise that in a career, you may be dropped many times [but] it's how you bounce back that matters. How you work through that disappointment – that's what makes you a better player, a better person.
>
> *Conor O'Shea – former professional rugby player; 35 caps for Ireland, 127 appearances for London Irish; head coach of the Italian national rugby team*

Perhaps even more so than getting injured, losing – a game, a match, a competition, a series – is inevitable in sport, an absolute given. Even the most consistently accomplished, talented and high-achieving sportsperson in the world will have had the experience of not being successful at times. No high-performing athlete enjoys losing, or indeed any athlete – but it is something that must be accepted as part and parcel of participating in the first place. Let's hear some top competitors talking very honestly about what it's like to lose:

> I never enjoy the feeling of losing, and I never want to lose in anything I do. I understand that it is all part of sport, but in the moment I can feel frustrated, and ask why I or the team were not good enough. In time, I learn the most from losses and it makes me reflect even more on individual and team performances . . . [which] drives me to be better.
>
> *Suzie Bates – captain of the New Zealand women's cricket team, the White Ferns; ODI player of the year 2013 and 2016*

> When I first turned professional, if I lost a game, I would lock myself away. I'd be on my own in London and lock myself away for a couple of days. I couldn't come out – I was thinking that the whole world was caving in on me. Because I lost a silly match. But I learnt to cope with it. I talked to people and gave myself that bit of confidence . . . It made me a little stronger, and I had to keep believing in myself.
>
> *Ken Doherty – ex-professional snooker player; snooker commentator; 1997 world snooker champion*

> Over the years, I have gotten better [at losing]. Before, it could take me a few days, weeks or more of constantly going over the errors I made and focusing on a lot of the negative parts of the game. I still [get] downhearted and disappointed, but I try to focus on the positives. There is no such thing as a perfect game; you are constantly making mistakes and learning from those mistakes. I like hanging around with the girls, maybe sticking on the kettle and just having a mini-rant together, or talking absolute rubbish. [We] just get together and laugh.
>
> Not winning the 2017 World Cup . . . to be honest I'm still not fully over it. We had an opportunity to play at home, competing in the biggest competition in women's rugby, and we didn't perform. That was hugely disappointing. I honestly want to delete a lot of it from my head – reflect and learn from it [first], and then on to something else. I am open about my feelings with some of my teammates, family or friends. It's OK for me personally to be vulnerable or to show vulnerability; it's OK if I get visibly upset after a game, and so on . . . You can pull something from the experiences you have, good or bad. As much as I didn't enjoy that World Cup, I still got something from it.
>
> *Jenny Murphy – professional rugby player, 28 caps for Ireland*

One factor that can make losing in sport even more difficult is not having the chance to get out there quickly after a defeat to prove yourself again, which can often be a very satisfying way of putting a bad experience behind you. Some sports, by their very nature, require players to have incredible patience and the extra fortitude of being able to put thoughts of failure to one side for an extended period of time. As former boxer Bernard Dunne explained to Brent, his sport is one of these:

> When I lost, I had a lot of time to think about it. That can be a bad thing in boxing. In other sports, athletes may get a chance to redeem themselves as early as the next week. In boxing, it may be eight weeks before you get another chance to fight.
>
> [Fortunately] I had a close family structure. I always asked questions of my father [and] my trainer; always took advice on what I should be doing better, how I could change things. I looked for their knowledge all the time.
>
> *Bernard Dunne – former professional boxer; WBA super bantamweight champion; European super bantamweight champion*

It is clear in all of the testimonies above that, while no one likes losing, these athletes learnt to deal with it better over time, and with the increased self-confidence that comes from having more experience in one's field. Ken Doherty and Jenny Murphy freely admit that at the very beginning of their careers, losing a game or a match was devastating for them – something from which it might take them a long time to recover; however, as time went on, they were able to bounce back from and overcome defeat more quickly and more easily each time. This capacity to bounce back from adversity is known in psychology as *rebound resilience*, and is a key quality shared by all those who achieve consistent and long-term success in sport – and indeed in any other field. As we can see, it is not necessarily something you either have or don't have – it can be acquired and built upon over time and with repeated exposure to challenging situations.

As we saw in the previous chapter with the experience of injury, the athletes above confirm that it helps to have a realistic view of losses and disappointments in sport: in the words of Jenny Murphy, 'There is no such thing as the perfect game – you are constantly making mistakes . . .' Keeping things in perspective in this way guards against unhelpful, perfectionistic ways of thinking, and helps us to avoid over-reactions and disproportionate responses to these kinds of setbacks. As well as this, we also see in these testimonies, yet again, the importance of connecting and communicating with trusted others – teammates, coaches, family and friends – as a means of recovering more quickly from disappointments. Being able to show vulnerability, connecting with how we are really feeling, is a much healthier and, in the long-run, more productive way of dealing with difficult experiences than the strategy of appearing strong at all times, which more often than not means we are simply disconnecting ourselves and denying what is happening in the 'here and now'.

Possibly the most important observation of all in the interviews above, and which all five of these high-performers reiterate, is the notion that losses, mistakes and failures are opportunities to learn more, about oneself and one's sport. In fact, these experiences tend to be the ones that present the greatest possibilities for growth in terms of both a player's abilities and self-belief. While it is not a good idea to constantly dwell on or become obsessive about mistakes, losses or failures, it is crucial to think about what went wrong, with a view to being able to improve in future performance situations. We can use it as research, as part of the strategies of measurement and evaluation. This is what will separate good players from really great players, as former Irish rugby star Ronan O'Gara highlighted when I asked him about the best way of dealing with mistakes:

> Being in each situation, I am always learning something from it: this mindset helped me a lot. You get pushed to the max with pressure, especially as a young kicker and [when you are] failing. It's from failing most of all. It's brilliant to know that from massive failings can come massive positives – as long as the right messages are received.
>
> [It's] taking those lessons on board . . . and having the capacity to know if you failed for technique or for a mental issue. This can be very, very harsh for young players to accept. What is good then is having another opportunity. The coach will not always give you that and you don't get picked sometimes, which is very frustrating – but that's out of your control.
>
> *Ronan O'Gara – former professional rugby player; rugby coach; 128 caps for Ireland*

As Ronan points out, it's being able to analyse past errors and losses in a measured, non-emotional way, and to work out whether the problem was down to inadequate technique or having the wrong mindset while playing, which means we truly embrace our failings in order to turn them around. This ability to analyse in a reasonable, thoughtful way is where so many of the mental skills we have been talking about really come to the fore.

CHOOSING HOW TO RESPOND

When we find ourselves worrying about a future performance, or fretting over past mistakes and mishaps and fearing they will happen again, it can be helpful to remind ourselves that this is a process that we signed up for; that it is all part of something that we agreed to be part of; that we chose this path to challenge and grow ourselves. In this way, we can take ownership of the experience, which in turn helps us feel more in control and reminds us that, in this context anyway, we are not victims of circumstances, but masters of our own destiny. This is true in sport and in business, and can be so in life too, where we are of course actively involved in many of our most important decisions – choices such as our life partners, our careers, our friends, the values we live by and so on.

However, this is not *always* the case. Sometimes we find ourselves in the middle of something that we hadn't signed up for, but that is happening right now, and that requires us to decide how we are going to react. These times can be exciting or terrifying, fun or gruelling, daunting and overwhelming or inspiring and uplifting – depending on how we manage ourselves and our approach as we face into such challenges; depending on where we choose to stand and what perspective we decide to take.

We live in a physical world in which there is a lot that we cannot control, both in terms of the external environment and the internal workings of our own bodies. However, again we need not be victims to this fact. There are ways in which we can influence the world around us, as well as our own physical health and, most importantly, we can always influence our thoughts and feelings – our attitude to what happens to us and the situations we find ourselves in.

VIKTOR FRANKL

In his ground-breaking memoir *Man's Search for Meaning*,[1] the distinguished neurologist and psychiatrist Victor Frankl speaks clearly to this, based upon the most evidential experience possible. In 1942, the 27-year-old Frankl, an Austrian Jew, was captured by the Nazis and deported to Theresienstadt concentration camp. Between 1942 and 1945 he laboured in four different camps, including Auschwitz, while his parents, brother and 24-year-old pregnant wife Tilly perished. Based on his own experience and the experiences of others he treated later in his psychiatric practice, Frankl argues that we cannot avoid suffering, but that we can choose how to cope with it, find meaning in it and move forward with renewed purpose.

While in the camps, in response to the relentless efforts of his captors to dehumanise him and his fellow prisoners, having robbed them of all their possessions, their families, their physical freedoms and even their names by way of an identification number tattooed onto their arm, Frankl came to this remarkable, and very clear, conclusion: 'Everything can be taken from a man but one thing: the last of the human freedoms – to choose one's attitude in any given set of circumstances; to choose one's own way . . . When we are no longer able to change a situation, we are challenged to change ourselves.' Against all the odds, Frankl survived his time in the Nazi death camps until 1945, when US troops liberated the subsidiary camp of Dachau in which he was then incarcerated. He would go on to achieve many remarkable things in the fields of neurology, psychiatry and philosophy, publishing over 40 books and being pronounced by experts in psychiatry circles as 'the most significant thinker since Freud and Adler', before his death in 1997 at the age of 92.

As Frankl's own very powerful testimony undeniably shows, even in the worst imaginable circumstances we need not regard ourselves as victims. The one essential thing that is ours, and not for the taking, is our ability to decide how we want to *respond* to any situation. We can always challenge ourselves to think, do, be and feel better about what is happening, regardless of how difficult our situation is. It is our human ability to self-reflect, and in so doing become more aware of ourselves, which allows us to work on and have control over our thoughts, feelings and actions.

To put it very simply, our attitude is one of the very basic things that *is* within our control. We can choose to influence it any time and in any place. In sport, this might be our attitude towards injury, non-selection, losing, winning, training, teammates, coaches, travel, etc. In business, it could be our attitude towards stress, pressure, deadlines, managers, colleagues, salary, being an employee, being self-employed, shift work, holiday time and so on. In life, our attitude towards family, intimate relationships, children, friends, health problems, inability to have children, status, our living conditions, financial hardship, bereavement and death, feeling unfulfilled, being happy . . .

Aspects of our modern lives can be very tough at times – especially psychologically. Challenging situations can often *feel* overwhelming and incapacitating. However, as we have seen, there are many ways in which we can face into these challenges more easily, and there is a wealth of resources and support we can call upon to enable us to cope better when times are very trying. In terms of safeguarding our mental health, it is essential to know that there are always things that we can influence, even in the most extreme of situations. Even when it seems that there is nothing we can do, we can always adapt our own attitude to what is happening, just as there are always things we can work on, influence and improve. It is key to remember too that no situation remains the same forever – even when we feel things are unbearable, we can have the certain knowledge that 'This too shall pass'. Change is one of the few constants in this life – it is always on the horizon.

PART 5

The Strength to Win

FIFTEEN

Dealing with Depression and Anxiety

'Our minds build our determination and our resilience. The most important thing when times are very tough is to be able to draw on the tools that are around us'

Brent Pope

Brent

All my life I have struggled with mental health issues – panic attacks and bouts of depression. They started when I was just a young boy and were mainly centred on catastrophe and failure – in relationships, in school, in my future. I had very low self-esteem and confidence, which I masked with humour. Even now, I feel that I don't deserve to be where I am, despite others telling me I have earned it. I get mired in negative thoughts – they enter my mind, like bullets from a Gatling gun: 'You are not good enough'; 'You will never succeed'; 'Life will not work out for you'. Despite learning to stop them, I slide back sometimes. Then it can feel like I am trying to drag an elephant across the room – it's exhausting.

I see the negative thoughts as real and that they are going to materialise – despite the fact that they never do. I would picture myself as being homeless, an unloved person never achieving anything . . . These thoughts lead me to not being able to just sit back and be happy with what I have achieved. I can never seem to just enjoy what I have done – like making that team, writing my numerous books, establishing a fashion brand, owning a nice house, having a loving partner.

I have huge regrets at times – such as not being confident enough to look back and be able to say, 'Hey, you did well.' That is a sad thing for me – I want to be able to enjoy how far I have come, a small-town boy that did something. I was ashamed that I suffered anxiety and that I felt I couldn't find the happiness others seemed to have. I felt guilty that others had real worries and that I should just be able to get over it – but mental health issues don't discriminate; the person with what we see as the perfect life may be the one that is in most trouble. Loneliness too is difficult for me. I think that it is the biggest factor many men of my generation still face, becoming increasingly more isolated as modern society strips us of communication skills. Years ago I was diagnosed as being dysthymic, which is a term for being in a chronic state of discontentment. Chronic as in always there, stealing any joy I might have. I'm not ashamed to say I see a therapist each week and that I have been medicated with antidepressants, even though I often found the side-effects too hard to handle.

Things came to a head some years ago, at a time when I hit rock bottom and became mentally and physically ill. I shut the doors to my apartment and locked myself away from friends and family. I had lost hope; I had nothing left to give. I felt ashamed and very lonely, and could not see any real future. I felt I had no one to talk to, no one to confide in. All my life I had lived by the code 'Real men don't cry'; 'Harden up, toughen up, and go to the gym', and so on. I saw myself as weak, as less of a man. A failure once again.

One night in desperation, I thumbed through the Golden

Pages, looking for helplines. I knew I needed help. I came across the number for the Samaritans, and decided to call. It was in the early hours of the morning, and I was sitting on the edge of the bed, hoping no one would answer – but also hoping they would. I was scared and alone, but the man who answered the phone had such a kind voice. He simply asked, 'What's wrong, friend?' Even now, that word 'friend' brings me to tears. I didn't know him, yet he was prepared to call me his friend – there was already something comforting about it.

This guy was such an empathic soul. He listened, he understood; he was gentle, and he told me not to feel shame anymore – that I was human. We talked for hours. The Samaritans guy, my friend that I never met, saved my life. The next day, I took small steps to change. I understood then that I had a choice – to make myself better or to continue drowning. Change the in to change the out. So, small steps . . . I started cleaning up my apartment, showering, going for a walk – little things that I could feel some sense of accomplishment about.

From there, things began to gradually improve. My brother Mark (who is a psychotherapist) helped me immensely. I learned ways to remind myself that when the negativity started, I needed to go easy on myself. I began to meditate, despite finding it hard to do. I exercised more and tried to eat well. There were lots of small things I did each day that helped – things I liked, such as going to the movies, reading a book or meeting a friend. The most important lesson for me was I did not need to feel ashamed to ask for help. I was not alone.

It started with that simple call to the Samaritans, when I was at my lowest ebb. I absolutely believe that one call saved my life. Over the years since then I have been brave enough to seek help each time I felt I needed it.

I look at things differently now. I still have panic attacks and I can still experience hopelessness and loneliness, but I talk about it. I journal, write down my thoughts, and I seek professional help. I'm still ashamed in some ways that, while my body has always served me well, my mind at times has not. I don't think the shame will ever entirely leave me, but maybe I have something to give too. I am learning to be grateful for my flaws. At the end of the day, they are a part of me.

I very much hope that people will read this book and understand that success is not all about just physical ability. That our minds build our determination and our resilience, and that the most important thing when times are very tough is to be able to draw on the tools that are always around us. When you need help – get help. When you feel anxious, or nervous, or under pressure, know that there are some processes that you can call upon. Meditate, relax, breathe and do whatever it takes to help you get through and be the best you can be in that moment. Don't try and measure up to others' standards. Set your own benchmarks for success, so that one day, many years from now, you will be able to look at yourself in the mirror and say, 'I gave it my best shot.' Even now, I am still in the process every day of learning how to say this to myself, and it is finally coming more easily to me – 'Brent, you gave it your best shot.' So, today, at 55 years of age, after all this time dragging the elephant across the room with me, on good days and on the harder days when I feel I am just putting one foot in front of the other, I allow myself to think that, 'Yes – I too am winning.'

Dealing with Depression and Anxiety

In the interviews we conducted for this book, we have seen how even the most respected, successful and well-loved athletes in the world have at times experienced a lack of self-confidence – or even chronically low self-esteem – as well as bouts of loneliness and feelings of isolation. And as Brent's account also attests, it doesn't matter who we are or the extent of our achievements, we can still be affected by depression and anxiety. Such problems are on the rise in Western society, with statistics getting more alarming each year, including, tragically, a very noticeable increase in the incidence of suicide.

We saw in the previous chapter how facing into, and living through, very challenging situations can actively help to build our resilience, meaning we are better able to deal with similarly difficult circumstances in the future. Research shows in fact that there is actually an optimal number of adversities we can be exposed to in life that will build our capacity for resilience to a peak level. But if we have too many setbacks to negotiate in very quick succession, or even all at once, we can feel overwhelmed. When this happens, we are in danger of burnout, and at risk of mental illness, of which the most common disorders are depression and anxiety. In this chapter we are going to look more closely at these conditions, and at ways to manage when suffering from them.

When a person is suffering from either depression or anxiety, or indeed both at the same time (which is also very common), their biological system is out of balance. As we saw earlier in the case of panic attacks, when certain key chemicals in the body are out of whack, distressing physiological and psychological symptoms can occur. An imbalance in brain chemicals such as serotonin and noradrenaline can drive a depressive disorder, while in the case of severe anxiety, a disruption in the normal interactions of chemicals such as adrenalin and cortisol will also affect the sufferer in distressing ways.

These imbalances can happen due to a build-up of stressful experiences over a period of time, or as a more immediate reaction to something life-changing or traumatic happening in the present. In the case of the former, the accumulation over time of the energy of stressful experiences and the associated chemicals in a person's system can tip over into depression or anxiety when a series of repeated experiences in the present can echo early but unprocessed instances of hurt, pain, fear, anger and loss. In the case of the latter, major life events such as bereavement, relationship breakdown, loss of employment, the diagnosis of serious illness, unexpected financial hardship and so on, can also trigger the chemical imbalances that lead to depression – this is 'reactive' depression. When external events overwhelm our coping strategies, we get pushed to our psychological limits and, if we do not or are unable to find additional support to help us get through these times, depression and anxiety can be the result.

Our individual susceptibility to these disorders is generally determined by the make-up of the psychological framework (or internal models) that we have developed about ourselves, others and life itself – our internal stories, as it were. When this framework and some of the associated stories are not helpful or healthy, we are more likely to be vulnerable to illnesses like depression and anxiety.

The good news is that our ability to talk, and so create new and meaningful experiences, allows us to change our stories and set down different frameworks. Developing the key skills of *emotional fluency*, *active reflection* and *assertiveness* enables us to influence our feelings and thoughts, and thereby gain more control over our experience and our part in it. Later in the chapter we will look closely at how and why talking – or talking therapy – works.

MOOD DISORDERS

Like our feelings and thoughts, our moods tend to come and go. As we said at the end of the last chapter, one of the key constants in life is change, and nowhere is this more true than with our mental and emotional lives. Our feelings are always changing, our thoughts are always moving in another direction, our moods are always shifting. We all know what it feels like to be a bit down in the dumps or on edge some days, feeling a bit depressed or anxious – these are both very common and completely natural mental states. This doesn't necessarily mean we are suffering from anxiety or depression in a clinical sense. Mood disorders set in, however, when we get kind of stuck in such feelings, when there is a longer timeframe involved. While feeling a bit down or anxious for a day or two is nothing to be concerned about, what we do need to be wary of is if these feelings persist for a longer period – say, beyond a week or so. For moods to be considered disorders, they must satisfy certain criteria, of which the time element is an important one. Below we will look at some of the other criteria.

DEPRESSION

The *clinical criteria* for depression (or 'Major Depressive Episode', as indicated in the Diagnostic and Statistical Manual of Mental Disorders, or DSM-4) stipulates the presence of a certain number of symptoms (five, to be precise) for a two-week period and beyond, as well as a clear change to our previous functioning.

However, there are certain general signs of depression we should look out for and take measures to prevent from setting in, including, most importantly:

- A persistent lack of motivation, or wanting always to stay at home or stay in bed.
- A lack of concentration and increased use of drugs such as alcohol.
- Often feeling overwhelmed, with bouts of sadness or feelings of guilt or shame.
- Easily frustrated or irritable, with oppressive feelings of doubt and low self-confidence.
- Frequently feeling indecisive, 'stuck', frozen and unable to clearly act.

- Persistent negative self-talk, such as: 'I am no good'; ' I am a failure'; 'I am useless'. Or negativity about the future, for example, 'I will never be happy/ successful/rich', and so on. Dark thoughts, such as 'I am better off dead'; 'It is too hard to go on'; 'Life is too hard'; 'Others would be better off without me'.

- Emotionally or psychologically fatigued, with a loss of appetite. Unusual weight loss or gain, and suffering from unaccustomed sleep disturbances.

ANXIETY

The *clinical criteria* for anxiety ('Generalized Anxiety Disorder', as indicted in the DSM-4) highlight the experiencing of an excessive degree of anxiety and worry about a variety of events and activities, on more days than not, over the last six months.

However, some general signs of anxiety to watch out for are:

- Feeling constantly on edge, wound-up, tense. Often panicky and having actual panic attacks. Finding it difficult to breathe at times, with rapid breathing or tightness in the chest.

- Finding it hard to sit still for long; quickly tired and easily irritated by things and the behaviour of others. Excessive worrying; agitated and fearful about straightforward things; frequently thinking the worst; catastrophising and overdramatising.

- Obsessive ruminating, or talking, about things. Talking oneself out of things, and continually avoiding situations. Finding it hard to stop thinking and relax; continual buzz of thoughts in the mind.

- Disturbed sleep – frequently waking; difficulty falling asleep; sleep which is not restful. Lying in bed looking at the ceiling every night, not able to wind down. Easy tasks seem hard, and even insurmountable.

- Suffering an unusual degree of aches and pains due to tension in the body: neck, shoulders, jaw, back, and so on.

- Thoughts of wanting to run away; being convinced that starting again will make it all OK.

HOW TO HELP YOURSELF

Fortunately, there are a number of practical measures we can take to help ourselves when suffering from anxiety and depression – in fact, there is a whole wealth of resources and support you can tap into at such times. The first and perhaps most important of these is to draw on your mental skills of *active reflection, clear decision-making* and *emotional fluency*, and simply talk to someone about how you are feeling. There are many other practical steps that can also help – and we will look at these towards the end of this chapter.

For now, let's focus on 'talking therapy'. Talking early on to those close to us, and also talking to a professional, are great ways of spotting quickly what is happening. Confiding in another person gives us a chance to clarify what our own thoughts are, as we express them out loud to someone else. Talking to a professional means knowing that anything we say will be kept confidential, so that we can feel more secure about opening up and being really honest about what is going on for us – we have the additional reassurance that, because of their training and experience, we need not worry about being judged by such a person. Just as when Brent made the call to the Samaritans, we should always feel accepted and safe.

WORKING WITH A THERAPIST

As a psychotherapist myself, I am privileged to have the chance to work with people who have all shown great strength of character and will by seeking support and guidance at times in their lives when they are feeling low, afraid, lost, distressed and struggling. To make this decision – to connect with someone and to show trust enough to open up and share what is happening – is not easy. There is the fear of being judged, and it feels scary to be vulnerable and to take this first step into the unknown. It is a decision however that very few people who have worked with a therapist who is showing commitment and integrity will ever regret.

I can say this because the moment a person walks through the door of my consulting room, we are both on a journey, a process of discovery, and we are in it together. We are both signing up for the process, and we are both agreeing to bring all we can to it. This is a key part of the role of a therapist, which can only be fully realised through the high level of trust, and high value, that is placed on the therapy relationship.

When a person makes the decision to see a therapist,

psychologist, counsellor or psychiatrist, they are taking a leap of faith. They are there because they want to believe that the work they do together will help them get better. The therapist equally has faith in this process. He or she also believes that the work they undertake together with their client will lead to improved health and wellbeing for that person. Yet neither client nor therapist knows exactly where the journey will take them. Together they will explore areas such as the thoughts, beliefs, feelings, relationships, past and present events and the wealth of memories that make up a person's experience. They do this to help make meaning and sense of the client's experience and try to identify what has contributed to their seeking support in the first instance.

Our lives are built upon a vast array of experiences. Many of these were good, healthy, loving experiences, but not all. Unfortunately, negative things happen to all of us in life, many of which are beyond our control. Like dealing with anything in life, it is how well prepared, and therefore how resilient, we are that contributes to how successfully we negotiate these challenges.

These good and bad experiences form the basis upon which we build our view of ourselves, our world and our place in it. To a greater degree, it is the bad or unpleasant experiences, and how we got through these, that hold more sway in our memory of early development than the really good ones. This is not a negative outlook, simply a pragmatic one. The unpleasant experiences from our past, those involving pain and hurt, have a stronger emotional force for us because they alert us to threat and danger, and our instinct is to remember these more clearly, so that we can avoid the recurrence of such hurt and pain in the future.

Many of our messages about hurt and pain are taken on board at a time in our development when our world is all about emotions and sensations, and when we could not yet bring our mind, logic or reason into play. Our early relationships can be healthy and secure but still we can hold onto or dwell on unpleasant experiences from the past and this can have a longer-term, unnecessary effect on our development – unless of course we get the opportunity to work through some of them. And this to a large part is what happens in therapy, as the client and the therapist explore some of the experiences in the past that may be currently holding a person back, hampering their future development. By working through the feelings, assumptions and unhelpful beliefs of the past, this person can come out the other side with a greater depth of understanding and self-knowledge, armed with better strategies and more helpful attitudes to help them manage similar events in the future.

BRIEF CASE STUDIES IN ANXIETY AND DEPRESSION

*Names have been changed to protect privacy of individuals.

JAMES*

Twenty-eight-year-old James came to see me because of worries about his ability to form close relationships with women. He was deeply afraid of getting into a relationship at all – but equally worried that he would miss out if he didn't at least try. His greatest fear was of letting a girl down, being a disappointment to her and not being able to handle the rejection he felt would inevitably follow. To side-step all of this, he told me, he had decided to simply avoid close relationships completely. The only kind of relationships he felt able to handle, he admitted, were long-distance ones, those conducted entirely online or the occasional brief fling.

James was a good-looking, physically fit, smart and fun guy. He was well liked by girls, with lots of acquaintances but not many close friendships. A lot of his peers were moving on with their lives, getting married or having children, and James was becoming very concerned about his own future. He too wanted to find someone, get married and have children, but was petrified of not knowing how to be in a close relationship, and crippled too by the sense of inadequacy he felt. The combined effect of all of this was that James was now suffering from anxiety. He felt particularly anxious about social occasions, where too many girls were showing an interest in him.

For James, the act of coming and talking with me in the first place was his first step towards experiencing a close, intimate relationship – one in which he would open up and allow himself to be vulnerable with another person. As our therapeutic relationship grew and developed, James would see that not only was he able to survive the experience of this kind of intimacy, but that he could come to trust, and actively enjoy, the process. In this sense, he and I were laying the groundwork to enable him to feel more confident about going out to find someone else, a woman he could trust and open up to.

In our sessions, James got the opportunity to learn and practise some key mental skills. Very importantly, he was able to develop a greater degree of *emotional fluency*, as he allowed the big feelings of fear and sadness to come up and be expressed, without being overwhelmed and consumed by them. For moments when he feared becoming completely engulfed by his emotions, we practised *breathing and grounding techniques* to help him manage this. By working on his awareness of negative automatic thoughts (NATs), we helped him build the confidence to challenge the imagined, illusory pictures about girls rejecting him which he had been carrying around in his head for so long. We were able to replace these with more realistic images, based on actual, positive experiences he had had in relationships. As he began to take opportunities to go out on some actual dates, we got the chance to recalibrate some of his negative ideas about how well he got on with women, by going through a process of realistic assessment about how things had gone on these occasions – which was often much more positively than he had expected, or was giving himself credit for.

By the time James's course of therapy with me was finished, he was feeling much more confident about himself, his potential appeal to girls and his ability to form a close relationship. In time, he was able to meet a girl he had a lot in common with, and they moved in together. James's inner story about himself and his relationships had dramatically changed.

JONO*

A very successful young rugby player, Jono had been tipped as a fantastic new talent and someone to watch out for. In the early stages of his career, he proved everyone right, moving rapidly up into the big leagues. He quickly became renowned for his explosive speed and his impressive agility, as he ducked and dived past opposition players, who were often left looking a bit dumbstruck.

After only two professional seasons, however, Jono's form dramatically changed. He was making a lot of handling errors, his speed had dropped and he looked uncertain on the pitch. Now so much less sure of himself, he became an easy target for the opposition tacklers. He moved from being a starter to being benched, and was finally relegated to the status of only being brought on as injury substitute or in the final minutes of a dying game, to give other players a break. Jono was asked to come and see me by the team's high-performance manager, which he very reluctantly did.

This once promising young player hadn't lost any of his ability, his talent or his health; he was still young and fit. Clearly, something else was going on. Pretty soon, as he began to speak with me, it became apparent that some off-field issues were draining his energy and throwing off his focus. His feelings of insecurity in another area of his life were making him feel uncertain and full of doubt about his abilities on the pitch – where he had once felt so confident. In a nutshell, Jono's relationship at home was not good.

It only took three sessions for Jono to open up and express how he was feeling – both on and off the field – and for him to figure out what he wanted to say, and do, about it. The areas we decided to concentrate most on were *communication*, *assertiveness* and *clear decision-making*. Pretty soon, following some constructive talks with his partner, Jono felt his energy and confidence coming back. Not long after that, he was able to show a return to form in training, and was soon being picked again as a starter player. He finished the season very well.

FURTHER STEPS FOR DEALING WITH DEPRESSION AND ANXIETY

We have seen, in the examples above, how effective the talking cure can be. Let's look now at some other helpful measures that have proven to be positive in dealing with depression and anxiety.

EXERCISE

There is lots of evidence to show that light exercise really helps with both disorders. Some research says it is as effective as medication. However, exercise can be difficult to do or even contemplate for someone who is suffering from severe depression and struggling to just get out of bed.

In this instance, a course of prescribed medication can really help change the chemical imbalance in the body as well as using mental skills such as realistic mini-*goal-setting*, *encouraging self-talk* and *centring* to create the psychological energy needed to simply get started – the energy to put into just one small task at a time, slowly building momentum in the body. This type of mental process helps to create the momentum to sit up, put your feet on the ground, breathe in and out, use your legs to lift your body, put one trouser leg on and then the other . . . Next task, next goal and so on. In this way, we can gradually build the psychological energy to set more goals – first small, moment-by-moment ones, then day by day, week by week, like Brent shared earlier in this chapter. Each day, each week, getting us back on the horse and out into the world again.

SOME PRACTICAL TASKS TO HELP

Here are some more small practical steps you can take that will help you on the road to wellness when suffering from depression or anxiety:

- Book in for a check-up with your GP, and let them know what is going on. There is no pressure to take medication, though a course of anti-anxiety or anti-depression medication can really help quickly bring the body's chemicals under control and into balance again. It is most important, however, to let your GP know how you are and to hear them out. They will often know of other sources of support available locally.

- Check the local resources out for yourself. There may be a support group nearby. There will also be free, 24/7 helplines in your area, such as the Samaritans, etc. It's a good idea to keep these numbers handy.

- Go online and check out some depression and anxiety websites in your country – some are listed in the back of this book. These offer a good overview of what is happening and have some great ideas of things to do.

- Keep a daily record of how you are doing each day, morning and evening if possible. Write down what you are feeling, and note the intensity of that feeling (out of 100). Which feelings would you like to heighten, and which would you want to reduce? You could set an alarm on your phone or watch to remind you to do this, twice daily. This is a good way of being able to track any progress you are making – when you are depressed, it's often very hard to see that you are progressing at all, so this log will help you see, in black and white, when there are times that you are feeling a bit better.

- Plan your days to try to heighten the feelings you want more of. Try to structure your day so that you have some things set up that you know will help – for example meeting a friend for a coffee, listening to music, going for a walk, meditating, watching a funny movie and so on.
- If possible, plan the night before, but allow yourself to review and update things in the morning. Don't be disappointed or harsh with yourself if you really don't feel able to stick to your plan.
- Try to plan some bigger activities each week, at least one of which involves others and that you will commit to.
- Set yourself a SMART goal to get well (see Chapter Two). Make yourself your most important project. But remember to be as patient with yourself as you would be with a good friend!
- Give yourself an incentive – write out one thing that you would really like, and make this your reward.
- Create your favourite list of mental skills, and have it visible in your bedroom. This will remind you each day to do at least one of them, also that they are all there for you to call upon at any time.

- Finally, unlock your creativity and your physicality. Get curious about the creative part of yourself – we all have one! Think back to what you loved to do when you were a child. The kinds of things you did for fun and play – singing, writing, building, designing, dressing up, play-acting, joke-making, running, cycling, basketball, soccer, playing with dolls! The list is endless. Just let yourself remember what you enjoyed. You could even ask someone from your family or a childhood friend to help. Look at old photos to jog your memory. Start doing some of this again!

One of the big challenges of mood disorders is that they can make us feel and think we are alone. They try to isolate and separate us from others, creating a mental picture, or telling us a story, that we are completely alone in this world and with our feelings. So we feel very lonely, and we believe we are powerless, useless and out of place. When our heads are clear, we know that we are not alone; we know we are capable and powerful; we know we are intimately connected to this world and the other people in it.

When we are emotionally or psychologically unwell, however, we are not thinking very clearly. Our body is out of balance; we are upset on a number of levels. At these times, the question, 'What is best for me?' is more important than ever. It invites us to see past the present moment, to try to take a bigger view of what is going on and how we can influence it. When we are out of balance, experiences can feel overwhelming – but we can still rise out of these moments and think from a different perspective. The higher perspective of, 'What is good for me? What will move me towards health again? What will help me get on a more even keel and feel more like myself again?' Step by step, little by little, we can make the most helpful decisions for ourselves and so find the best way forward . . . For example, what is best is getting out of bed and achieving this single task; what is best is making sure to eat something every day. Locking ourselves away from others is not good for us – talking to someone is better; going to see a friend, a teammate, the GP. What is best for us is telling others how we feel, and what is going on. It is hard but it is the best thing to do right now.

We all struggle at times, but none of us is alone in suffering. Just as in sport, our own personal team is in the challenge with us and there is support available if we need it. Our job at these times is to get back on task and get back on track – get back to who we really are. To get well, to be well and continue to focus on living well, for ourselves and for those we care about and who care for us. This is winning too.

SIXTEEN

Resilience

'Surrounding yourself with people is essential. Find one or two people that you trust . . . Then, when you're feeling low, call on these people'

Derval O'Rourke

I looked at my career broadly, placing the loss[es] into a bigger picture of achievement. Don't get me wrong, winning became increasingly important to me as my career went on. At times it was the number one reason I liked to play – loving the moments of extreme joy that are particular to sport. I did however recognise that sport is one part of my life and it didn't define me, nor did one loss or one win. I acknowledged to myself that my sporting career is finite, and [that] the highs and lows of sport will not continue forever. What really helped with the lows was communicating with friends and family. Increasing the communication on and off the pitch really helped at these times.

Shane Horgan – former professional rugby player; 65 caps for Ireland, 203 appearances for Leinster

Unpredictable and tragic events can and do happen in life. Most of us have had some direct experience of tragedy, or know of it indirectly, through the experiences of those close to or in some way connected to us. In 2003 I was part of an envoy sent to Bali on behalf of the New Zealand government for the first-year anniversary of the Bali nightclub bombing, supporting the families and victims of this devastating tragedy. Some 202 people died in this terrorist attack, with victims from 88 countries. Many of the victims and I walked through the bombsite talking about what happened that night and how this trauma has affected them and their lives since.

In 2016 my family and I moved to Stockholm, where we would live for 18 months. Within the first six months a terrorist attack involving a truck on a busy shopping street in the daytime resulted in the deaths of four people, with another 15 people injured. Just one hour before, my wife had been on this street, as were many of her colleagues, one of whom, very sadly, was among the victims who died.

Few of us know how to cope when faced with such tragedy. However, by building our resilience in a more general, long-term way and learning from the shared insights and experiences of others, we can help ourselves and those in our circles to cope better when the worst-case scenario does actually strike.

I was lucky enough to meet New Zealand-based writer and psychologist Dr Lucy Hone at a national cricket workshop where she presented her latest resilience research. While Lucy was studying resilience she tragically lost her 12-year-old daughter Abi in a car accident. She shared how her resilience training helped her manage better during this time, in a very real way. Her research in the post-quake environment of Christchurch helped her and her family cope with their terrible loss. Lucy received top-level resilience training from the University of Pennsylvania, the same training that 1.1 million US soldiers have received. Specifically for our book, Lucy recommended five strategies when faced with adversity, and we share them here:

- Ask yourself, is what I am doing, or going to do, or thinking, *helpful* or *harmful* in my getting through this current challenge?

- We all get to choose what we focus our attention on and we can choose to put things in perspective by deliberately seeking to discover what is still good in our world. Don't see any present adversity as permanent or pervasive: 'While death *is* permanent, I forced myself to recognise that the feelings of loss and misery wouldn't be permanent, and the grief wouldn't write my life off forever' – Dr Hone.

- Know, appreciate and continually use your personal strengths.
- Use the power of distraction to give your mind, body and soul a rest from the exhausting work that is grieving.
- Finally, remind yourselves that you get to say 'no' and you get to say 'yes' to what you want or don't want.

Difficult times invite us to *slow down* and look at what is happening right now, and to acknowledge that what has happened in the past is now part of our life story. They offer us an opportunity to bring in *perspective thinking.* To take a look at our lives and how we are living, to ask the important question: 'What changes could I make to improve my life and wellbeing moving forward from here?' These experiences can help us evaluate what is *really* important and what is not. What is good for us and what is not. What will help and what will not.

When it comes to reducing acute stress, negative, anxious or depressive thinking does not help – what is needed is *optimistic thinking*. Inherent in optimistic thinking is hope, the hope that we will grow from this experience as we do from all our life experiences. To be hopeful is to err on the side of *positivity* as opposed to negativity. To decide to be optimistic and to believe things will get better: 'Things always get better and I will be OK, no matter what happens.' Tapping into our inner experience and reminding ourselves that we have been through many challenges already, big and small, and we have made it through and we will again, in moving into a new stage of life.

Dr Lucy Hone says that resilience can be learned. It requires only very ordinary processes, such as having strong supportive networks to rely upon, being able to communicate our needs to these people when times are tough, and focusing our attention on the things we can change and accepting those we cannot. In addition, it fosters hope that we are able to get through these tough times, based on our own real experiences.

She acknowledges that 'death, divorce, redundancy, mental illness and physical impairment don't discriminate, they can happen to us all', but understanding what boosts and what derails our personal capacity for resilience is a key skill for health and optimal functioning. Her advice is that the mental skills in this book such as *grounding, centring, meditation, active reflection, talking, goal-setting, clear decision-making* and *emotional fluency* all help, especially with regular practice. Lucy shared with me that this makes us more resilient and improves self-function by:

- Helping us to overcome childhood adversity like physical trauma or emotional neglect.
- Allowing us to navigate the stresses and strains of daily living – the printer breaking down, employees not showing up for work, your partner failing to return your call, someone stealing your parking space.

- Steering us through life's big challenges such as death, divorce, sickness.
- Enabling us to reach out and try new things like talking to new colleagues, visiting new countries, tackling new software systems, learning new languages, asking someone out on a date.

When times are hard and we feel like giving up, determination and personal inner drive will successfully see us through. All of us have experienced times when we struggled but came out the other side. Reflecting on these times is important, as resilience is a process in the moment and also over time.

ROBUST RESILIENCE

In Chapter Fourteen we looked at *rebound* resilience, but in sport there is also 'robust resilience'. This occurs when preparing for performance pressure, usually through repeat exposure to pressure situations and in so doing building resilience – actively choosing to face into a challenge and becoming more resilient for having done so.

Robust resilience is about developing an experience protectiveness – the protection coming from a person maintaining their wellbeing and performance when repeatedly put under this pressure, such as elite athletes and elite military teams, where individuals actively choose to put themselves in pressurised, stressful and challenging situations, through training, games or manoeuvres.

In a nutshell, rebound resilience is about bouncing back

because *we have to*; robust resilience is about facing and experiencing challenges because *we want to*. In both cases we learn a lot about ourselves and we always grow *through* the experience.

IN THE MOMENT

Both types of resilience work best when mental skills are actively being employed, and a combination of such skills allows a person to be psychologically stronger, knowing they have techniques available to help them in any given situation. Like layers of protective clothing, mental skills help safeguard the mind by activating a skill suitable for any particular challenge, in the moment.

Mental skills will prevent us from losing ourselves in the overwhelming emotion of the moment or disconnecting ourselves so much that we deny what is happening in the here and now. Instead, we will be practised enough to manage our way through any situation. It's OK to experience emotions while not getting stuck in them. With *encouraging self-talk*, for example, we learn to hear ourselves being motivating. We can train our mind to use language like 'come on', 'get up', 'get going', 'move forward', 'keep moving', 'you are able to do this', 'focus on the next bit', 'get through that', 'keep moving forward', 'lift yourself', 'lift your energy', 'head up', 'eyes forward', 'keep talking', 'keep connecting', 'push on through', 'next task, next task'.

RESOURCE RESILIENCE

In terms of managing stress, if I could revisit my career, I would probably go home and tell my wife how I'm feeling after each game. I think, for me, that would have helped manage stress, by helping to stop more stress being created . . . Because your partner doesn't know what you are thinking, and doesn't know why you have shut down, but if you can explain to her where your head's at and why you're feeling like that and that it's not her fault . . . You know – it's not their fault but that you're just processing this [loss]. So, probably, being able to just open up to your partner and then really trying to focus on the good stuff you have done [in the game] . . . Yeah, and having a mentor as well. Someone that you can just pick up the phone and talk to, who will almost be there 24/7 if you need them. Being able to just have that person you can trust, who doesn't have to be your family or your girlfriend – a person who is in a sort of neutral ground.

Ben Sigmund – New Zealand footballer; 31 caps for New Zealand All Whites; 181 appearances for Wellington Phoenix

I always had a tight group of people around me that I trusted. Like-minded people to pull me back from being low. I think this is hugely important. Surrounding yourself with people is essential. Find one or two people that you trust and are willing to be very honest with. Then, when you are feeling low, call on these people for a cup of coffee – sit down and tell them exactly how you feel.

Derval O'Rourke – former Irish sprint hurdles athlete; Irish national record holder in 60 and 100 metres hurdles

There is a third type of resilience that I like to talk about with individuals and teams, which I call *resource resilience*. The first two types of resilience are about responding to an obvious challenge – accident, emergency, loss, natural disaster etc. – or actively engaging in a challenge, such as high-level sports, adventure sports like skydiving or taking on a difficult competition like an Ironman or marathon.

For many of us, these experiences may not occur too often in our lives. However, many people today are struggling and in need of resilience skills, just to manage themselves while living day to day.

Resource resilience is the psychological ability to seek out, call on and tap into resources that help us in the moment and over time. To figure out how to get through the many minor challenges that we face in a typical day, week, month or year – minor challenges that can gradually build up in our system. To activate these resources when we feel psychologically vulnerable or emotionally exposed, with so much going on. To be able to slow down, breathe, ground ourselves enough to answer the question: 'What are the resources I can call upon to help me with what I need to do next?'

Who can help me, where can I go for support, what can I do right now that will help me get through this, how can I make this easier on me? What do I know will lift me? Who can I talk to?

At the heart of resource resilience is the knowledge that

we are never alone, even though at times we may think we are. Lucy also shared this view when I talked to her: 'The standout finding of resilience research is that nobody goes it alone, everybody needs a tap code' – referring to the 'tap code' or Morse code used by American war veterans held captive during the Vietnam War, which was a vital link to connect, acknowledge, communicate and support each other.

We all have tap codes! We just need to know them better.

It is also the psychological realisation that within all of us there are lots of our own personal resources open and available, our personal arsenal of resources with many mental skills that we can learn, practice and continually integrate. Our on-board survival kit.

TEAM RESILIENCE

In any team there is always a wealth of knowledge and experience that exists. Winning in sporting relationships can be done by communicating well, sharing these experiences and sharing the tasks. Lack of communication or too much negative currency puts teams into the red. Teams that go too quiet and clam up, or get too loud and urgent – shouting, blaming, witch-hunting and criticising – are not winning but losing. This is the opposite of the successful behaviour of communicating well and sharing the load. What is helpful, and success driven, is problem solving, helpful observations, suggesting new or adapted plans and strategies. Teams that share together, care together and fare well together. Teams and athletes who know how to share energy and bring intensity during a game, a competition or a tournament are already winning.

LIFE SUPPORT

In competition, as in business, or indeed any aspect of life, we all face times when we are out of our comfort zone – when we are stretching ourselves. Think about this expression for a moment: we are literally stretching our sense of self and we are growing bigger through the process. Like clothes getting too small for us, we are busting at the seams with the challenge of the task. Such times can be very uncomfortable and stressful.

Sometimes we feel out of our depth and we need to make some *clear decisions* to move forward. Other times we realise that, actually, we aren't out of our depth but that we are just *feeling* the challenge of the task. It is within this *uncomfortable zone* that we learn most about ourselves, about life, about success and about what it is to be winning. These wins are all about doing what we can with these moments, truly potentialising them and growing through the process.

When we succeed we have grown with the task and we cannot un-grow again. In the same way we cannot turn back time. These experiences are now part of us and we need to always remember and respect them, these tough times we have already successfully experienced and overcome, and that cannot ever be taken from us. In these times we are already winners, we have beaten the experience.

This is why many people respond to life-threatening illnesses or life-altering events with a renewed sense of purpose. A new sense and focus on what is important in life. Faced with the reality of what has happened, we are inspired to want to do more.

WINNING IN LIFE

Today more than ever we all have access to so much knowledge that is freely being shared, with just a few clicks of a mouse. Winning in life comes through using this knowledge and activating our successful behaviours more often. Through understanding what we need to do to satisfy the energy associated with our successful behaviours. To let go and let it flow – not interrupt or divert it. For all of us there are some common successful winning behaviours for life and mental health, as follows:

- having fun and driving enjoyment
- laughing often
- caring, sharing and relating
- creating and completing
- setting and achieving a mission
- purposeful reflecting
- self-challenging
- positivity and optimism
- listening and understanding

This list is not ground breaking but these things are exceptionally important for our health and wellbeing. They can easily be neglected, so we need to actively drive them to succeed. We need to potentialise them more often.

SEVENTEEN

Conclusion

Driving Happiness

'I love winning. Winning is great, there's no better feeling'

Dane Coles

'I love winning. Winning is great, there's no better feeling after the game – especially in the sheds after. I never think about it during the week when I prepare. I just think about what I can do to prepare the best I can to help the team to win, and, for me, that's about taking pride in my performance. It's never a main priority, but I do love winning.'

Dane Coles – All Black hooker with 56 caps; plays club rugby with the Hurricanes

As All Black Dane Coles highlights in the interview on the previous page, winning makes us feel really happy. While our bodies are capable of letting us feel happy as much as they are capable of letting us feel sad, angry or afraid, to achieve greater happiness we need to make it a goal – setting our mind, our body and our abilities towards achieving this feeling more often and feeling less of the negative emotions. Such a goal is realistic, and there are many people in the world today who are pursuing this goal and using various mental skill routines to achieve it. Perhaps the best known is the Dalai Lama.

The Dalai Lama discusses his continual pursuit of happiness in his book *The Art of Happiness*, co-written with Howard C. Cutler. Here he outlines the determination he puts into his daily practices, in his pursuit of happiness. It is a blueprint that all of us can follow.

The Dalai Lama talks about the *limits* we impose upon ourselves when we try desperately to explain *everything* using our own minds. This is automatically limiting because there is always a larger picture at play, things bigger than ourselves. Things we do not know and may never truly know. We need to activate *perspective thinking* to know we cannot fully know everything.

The Dalai Lama believes we all have a unique happiness 'baseline' that at any time we can return to, by using various mental practices. We can also actively grow and develop this baseline happiness to enjoy life more. These mental skills are essential, as our mental state or 'attitude' plays a predominant role in our daily lives and we therefore need to train these mental states if we are to enhance our happiness.

For example, we can train our minds specifically with calmness and with our innate ability for compassion and affection. He sees these as being at the heart of the energy associated with human happiness. The mental skills we practise throughout our day will bring about calmness of body and mind – skills such as *grounding, centring* or *encouraging self-talk* – and if we wish to enjoy a continuously happy life this requires discipline and determination.

CONNECTING WITH AFFECTION

The Dalai Lama outlines how true self-worth is enhanced by investing in relationships with others, in human connectedness, and it is within relationships that we 'anchor' ourselves. It is through this connectedness that we guard against a false sense of worth and against illnesses such as depression and anxiety – by accessing the healing value of human warmth and affection.

Lasting happiness also comes within our mind and heart through the reduction of suffering. It is our mind that helps us grow our daily happiness (or conversely can detract us from achieving this goal), so, where possible, we need to train our mind to reduce suffering and therefore increase happiness. Just like any athlete needs to *continually* train their body to achieve greater sporting success.

Through practising such skills as *active reflection* and *clear decision-making*, we can learn to identify, nourish, cultivate and drive those things that enhance our mental wellbeing and are psychologically helpful to us. At the same time we can get rid of those that are harmful and undermining, by identifying and reducing their negative influence, recognising that they are detracting us from our happiness goal.

We must really appreciate the intrinsic value in limiting negative thoughts and what the Dalai Lama calls 'negative emotions', while driving the positive thoughts and positive emotions, but especially doing this when it is *hard to do*. We must clearly distinguish in our own minds what leads to happiness and what does not, similar to Dr Lucy Hone's suggestions earlier. The Dalai Lama points out that hatred, jealously and anger are harmful and do not lead to happiness, whereas compassion, warmth and kindness leads to communicating with others much more easily, which in turn paves the way for happiness.

Doing these things allows us to determine, take charge of and change our feelings from negative to positive, and the secret to achieving this is knowing that this process puts happiness within our reach. Understanding that these are successful winning behaviours worth driving and maintaining, we then each day put happiness more within our own self-determination and our own capable hands.

Brent: We wanted this book to be for everyone – but especially for young people. To help them understand that, no matter what hits us in life, it is manageable. Our interviews have shown that even the most respected, successful athletes in the world have struggled with self-doubt and negative beliefs about their abilities at times; they too have sometimes felt lost and alone. Not one person in this book has had it easy. They have all had times when they wanted to throw their boots or running shoes away, to simply give up – but they didn't. One of the other things they all have in common is that they kept going, even when things were difficult. They pushed themselves, they trained hard and they sought help, they talked to others when they needed it; they recovered, and they succeeded. To all of us, they are an inspiration. They found the drive to say, 'I will win, I will succeed' – and, most importantly, they achieved success on their own terms.

If you would like to learn more about the exercises in this book, be supported or coached, or would like to share any comments and stories on how this book has helped you, please visit www.thewinningmind.net – we would love to hear from you.

Brent Pope and Jason Brennan, January 2018

Glossary of Mental Skills

*Technique (T)
*Process (P)

ACTIVE REFLECTION (P)

This skill involves taking the time to actively think about and process our experiences, which in turn leads to a greater level of *self-awareness.* Good times to reflect are usually when we are feeling rushed, pressured or close to our stress threshold.

This is best done in a quiet place if possible. Begin by taking a few deep breaths, and then start to 'zone out' of the external environment, as you bring your energy and attention inwards, to what you are feeling and thinking. Now ask yourself these questions:

- What do I specifically want to reflect on?
- What are the key questions I need answers to?
- What will I gain from this time?
- What will I do following this reflection?

If, for example, you are visualising a difficult conversation, start with the type of conclusion you ideally would like, and work back from there, keeping this end goal in mind. Be sure to imagine the situation from the other person's perspective also, and reflect on what language and approach will work best to achieve the most desirable outcome.

ADVERSE PLANNING (T)

This is the process of having a plan for when things don't go as expected or hoped and is widely used in the military in preparing for worst case scenarios or to mitigate unforeseeable events. In adverse planning, we need to focus on the type of behaviour we *want* to exhibit when faced with challenging circumstances. When we experience something outside of our control, for example, we learn to focus on how to stay calm, deal with and work on what is controllable. By developing this mindset, we can prepare for unfortunate events and move forward in small manageable steps and regain momentum i.e. movement forward.

ANCHORING (T)

Pick a specific activity or skill you want to get better at or feel more relaxed about. The next time you are engaging in this activity, begin as you normally would. Now, stop and think about how you would specifically like to improve in this area. Imagine how it would feel and what it would look like if you were able to do this better. As you bring these images and sensations to mind, slow your breathing and become aware of your body relaxing. Continue to imagine doing the activity well, as you feel the tension draining from your neck and shoulders, and you should feel a pleasant sense of weight in your belly, lower back and tailbone as you begin to relax. Feel the energy flowing freely through your body, up and down your spinal cord and into your limbs.

Once you begin to feel this effortless movement of energy, and when you are ready, choose a physical gesture or movement that you will use to remind you of this feeling, this flow, these sensations. This should be a gesture that you would not normally use – one that is unique and can be *anchored* to this experience. Examples might be putting two fingers together that don't usually sit together, or brushing or tapping a part of your body – your shoulder, your head/ temple, your chest, etc. Now practise making that gesture when you are in this state of relaxation and free-flowing energy. Repeated practice is very important to help this association between the gesture and the feeling to take hold. In time, you will be able to evoke this relaxed state or desired image easily, by simply making this gesture. *Anchoring* techniques also work well with *trigger words*.

ASSERTIVENESS (P)

Assertiveness is a healthy form of expression and essential to success and winning. It is an Adult Ego State process (see PAC model) in Chapter Three because it involves: problem-solving, showing balanced respect, logic and reasoning, analysis and observation, employing listening skills and openness to understanding, empirical skills and experience, empathy, and focus on the here and now.

The Adult Ego State Energy is the best place to be assertive from because it is very grounded and balanced. It provides a high level of security from which to communicate as the experience held within it is reliable, tested and open to being updated if proven incorrect.

It is also a resilient process as assertiveness centres on expressing what, from our point of view, is okay and not okay.

Let's remember what the Adult Ego State in use is like by asking ourselves:

- What do I feel when I am talking in a confident way about something I'm knowledgeable about?
- What are the words I associate with speaking confidently?
- If I was thinking something was incorrect and wanted to tell someone, how would I like to do this?
- If I had a good idea, but were afraid to tell someone, how could I encourage myself to speak up?

CENTRING (T)

This is a breathing technique that focuses on our diaphragm – our centre. It is great for focusing the mind and body in times of stress and challenge, and helps us dissipate pressure by giving us a greater sense of control over our physical and emotional state.

Begin by simply saying, 'I am breathing in; I am breathing out', as you feel the sensation of the breath entering and leaving your nostrils. Note how the air feels colder as you breathe in, and warmer with each out-breath.

Now move the focus of your attention to the centre of your body – your diaphragm. Feel the powerful muscle in the diaphragm as it controls the influx and exhalation of your breath. As you breathe in, your belly should expand outwards like it is filling with air, then push back with this muscle, towards your spine like you are emptying the air from your belly. When you are comfortable with this motion, try holding the muscle and your breath as you breathe fully in or fully out – like the belly is either full of air or empty of air. This technique is about gaining greater control and mastery over your breathing and, consequently, over the physical symptoms of nerves. Long, slow breathing in particular brings a greater sense of calm throughout our nervous system and more oxygen into the body will clear the head and help to disperse stress chemicals. When finished, just let go and breathe naturally again.

CLEAR DECISION-MAKING (P)

We make decisions, large and small, all the time – however, we are often not clear on our motivations in making these choices, and many of our reasons may be unconscious ones. To think clearly means to understand *why* we are making a particular choice, what the desired outcome is and what it might mean if we were not to make it. If, for example, we decide *not* to do something, what is the reason, the underlying motivation? It may very well be fear. In this instance, deciding to do something, then, is a *potentialising* move forward. Deciding also means being able to follow something through, putting it into action.

Clear decisions, made from a positive, forward-looking standpoint, are *congruent* decisions (see below). Since they reflect what we are really thinking and how we really feel, these types of decisions help to generate *confidence* and *assertiveness*. Unclear decisions, or those which come from low-quality and negative thinking, are not congruent and lead to negative, undermining outcomes. Practise exploring your motivation by asking:

- What is the choice I have to make here?
- Why might I choose either option?
- Why would I *not* do either?
- Which option is the escape clause?
- Which option will help me to grow more?
- What decision will I now take?

CONGRUENCY (P)

Congruency is when a person's actions match what it is they say they will do, and what they actually want to do: when what they are doing lines up, or is *congruent* with, what they are saying, thinking and feeling. Congruency is important when it comes to high performance and success – when our thoughts, feelings and behaviour are in agreement, the natural energy of flow, or physis (growth energy), kicks in and things fall into place more easily.

Incongruent behaviour is the opposite. This is when what someone does is not matched up to what they are saying, thinking or feeling – there is conflict in the system. They are not 'practising what they preach' – doing things they don't want to do, or *not* doing something that they would like to do.

Congruency enables trust, a sense of integrity, assertiveness and respect.

CONNECTING (P)

Being able, and willing, to connect and communicate with others regularly and especially at difficult times is invaluable in all areas of life and sports, and a vital part of a mental health skillset. In team sports, it can enable a player to lift the energy of the team, through consciously connecting with his or her teammates – verbally and through body language. Away from sport, it means making a real and consistent effort to go out and connect with friends, family and groups. Connecting is a key skill when it comes to building our resilience (see Chapter Fourteen).

CONTRACTING (T)

Contracting means putting an agreement in place. Contracts are very useful in helping to delineate boundaries and responsibilities (especially when allocating work), and in avoiding confusion. The clearer the contract, the easier it will be to identify individual responsibilities and to recognise when agreement has been fulfilled.

Contracts need to specify the desired outcomes and the actions required to achieve these.

An example of a very simple contract someone could enter into with themselves might be a 'hold off' agreement – i.e. 'I will not do X (e.g. watch my favourite soap on TV; eat a bar of chocolate; go out for a coffee, etc.), until I have completed Y (e.g. make a phone call I've been putting off; finish answering the morning's emails; clean the bathroom, etc.).' A simple contract with another person might be around the issue of giving feedback on something they have done or said, or on an ongoing basis. This would involve first asking them if it is OK to provide some constructive feedback, pointers or advice. If they say yes and you explain your motivations – the reasons you want to do this – then there is a contract in place between the two of you. Giving feedback without asking, or not having such a mutual agreement in place, is not conducive to good communication, and risks the other person being closed off to what you have to say, or even offended.

COMPETITION MINDSET (T)

This is more focused on a specific game or competition. In business this might be getting in the right frame of mind for a presentation or interview. What helps most with this type of preparation is an outline of specific actions and desired results. Questions to explore are:

- What is my role here?
- What do I specifically need to achieve to be successful in this role (behaviours/actions)?
- How well do I personally and specifically want to perform?
- What do I need to tell myself and keep in mind during the competition (or interview etc.), that will help me focus on performing my role?

CURIOSITY (P)

Curiosity is one of our strongest natural traits, but one which we can unconsciously block. It is a mental skills process, in that it can be developed and enhanced. The energy of curiosity allows us to learn more about ourselves and what we are capable of, enabling us to grow and evolve. We can foster our curiosity and encourage our 'growth mindset' by asking ourselves these kinds of questions when we are faced with the opportunity to try something new:

- What can I gain from giving this a go?
- How will I feel after I have done it?
- What's the harm in trying?
- What's the harm in *not* trying?
- Why am I *really* stopping myself from doing something new?

DISCIPLINE (P)

Everyone knows that in order to gain mastery over – and continually improve in – a particular skill, repeated practice and preparation are a big part of the equation. Discipline comes into play when we feel our motivation flagging, when we are fed up of practising or discouraged because our progress is slower than we might have hoped. Discipline is our inner mechanism, or inner consciousness, which helps us make the best choice in continuing to work on our goals. By practicising discipline, we can maintain focus once the initial excitement of doing well begins to wear off and the reality of the work sets in. (See 'The Four D's' in Chapter Two)

DISCUSSING A PLAN WITH YOUR COACH OR LEADER (P)

This involves *talking* and *goal-setting* and using *active reflection* before a meeting. Write out what you want to work on and need help with. For example, what questions you want answered and why. Preparing will help your coach or leader help you get answers to your questions quickly, and structure the meeting to keep it on track.

Ask for a meeting. Book a time with your coach or leader. Suggest a timeframe also, to help them understand what you are looking for, for example ten minutes, fifteen minutes, half an hour. Let them know briefly what you want to talk about to help *them* prepare. Bring your plan. Ask them to fill in the blanks or identify the holes, or which area needs developing. Ask them how they can help you be successful. Set tasks going forward.

EMOTIONAL FLUENCY (P)

This simply means having the ability to identify how you are feeling and a willingness to share it with others. Emotional fluency involves being able to identify and *label* your emotions to help express them verbally to others. The way to develop this skill is by consistently checking in with ourselves, and acknowledging how we are feeling, and then making the effort to name the emotion that is rising within us. To make this easier to do, we can narrow our feelings down to four primary ones, and then identify which of the four is being felt and making the effort to name the emotion that is rising within us – is it happiness, sadness, anger or fear? When we are able to name it, we are able to say it. This is key when it comes to expressing ourselves and sharing our feelings with others, so that they can understand us better. Of course, feelings can sometimes come in pairs and being able to express both of these basic feelings really adds to the level of communication.

FATIGUE MANAGEMENT (P)

In sport and exercise, pain and fatigue are part and parcel of performance and how we manage them can be greatly enhanced by drawing on a range of mental skills. Pushing through the barrier of physical fatigue is something all top-level athletes must practice at some stage. Much (but not all) of what we consider to be fatigue is actually generated by the mind: a tired mind will produce symptoms of fatigue in the body. None of us knows what our bodies are really capable of. Our minds have the power to hold us back or drive us forward. Skills such as *self-awareness* and *assertiveness* are important in this context, in helping us spot and shut down the negative self-talk of fatigue which kicks in when we are feeling tired. Mental skills techniques such *grounding, centring, meditation* and *visualisation* help in overcoming physical pain and in managing physical tiredness or burnout. *Encouraging self-talk* is also a great skill to develop to help the mind combat negative fatigue inducing thoughts.

FLOW (P)

Flow, or *flow state*, is an intensely energetic concentration on a task, to the point where it is the sole focus of our attention. Nothing else matters; there is a feeling of calm, and an enjoyable sense of absorption; also the knowledge that we are performing the task really well, or optimally. This experience, of time passing with a continual, uninterrupted flow of energy and intense focus on the task, gives rise to a deep sense of satisfaction.

FREE ASSOCIATION (T)

This exercise is designed to tap into the *unconscious* mind and reduce any resistance caused by the *conscious* mind. Start with a few long, deep breaths. Preferably sit somewhere with few distractions. Name clearly the experience you want to find out more about – be specific. Name clearly what you would like your mind to do for you.

Without trying to force yourself, let your mind start wondering about this experience. Come up with as many words, ideas or associations as you can. *Do not* censor or judge these ideas. This is an exercise in *creativeness* and *openness*. See where your mind goes. Use single words first. Capture them, write them out or draw them. Free association is a bit like *mind mapping*. Then start branching off ideas.

After a set period of time, go through each one of these words and rate their quality. Some of the words you can expand on with sentences and then even actions which you can decide if you want to follow up on. All such associations are significant, as they come from your unconscious. The more you explore them, the more you will find out about yourself and discover what is important to you.

GOAL-SETTING (T)

This is essential for all types of performance, a key skill to develop if we want to achieve results. Our minds like to be put to work, to focus on achievable goals, to feel a sense of satisfaction when they are completed. Figure out what you want to achieve, and create a picture in your mind of the successful result. Your goals can be big or small, can take hours, days or months. They can lead into each other – like stepping stones. Each goal needs to fulfil the criteria for SMART goaling:

S	Specific
M	Measurable
A	Achievable
R	Realistic
T	Time-bound

Write out where you are starting from and where you hope to finish, including timelines and dates – what specifically will be achieved by when. Outline what will happen, what will be different. Write out the steps that you can think of. Write out how you will acknowledge the achievement of each step. Track your progress and plan for setbacks. Plan for what will get you back on track and keep you going.

GROUNDING (T)

This is the skill of consciously shifting energy in our body, with our minds. It is very effective if the brain is overactive, with too many stress chemicals. With too much energy in our head, the best place to go is the furthest place away from that – our feet, and specifically, our big toe. Send energy to the big toe by listening to the sensations this toe is giving. Is it hot, cold, tingly, painful? Can I feel the sock or shoe? Then shift the energy to the other toes by moving them. Next the sole of the foot – what can this tell me? Then the heel and then the whole foot, by rocking them back and forward. I am *grounding* myself because I am connecting with my *ground*, my pillars of support. By spending time in my feet and later checking in with my legs (calves, knees, thigh muscles), I am energising my trunk and dispersing the energy and chemicals from my head, which then starts to 'cool down'. A good way to help the body quickly get the energy into the feet is to walk around on grass, sand, water or snow and be able to quickly recall these physical sensations again later. This is very effective in the heat of competition, in an office with feet under the desk or when commuting.

MOOD-ENHANCING MUSIC (MEM) (T)

To use music to enhance your mood, create a playlist of the songs that you know lift your energy or help you to relax. These can be timed to bring a much-needed boost to training or to brighten a day that is stressful. Music is a mood enhancer, in that it affects the chemicals in our body to bring positivity to how we feel and what we think.

OPTIMISTIC MINDSET (T)

When it comes to managing challenges and reducing stress, negative, anxious or depressive thinking does not help. What is needed is an *optimistic mindset* or *optimistic thinking*. Inherent in optimistic thinking is hope – the hope that we will grow from the negative experience as we do from all our life experiences. To be hopeful is to err on the side of *positivity* as opposed to negativity. We can decide to be optimistic and to believe things will get better: 'Things always get better and I will be OK, no matter what happens.' Tapping into our previous experiences and reminding ourselves that we have been through many challenges already, big and small, and we have made it through and we will again, in moving forward. Optimistic thinking is about believing it will work out – no matter what.

PAIN MANAGEMENT (P)

Psychological pain management is the ability to use our minds to overcome or distance ourselves from physical pain. The job of physical pain is clear – to alert us to the fact that we have received an injury or that some part of the body is otherwise under duress and that it will need attention at some stage. In many cases, we have a choice as to whether to dwell on this pain, or temporarily postpone placing our focus on it. We are able to turn off the thoughts connected to pain, like a tap, and instead simply breathe through the pain or distract ourselves from it, placing our attention elsewhere. The power of mental training is to help turn off, or at least turn down, pain receptor sensation. However, it is always important to listen to your body and know when the pain is too much and requires urgent attention (see Chapter Eleven).

PERSPECTIVE THINKING (T)

This is thinking about a situation from a different angle. Taking an alternative viewpoint and seeing how it fits into a bigger picture. We do it with questions like:

- In the grand scheme of things, how big is this really?
- Are there more important things happening in the world?
- Are there others worse off than me?
- Have I experienced bigger things before?
- How does this fit into my overall picture of who I am and where I am going?

POSITIVE ATTITUDE (P)

This means consciously harnessing our ability to *choose our attitude* in any given situation – even before we go into that situation.

It involves recognising that negative thoughts and negative language simply create negative energy. Stopping this, and turning it into positive energy, is far more productive. Our attitude is displayed in how we think and how we behave. It is obvious to others.

We can drive a negative attitude through what we say and how we say it (tone, emphasis etc.), or we can choose a positive attitude. To do this, we *actively reflect* on what we are saying or are about to say, and remove any negativity. Instead we put in place a more positive version – in our tone, choice of words, language and even physical behaviour (e.g. palms open and body turned more towards others). Sometimes it can be challenging to always see the positive in things, and it's not realistic either, so a good way to simply avoid the negative is to have a more neutral or balanced attitude, but with a positive tone or open body posture.

POTENTIALISING (P)

This means making a decision to do something that will release energy to grow a person's experience, furthering their abilities and increasing knowledge of their performance – what they can actually achieve. This happens through an in-the-moment decision to act on something that is challenging to do, rather than simply not doing it – harnessing the mental skill of *clear decision-making* and combating doubt, fear and negative overthinking. The best-known potentialising phrase today is 'Just do it'.

PROCESS MINDSET (T)

This is a healthy way to engage in any activity, by focusing on the *process* and not just the outcome. The process is the actual doing of the task – engaging in it and allowing yourself to focus solely on that task. Putting too much emphasis on the outcome can often be distracting and can undermine our process. The key factors in a process mindset are repeatable *routines*, practised *preparation*, prediction *planning*, *self-assurance* and *confidence*. Knowing a process means having created a process that works, that we know well, that helps with focus, relaxation, anxiety reduction and successful actions. Being able to write these processes out also helps. Whenever in doubt, think of our processes – go back to what we know works for us.

PROGRESSIVE THINKING (T)

We do this by letting our imagination follow through to a conclusion. If we are worrying about a future event, we can allow our mind to play it out, to keep on working it through bit by bit, following the event to reach a conclusion that is less anxiety-provoking. With questions like, 'And then what will happen? And then? And after that?' – eventually reaching a more realistic and usually less emotional outcome.

REFRAMING (T)

This means looking at a situation through a different lens, framing it differently to our initial take on it. We can frame it up using a *positive lens*, a *rational lens*, *enhancing lens*, etc. It is an excellent technique to get the most out of a situation. It reduces emotional reaction and invites problem-solving, balance, understanding, building new neural networks by breaking away from familiar emotive thinking.

1. Pick a situation that is worrying or frustrating you, that you are thinking negatively about.

2. Score the feeling out of an intensity level of 100.

3. Ask yourself, 'How can I look at this situation from a different perspective?'

4. 'How could I learn from this situation? What am I finding out about myself?'

5. 'What's the opportunity being presented here? How could I make the *best* of it?'

6. 'How might this experience help me in the future?'

7. After following these steps, once again score the intensity of your feeling out of 100. You should notice that it has reduced and that other sensations, such as calmness, are produced.

RESILIENCE (P)

The capacity to bounce back from adversity is known in psychology as *resilience*, and is an absolute key quality shared by all those who achieve consistent and long-term success in sport – and indeed in any other field. It is not necessarily something you either have or don't have – it can be acquired and built upon over time and with repeated exposure to challenging situations. Mental skills such as *reframing, optimistic mindset, perspective thinking* and *centring* all help the mind and body cope better and respond to adversity quicker – responding to errors, loss, disappointment and frustration in a more productive way.

SCRIPTING (P)

This is a story we tell ourselves about an experience or situation. Our stories are heavily influenced by our past learnings, which become unconscious scripts driving our behaviour. We develop scripts based on how we see ourselves, others and the world – in particular, around performance. We update these scripts through mental skills training and repetitive mental script writing – storytelling – and by influencing our *frame of reference* – the way we frame up things psychologically. (See PETS)

SELF-AWARENESS (P)

This skill is invaluable if we are to grow and develop throughout a lifetime. The core mental skill is *active reflection* – taking time to slow down and ask ourselves, 'What is going on for me *right now*?' Regularly do an inventory of what is happening internally for you, making yourself a source of interest:

- 'What am I thinking?'
- 'How am I feeling?'
- 'Why might I be feeling or thinking this way?'
- 'Why have I reacted in this way?'
- 'Do I want to continue to react this way?'

This process creates a deeper understanding of our behaviour, piecing together a story or variety of stories (as we are complex) that help make meaning, explaining some of what is happening in any given moment and understanding more of our internal self, to make better sense of our externally projected self and how we want to be in the external world.

SELF-DETERMINATION (P)

This is how we direct our energy in any given way. It begins with a clear understanding of what we want to achieve and whether this is beneficial for us. This is helped by formulating a SMART goal. If it is of positive benefit, then the psychological energy connected with focusing on the outcome will help drive our determination to achieve this outcome. To break it down into its two parts –

determination is the drive energy we invest and decide to engage in; self is the clear understanding in ourselves of *why* we want to achieve this so much, asking:

- 'Why is doing this so important to me?'
- 'Why *must* I complete this goal?'

SELF-MOTIVATION

All mental skills require self-motivation to enact them because we need to be motivated within ourselves. Self-motivation then is a decision to put energy into achieving a result. Turning psychological energy into action. De-motivation then is the opposite – not doing or achieving something. We enhance our self-motivation by using mental skills such as *encouraging* and *focused self-talk*, *clear decision making* and *goal setting*.

SELF-REGULATION (P)

This is the ability to cool down our own feelings and our bodily reactions. When we feel sad, angry or scared we feel these with different intensity levels. When we are *over-feeling* them the intensity levels are very high. We need strategies to help lower the impact of the intensity of these emotions, bringing our system back into balance – homeostasis. We need to regulate our body and ourselves using a variety of mental skills.

SELF-TALK (T)

Our mind is always active, with lots of conversations going on. This skill is about becoming *more conscious* of these conversations and the quality of them. Are they encouraging or are they negatively driven?

- Slow down and listen to what your mind is doing.
- What is the type of language being used?

- Is it encouraging or is it undermining?
- Decide how you want it to be.
- Create a better story about what you are telling yourself.
- Encourage yourself more, stop listening to thoughts that hold you back. Tell them to stop.
- Tell yourself to go ahead.

ENCOURAGING SELF-TALK

This involves ensuring that the conversation going on inside us is positive and encouraging, nurturing and growth-worthy; as opposed to negative, excessively critical or undermining. Phrases here include:

- Well done, good job
- You got this
- You know how to do it, you have lots of experience
- This will help you grow, and make you better for it
- Focus on what you know, not what you don't

FOCUSED SELF-TALK

This is about creating a particular story about something we want to achieve. This works well with our *list of strengths*. (See SBT) It is *focused* because it is about telling your mind what the actual behaviours are that you want to achieve, for example I want to start off really well and I will do this by, say, slowing down, concentrating, focusing. Or by getting a good first touch, first clear sentence out, a good question prepared, etc. The focus then is on an actual behaviour to be produced.

SENSE OF BELONGING (P)

This is fundamental in developing and growing skills such as *confidence, team spirit, engagement, participation* and *experience.* We all belong to many groups – families, friends, clubs, teams, organisations and so on. How we acknowledge how we belong helps us build a sense of *unity* and *affinity* within these groups. Knowing how we can contribute helps build connections and makes teams stronger. How much we care for a group will determine how much we are willing to give to a group, how much we are willing to fight for that group.

SENSE OF EQUALITY (P)

This is a belief that everyone is created equal. It forms the basis of all human rights. Regardless of age, experience, wealth, gender, colour, etc. everyone is equal. What is important to keep in mind though is that not everyone has equal *knowledge* or *experience.* However, a sense of equality can be understood based on *process,* not on experience. For example, a person may be on a team or at a meeting who is less experienced, but because they are *there* they have a *right* to be there, and will feel a sense of equality based on this right. Team members are members for a reason. They have been chosen and have a right to participate. Meeting invitees are there for a reason. A sense of equality encourages *self-confidence.* If I have worked my way onto the team, onto the field or into the meeting, then I have a right to be there. I can decide to show what I am capable of. It's about being respectful and generating respect.

STRENGTH-BASED THINKING

SBT is a powerful routine to engage with, especially prior to a performance, and all it takes is a little time and a little reflection. Any person can do this by following the simple instructions below. If routinely practised it will help with all types of performance –

sport, business and personal, not to mention confidence and self-esteem.

Step 1 – write out what you are good at.

Step 2 – write out what else you are good at, what your personal assets are.

Step 3 – write out how you know you are good at these things.

Step 4 – write out who you would ask (in your mind), that you trust – who would confirm that you are good at these things.

Step 5 – write out what you think others would also say you are good at.

Step 6 – rate how good you are at these behaviours (0–10, 10 being exceptional and 0 not actually having these behaviours).

Step 7 – check your score: are you being too harsh, too generous or just right?

Step 8 – write out how you can actually use and build on your assets.

This list is the foundation of your SBT process. For the process to work well, you must look at this list often, but especially before a stressful or tense situation.

TALKING TO SOMEONE (P)

This is a pretty straightforward thing to do, but it is something that needs to be practised. Some conversations are difficult to have and are easily avoided. It can take *will power*, *clear decision-making* and *determination* to follow through. Opening up and allowing ourselves to be vulnerable is a key to recovery and growth. We do it by making *that* phone call, *booking* the time, *preparing* ourselves with *positive encouraging self-talk* and by turning up. The talking cure has been around a long time, and it works.

THOUGHT WRITING (T)

This helps slow the conscious mind down and give the unconscious mind time to put together helpful information around *motivation*, *understanding*, *awareness* and *desirable outcome*. Having a pen and paper handy in the bedroom to capture thoughts is useful, as is downloading an app on your phone to capture notes, even verbally recording them and then transcribing them.

TRIGGER WORDS (T)

These are similar to *anchoring* techniques, except instead of just using a physical gesture, a word is used. Trigger words can be used to imagine an experience solely in the mind, for example the energy associated with *confidence* or *strength*. Pick an activity or a concept (like confidence) that you want to improve on. Practise that activity as you normally would. Then start to imagine in your mind how you would like to build on this activity. Imagine doing it better and what this feels like. Sense how it is in your body. While feeling these sensations, start to slow your breathing down. Become aware of your body relaxing and any tension dropping from your neck and shoulders, your head and neck lifting and a sense of weight being more in your belly and tailbone and lower back. Energy free-flowing through your body, moving easily and unimpeded. When you are ready and feel this effortless movement of energy, pick a word that best describes this sensation and is connected to the activity you wish to be better at. Some common words might be 'strong', 'confident', 'focus', 'powerful', 'fast', 'success'. This word needs to be repeated over and over until it is fully connected to the experience. It can be tested by doing something else and then thinking of the word again to see if it recreates the sensations.

VISUALISATION (T)

This involves creating in your mind a visual image or picture of an action or series of actions that you want to execute well – a mental story that helps your body 'see' success. Imagining it activates the same neural pathways and chemical releases as actually doing it. Helping the body more easily prepare, getting it used to doing. Our 'internal model' is wired for pictures and images.

Decide where you want to practise your visualisation – in a quiet place like your bed, or where you actually perform the activity in question, for example on a training field, at the gym or in the office. Decide how often you want to visualise – we respond well to regularity and habit-forming. When creating images, real is best (unless using metaphor), and your body will respond best if all the senses are activated. Imagine what your body will feel like, what the smells and sounds are, what you would hear doing this activity, etc. Start with yourself – imagery works best from the first person, seeing through your own eyes.

Visualisation is a story and needs a start, middle and end – like in real life. No story happens in a singled rushed moment. Visualisations need to be staged – bit by bit. Follow some real timings as much as possible. A suggestion to help slow down the mind is to write out what will happen, bit by bit, breaking it into short set pieces. This can be done with a presentation, a challenging conversation or goal-kicking, etc.

Get into the moment by using a *grounding* exercise, to relax your system to really enter the experience. Start by tapping into your previous real-life positive and successful experiences of this activity. What it felt like in your body and mind. It might help to close your eyes to see yourself doing the *best version* of it. Get an image in your mind before working through the story. Picture how you were moments before you took your best shot, best hit, before you walked on to give your best talk, or best meeting.

Talk yourself through what it is you are doing: 'I am breathing slowly in and out, I am lowering my head and looking down at the ball. I breathe slowly out and I am raising my head slowly. I am looking at where the ball will travel to. I pick a spot in the distance. I look there. I look down again and pick an exact spot on the ball where my foot will make contact. I see my foot following through the ball, it lifting. I see it flying through the posts. I am imagining it going there. I breathe in slowly and I am lowering my head to look at the ball again . . .'

Practise, practise, practise.

AVATAR VISUALISATION

This type of visualisation, based on imagination, is designed to activate body parts and chemical reactions, using *metaphor*. Our minds respond to pictures and images, but also to metaphors and symbols. The two most common *avatar visualisations* are for speed and strength, but they can be for almost anything relating to a physical action such as jumping, punching, throwing, etc. Decide what action you want to get better at.

Think about which animal or image best reminds you of this action. The fastest animal, the strongest animal, the toughest character (whether a real character or an action hero), or an object such as a tank or a hammer. As the image is a *metaphor*, it is up to each person to choose their own, but it must be the *most powerful* associated image. Selecting one will help generate adrenaline, giving an extra boost of speed, strength or confidence.

In training, just before doing an exercise, call the image up in your mind. If it's an animal, take note of what it looks like, what it is doing. While imagining the animal, try and breathe into the experience, picturing it running (if your goal is speed) or fighting (if your goal is strength), etc. If you are feeling the experience enough, you should start to notice the effect of adrenaline in your system, for example heart rate, breathing, body heat – even if you are only sitting down. Say the animal's name to yourself or in your mind. The experience your body is having should then *anchor* to the word you are saying. In training, to bring an extra burst of energy, think of this animal and say its name. Allow your body to flow with the image of the animal. Measure how you are going normally, then use the *avatar imagery* to see if you go faster, stronger, higher, etc.

Tips for Getting a Good Night's Sleep

Sleep is unbelievably important for our health and wellbeing. It is one of the first indicators that we might be overly stressed (dis-stressed) and that our wellbeing is being affected. That something is getting out of balance. At different stages in our lives, our need for sleep varies. Newborn babies can sleep up to 18 hours a day (wow!); this shifts to 11 hours for pre-pubescent children, 10 hours for teenagers and then around 8 hours for adults.

Present-day studies show eight hours for most of us is pretty good, and is the average amount we need as adults. Although variance of six to eight does occur, for most of us if we are sleeping less than seven or eight hours a night it can start to impact on our health. Getting enough sleep is really important, and helps to:

- psychologically process material from our day or week (learning).
- heal and repair (muscle, tissue, hormonally).

- grow (physically, emotionally and psychologically) at different stages of life.

Not getting adequate sleep can be damaging for our health. If, say, we only get four hours' sleep a night on a regular basis, which can happen with today's hectic schedules, research shows that we are at higher risk of conditions such as cardiovascular disease, high blood pressure, diabetes, heart disease and obesity.

Chronic pain experts see a vicious circle associated with lack of sleep: excess stress leads to sleep disturbance, which leads to less healing and more physical pain, which in turn leads to more stress, which of course results in less sleep.

In order to perform well, therefore, adequate sleep is essential. Indeed, getting regular, good-quality sleep is a successful behaviour and when we achieve this it means we are winning more often.

Here are some of the things that can help us achieve better-quality sleep:

- If you find your sleep is disrupted because of a racing mind, get rid of some stress chemicals from your body by having a hot bath a couple of times a week. Just sit and sweat the chemicals out. Even better, use the sauna or the hot tub at your local gym.

- While in the bath, use the mental skill resource of *mood-enhancing music* (MEM). Put on some of your favourite relaxing music. Get your body in the mood to relax by letting go of the tension in your muscles. Let the stress chemicals leach out slowly!

- Avoid electronic stimulus for at least half an hour

before bedtime. Turn off the TV, don't check emails; instead prepare your mind for rest. If possible, ban all devices from your bedroom. Use the mental skill of *clear decision-making* to help you prepare yourself for good quality sleep.

- Darker bedrooms help the mind get the picture that the sun is firmly down, and that it's time to sleep. Blackout curtains are perfect. If you don't like too much darkness, put a light on outside the bedroom, with the door closed. This will frame the cracks of the door, so you can find the exit if need be.

- In the half-hour before bed, go through a regular bedtime routine – brushing your teeth, washing your face, laying out your things for the next day, getting into comfy bedclothes and so on. Then sit down on the bed with your feet firmly on the floor and use the mental skill of *meditation*. Find your feet with your mind first, and then focus on slowing down your breathing. Inhale through your nose, and breathe out through your mouth. Move into your preferred *meditation* or mantra. This will only take five or ten minutes, but will give great results.

- If using a phone to listen to a *meditation* app, do so with the screen face down. When finished, put the phone on silent and into a drawer – or even better, out of the room completely.

- Needless to say, alcohol and caffeine just before bed will not help with a good bedtime routine.

- Try and go to bed at the same time each night – our bodies like habit.
- While lying in bed before falling asleep, imagine something that would be fun to think about, or somewhere you'd like to go, while you are asleep. Or maybe create a *dream project*. This could involve taking a trip to a place you've already been to, or have always wanted to see. Or perhaps even an interesting, unique building or monument that you would build yourself. Make this your dream project by going back and revisiting it every night, creating or adding to it a little more each time. Bit by bit, detail by detail. Or you might want to imagine being in a particular setting – like a warm tropical beach or a cosy winter cottage, a huge, soft armchair in a forest or even in a spaceship floating in the upper atmosphere. You could even make up a story or a play with characters and a plot, elaborating on it every night before you fall asleep. It is your world and your imagination, so use it and enjoy it!

Useful Resources

Meditation Apps:

Headspace

Insight Timer

Calm

For free yoga and Tai Chi lessons online, check out YouTube

Websites:

In Ireland –

www.thewinningmind.net

www.thinkwell-ireland.com

www.aware.ie

www.yourmentalhealth.ie

www.hse.ie

www.pieta.ie

In the UK –

www.mentalhealth-uk.org

In New Zealand –

www.depression.org.nz

In Australia –
www.beyondblue.org.au
In the US –
www.adaa.org
www.algy.com/anxiety
www.anxietynetwork.com
www.ocfoundation.org

RECOMMENDED READING

Berne, Eric. *The Games People Play*. New York: Grove Press, 1964

Covey, Stephen R. *The Seven Habits of Highly Effective People*. New York: Free Press, 1989

Csikszentmihalyi, Mihaly. *Flow: The Psychology of Happiness*. London: Rider, 2002

The Dalai Lama and Cutler, Howard C. *The Art of Happiness*. London: Hodder, 1998

Dweck, Carol. *Mindset: the New Psychology of Success*. London: Robinson, 2012

Frankl, Victor. *Man's Search for Meaning*. London: Rider, 2004

Gallwey, W. Timothy. *The Inner Game of Tennis*. London: Pan, 1986

Goldstein, Joseph. *Mindfulness: a Practical Guide to Awakening*. Louisville: Sounds True, 2013

Goleman, Daniel. *Emotional Intelligence: Why It Can Matter More Than IQ*. New York: Bantam, 1995

Harris, Thomas A. *I'm Ok, You're Ok*. New York: Harper, 1967

Hawkins, Peter. *Leadership Team Coaching: Developing Collective Transformational Leadership*. London: Kogan, 2011

Recommended Reading

James, Muriel and Jongeward, Dorothy. *Born to Win*. New York: Perseus Books, 1996

Kahneman, Daniel. *Thinking, Fast and Slow*. New York: Farrar, Straus and Giroux, 2011

Kerr, James. *Legacy*. London: Constable, 2013

Lencioni, Patrick. *The Five Dysfunctions of a Team*. New Jersey: John Wiley and Sons, 2002

Maxwell, John. *How Successful People Lead*. New York: Little, Brown and Company, 2013

Pink, Daniel. *Drive*. New York: Riverhead Books, 2009

Rogers, Carl. *On Becoming a Person: a Therapist's View of Psychotherapy*. Boston: Mariner,1961

Seligman, Martin. *Flourish*. London: Nicholas Brearley, 2011

Toffler, Alvin. *Future Shock*. New York: Random House, 1970

Tolle, Eckhart. *The Power of Now*. London: Yellow Kite, 2001

Wooden, John. *Wooden: A Lifetime of Observations and Reflections On and Off the court*. McGraw-Hill: Columbus, 1997

Acknowledgements

To all the sporting greats who graciously contributed their time and their openness to the successful completion of this book – a huge thank you. There are too many people to name individually but this book could not have been written without all your achievements, your hard work and your willingness to openly share this with us and with others. We hope that giving back is as rewarding as your many successes, and know that by sharing in this way you are inspiring others to move forward with success and through disappointments in their lives. Thank you all graciously and humbly.

In New Zealand, a big thank you to the Wellington Hurricanes and the All Black players who so willingly provided their time and their great insight. A special thank you to Steve Symonds and Chris Stirling for all the support they provided Jason in his role as mental skills coach and in supporting this book. A big thanks to Haidee Tiffen, the coaching team and the great women of the NZ White Ferns team. Thanks to Tracy Street and Pat McShane from the Centre of Vision and Leadership (CVL) for all the great work completed together with Jason over the many years: this book is richer for it. To Jerri Bassi, Pete Roe and the Thinkwell team, Liz Pennington and the Vitae team, many thanks for all your years of fun and support of Jason. To Rod Sandle and Annie Rogers, thank you both for your continual input and support of Jason as a psychotherapist.

To Murray Kinsella, Adrian Russell and all the team at the42.ie – a big thank you for all the support and help with Jason's articles and information for our book.

In Sweden, big thanks to Markus Karlsson, Jocke Ryder and all the team at IFK Lidingo football club. Thanks also to Marcus Hammerberg and the coaching team at Spotify, for all your help and support for our book.

In Ireland a great big thank you to Ciara Doorley and all the team at the Hachette Group for investing in and making this book happen. A big thanks to our editor Susan Feldstein for all your hard work in bringing it all together.

Finally, a big, big thank you to our families and friends, all of whom backed us in bringing this project together. From Jason, thanks to my dearest loves Vanessa, Ella and Killian, to whom this book is dedicated. To the Brennan Boys, Greg and Colleen Brennan; the Regan clan, Angela and Des Regan for all their unending love and support. Thank you all for supporting our vision for this book.

A special thanks from Brent to Mark Pope, always a supportive voice in an often difficult journey to wellness – 'I know I don't tell you enough but I love and respect you, bro.'

Jason Brennan and Brent Pope, January 2018

Visit us at www.thewinningmind.net

Endnotes

Chapter 2

1 John Wooden (with Jay Carty), *Coach Wooden's Pyramid of Success: Building Blocks for a Better Life* (Revell, 2005)

Chapter 3

1 Carol S. Dweck, *Mindset: The New Psychology of Success* (Ballantine Books, 2008)

2 Carol Dweck, 'The Power of Believing that You Can Improve', TedTalk (2014)

3 Eric Berne, *Transactional Analysis in Psychotherapy*

Chapter 4

1 www.businessdictionary.com

Chapter 5

1 Gilbert Enoka, 'Make Mental Strength Your Strongest Skill – the All Blacks Way', www.gameplan-a.com, 1 March 2017 [accessed 15 January 2018].

2 https://www.youtube.com/watch?v=YNRQYT8IQDQ [accessed 15 January 2018].

Chapter 7

1 Shauna Shapiro and Roger Walsh, 'An analysis of recent meditation research and suggestions for future directions', *The Humanistic Psychologist*, vol. 31, nos 2 & 3, 2003, pp. 86–114.

Chapter 8

1 *Conor McGregor: Notorious* (dir. Gavin Fitzgerald, 2017)

Chapter 14

1 Viktor Frankl, *Man's Search for Meaning* (Verlag für Jugend und Volk, 1946).